Social and Economic Modernization in Eastern Germany from Honecker to Kohl

SOCIAL AND ECONOMIC MODERNIZATION IN EASTERN GERMANY FROM HONECKER TO KOHL

Mike Dennis

Pinter Publishers
London
St. Martin's Press
New York

Pinter Publishers Ltd.
25 Floral Street, London, WC2E 9DS, United Kingdom
and **St. Martin's Press**
175 Fifth Avenue, New York, NY 10010, USA

First published in 1993

© Mike Dennis, 1993

British Library Cataloguing in Publication Data

A CIP catalogue record for this book is available from the British Library.
ISBN 0 86187 166 9 (Pinter)
ISBN 0–312–08569–9 (St. Martin's)

Library of Congress Cataloging in Publication Data

Dennis, Mike, 1940-.
    Social and economic modernization in eastern Germany: from Honecker to Kohl / Mike Dennis.
        p. cm.
    Includes bibliographical references.
    ISBN 0–86187–166–9, – ISBN 0–312–08569–9 (St. Martin's Press)
    1. Germany (East) – Social conditions. 2. Germany (East) – Economic conditions – 1945–1990. I. Title.
HN460.5.A8D46 1993
306′.09431 – dc20   93–8747
                                                                      CIP

Typeset by Florencetype Ltd, Kewstoke, Avon
Printed and bound in Great Britain by Biddles Ltd., Guildford and King's Lynn

Contents

To my parents

List of abbreviations

BDI	Bundesverband der deutschen Industrie (Confederation of German Industry)
CAD	Computer-aided design
CAM	Computer-aided manufacturing
CAP	Common Agricultural Policy
CDU	Christlich-Demokratische Union (Christian Democratic Union)
CIS	Commonwealth of Independent States
COCOM	Coordinating Committee for East–West Trade Policy
COMECON	Council for Mutual Economic Assistance
CSU	Christlich-Soziale Union (Christian Social Union)
DA	Demokratischer Aufbruch (Democratic Awakening)
DGB	Deutscher Gewerkschaftsbund (Federation of German Trade Unions)
DM	Deutsche Mark (German Mark)
DIW	Deutsches Institut für Wirtschaftsforschung (German Institute for Economic Research)
DJ	Demokratie Jetzt (Democracy Now)
DSU	Deutsche Soziale Union (German Social Union)
DVU	Deutsche Volksunion (German People's Union)
EC	European Community
EMS	European Monetary System
ERM	Exchange Rate Mechanism
ERP	European Recovery Programme
ESS	Economic System of Socialism
FDGB	Freier Deutscher Gewerkschaftsbund (Confederation of Free German Trade Unions)
FRG	Federal Republic of Germany
GDP	Gross Domestic Product
GDR	German Democratic Republic
GEMSU	German Economic, Monetary and Social Union
GNP	Gross National Product
IFM	Initiative Frieden und Menschenrechte (Initiative for Peace and Human Rights)

IfW	Institut für Weltwirtschaft (Institute of World Economics)
IMF	International Monetary Fund
KPD	Kommunistische Partei Deutschlands (Communist Party of Germany)
LPG	Landwirtschaftliche Produktionsgenossenschaft (Agricultural Cooperative)
MAK	Material-, Ausrüstungs- und Konsumgüterbilanzen (Material, equipment and consumer goods balances)
MBI	Management buy-in
MBO	Management buy-out
NATO	North Atlantic Treaty Organization
NES	New Economic System of Planning and Management
NPD	Nationaldemokratische Partei Deutschlands (National Democratic Party of Germany)
OECD	Organization for Economic Cooperation and Development
PDS	Partei des Demokratischen Sozialismus (Party of Democratic Socialism)
R & D	Research and development
SDP	Sozialdemokratische Partei in der DDR (Social Democratic Party in the GDR)
SED	Sozialistische Einheitspartei Deutschlands (Socialist Unity Party of Germany)
SPD	Sozialdemokratische Partei Deutschlands (Social Democratic Party of Germany)
UNO	United Nations Organization
VEB	Volkseigener Betrieb (Nationalized Enterprise)
VEG	Volkseigenes Gut (Nationalized Estate)
VM	Valuta Mark
VVB	Vereinigung volkseigener Betriebe (Association of Nationalized Enterprises)

Introduction

In 1989, 'real existing socialism' imploded both economically and politically throughout the Soviet imperium, and the countries of Eastern Europe were obliged to seek some form of incorporation into a world system dominated by the advanced capitalist powers of Western Europe, Japan and the United States. Nowhere is this transformation more dramatic than in Germany, which had been separated for over forty years by competing ideologies, rival political elites and divergent socio-economic orders.

Since the late 1950s, convergence between the two world systems had been predicted by many industrial society theorists. Some presupposed that scientific-technological development and bureaucratic rationalization created the social-structural and cultural preconditions for the dimunition of inter-bloc political conflict and the emergence of similar, though not identical, political systems. In a kind of double convergence, capitalism and Soviet-type socialism would draw together, possibly culminating in some form of democratic socialism. Other analysts, in contrast, predicted that, given its much greater adaptive capacity, Western society, in particular the United States, was the model towards which all contemporary societies were striving and that the Western pattern of modernization would eventually lead to the development in the Soviet bloc of political pluralism, a high level of social differentiation and freedom of thought. This optimistic scenario was not shared by those who, like Ellul, perceived a trend towards authoritarianism and centralization (Hirszowicz, 1981, pp. 13–14). Their argument was that industrialism rather than fostering a democratic polyarchic system promotes the bureaucratic organization of total society because of the growing need for coordination and information management, the irresistible trend towards rationalization and the urge to monitor the performance of every individual (see Meyer, in Johnson, 1970, pp. 319–33).

In fact, double convergence did not take place: the Soviet-style model, rather than converging with Western capitalism, developed its own norms and characteristic *modus operandi*, offering what was in essence an alternative modernization route. Modernization is usually interpreted as a process whereby one society seeks to attain the standards set by a reference group or pace setter. The standards concern those patterns of behaviour and ways of thinking which are regarded as more up-to-date, more rational and more profitable (Chodak, 1973, p. 257). The major referents emerged as the administrative-command system of the Soviet Union and the free-market economies of Western Europe and the United States.

Modernization has long been a controversial concept and theory, with its earlier critics accusing it of ethno- or Westerncentrism, of an oversimplified polarism between the 'traditional' and the 'modern' and of an assumption of a linear three-stage traditional–transitional–modern progression. Once 'modernity' has been reached, further or continuous modernization, it was implied, was ruled out. Many of these criticisms were taken on board, and later models of modernization have sought to take account of breakdowns, the existence of hybrid systems comprising elements of the 'referent' and the 'follower', dynamic variables such as innovation to account for regeneration and the possibility of alternatives to the dominant Western blueprint of modernity. Even so, the revision of modernization theory and models fails to satisfy many of its critics who continue to regard it as an ideological weapon brandished by the Western capitalist system for rolling back diverging systems. The numerous sceptics, many of whom were located within the alternative political culture of the two German states in the 1980s, insist that alternatives must be sought to the dangers and risks inherent in modernization. These hazards include environmental degradation, the prioritization of material over spiritual-cultural needs, the misuse of scientific research in nuclear and biological programmes and the alienation and anomie associated with job losses and rapid structural changes in the economic system. However, as Wolfgang Zapf has observed, the fall of the Soviet bloc undoubtedly gave a powerful boost to the modernization paradigm of Western societies, and the massive transformation problems have once more quickened interest in the relevance of modernization theory as part of the search for real solutions, in contrast to the esoteric subtleties of postmodernism (Zapf, in Giesen and Leggewie, 1991, pp. 46–7).

Although reaching agreement on what constitutes the characteristic features of modernity is rather like the quest for the Holy Grail, the idea is usually associated with a syndrome characterized by self-sustaining economic growth; the widespread utilization of technical innovation and science; the provision of basic social welfare and a commitment to a reduction in inequality; systemic and individual flexibility and readiness to promote change; urbanization; a secularized culture; a high rate of literacy and the continuous spread of formal education; and the placing of a high value on achievement. While modernity is associated with an appreciable measure of public participation in the polity, or at least some democratic representation in defining and choosing policy alternatives, it also connotes a high level of regulation by a bureaucratic, institutionalized state.

Since the development of the Stalinist administrative-command system in the later 1930s, the Soviet Union had offered an alternative path towards modernity, one which the GDR was obliged to take in the late 1940s (see section 1.1). Like the Western model, the Soviet model, designated as 'real existing socialism' in the Brezhnev era, accorded a high priority to economic growth, advanced technology and a basic standard of living; and Soviet and GDR leaders professed to be committed to social equality as well as to extensive political mobilization. In practice, the ideals of equality and democracy were subverted by some of the steering instruments regarded as fundamental to social and economic modernization, notably the principle of democratic centralism and the all-pervasive control exercised by the ruling party and its army of bureaucrats. Marshall Goldman has characterized this as Stalin's Faustian bargain. Rapid industrialization and economic growth in the short run were exchanged for what would become serious impediments to modernization and growth in the future (Goldman, 1992, p. 34).

The aspiration behind the Soviet-type system was that the elaborate steering instruments of the central state-party apparatus would ensure the efficient management and allocation of resources for the fulfilment of critical societal goals. During the 1950s and the 1960s, the Soviet Union was able to keep in step with the USA in such fields as nuclear energy and to score a spectacular technological success with Sputnik. And the rapid expansion of industries such as steel, petro-chemicals, machine tools and motor-vehicle manufacturing underlined the belief that the administrative-command mechanism might continue to have some value, especially if it could be made more flexible through the incorporation of discreet borrowings from the capitalist armoury or by the application of more efficient management techniques developed from systems theory or from computer sciences. The New Economic System of Planning and Management introduced in the GDR in 1963 was one of the earliest attempts in the Soviet bloc to amend, through the operation of indirect levers, the existing mechanism in order to promote efficiency and innovation in management systems and in key industrial branches such as electronics and machine tools (see section 1.2).

Innovation proved to be the Achilles heel of 'real existing

socialism'. The administrative-command system was ill-equipped to respond to the specific requirements of industrial innovation in the age of the micro. From about the early 1970s, the Soviet-style road to modernity was becoming littered with the wreckage of obsolescent machines from the earlier period of accelerated industrialization. By contrast, the advanced economies of the West, though beset with many structural problems of their own, exhibited a greater capacity to develop and utilize key basic technologies such as microelectronics, flexible automation, industrial robots and biotechnology. By the turn of the decade, it was patent that, despite imports of Western technology, those countries employing some variant of the administrative-command mechanism were experiencing the utmost difficulty in responding to the challenge of rapid innovation posed by the scientific-technical revolution. Innovation is vital to the quality of life and prosperity and essential for any society wishing to remain or attain a position among the international pace-setters. Despite the many risks and hazards, not to innovate is to stagnate, even wither.

Innovation is usually defined as the process whereby an invention, that is, a new product, process, system or device, is introduced into the economic system, although the term is sometimes utilized in a broader sense to describe the whole process of invention, innovation and diffusion. The success or failure of an innovation depends upon an array of variables whose significance varies according to time, country and economic sector. In general, much will depend upon striking a judicious balance between the pull-demand of the market and the push effect of scientific-technical research within a social and political environment which is congenial to risk-taking and to rapid organizational and social change and which enjoys good communications with the international scientific community.

Various innovation strategies may be pursued (see Freeman, 1982, pp. 172–83). An offensive strategy centres around radical innovations which are designed to give a firm a competitive lead. This course requires a high investment in R & D and marketing and is attended by a very high risk of failure. Similarly research intensive is the defensive strategy employed by companies which, while not wishing to be encumbered by the risks of the pioneers, are intent upon obtaining a share of the market through significant technical improvements in the original innovation. An imitative strategy is not so geared towards being a product leader and is less research intensive than the other two. Conceding the role of pacemaker, a firm pursuing this strategy seeks to derive cost and other advantages from its late entry and concentrates on the 'captive' market of its own firms and satellites. Finally, firms or branches may be engaged in dependent and traditional strategies which involve no more than minor improvements to existing products or processes. These strategies basically correspond to the implementation, rapid growth, maturation and saturation stages in the innovation cycle.

In the Brezhnev system of 'real existing socialism' pursued in the GDR during the Honecker era, innovative ideas and initiative were stifled by the obligatory fulfilment of planning targets, in particular the quantity of production, by the monopoly position of many enterprises and combines in a 'secure' market which absolved them of the need to respond quickly to customer pressure and by the aversion of many bureaucrats and some sections of the labour force to the disruptive effects of basic innovations on existing qualifications, functions, experience and structures. The workforce was kept quiescent by a high degree of job and social security and by the central authorities' toleration of slack in the production process. The risks inherent in and the experimentation required for basic innovations were difficult to accommodate within planning periods, and the failure of a high-risk innovation threatened management and work-force with a loss of bonuses and prestige.

As the economic mechanism rewarded minor improvements which did not disrupt the production units and bureaucracies, GDR enterprises tended to opt for traditional and defensive strategies rather than the pace-making offensive and defensive strategies. Even where an imitative strategy was adopted, as in the case of the state's forced development of microelectronics from the late 1970s onwards, a lag with the international pace-setters was inbuilt as GDR enterprises lacked not only competitive incentives, both domestically and within COMECON, but also the stimulus of unimpeded links with scientists outside the Soviet bloc, Instead, managers found it safer to concentrate on standardized mass products such as steel, cement and shipbuilding. The disadvantages of this strategy are exemplified by the Trabant car. GDR citizens had to wait for up to fifteen years for a new Trabbi, by which time it was technically two decades out of date. It was also a model which exacted a high price in terms of fuel consumption and pollution.

It fell to Gorbachev to try and arrest the economic stagnation of the Soviet Union and through a gradual dismantling of the planned and administrative system to overcome the impediments to modernization and innovation. The controlled pluralization of society, an expansion of enterprise autonomy through the reduction of obligatory targets from above, a shift in investment to the consumer, greater opportunities for leaseholders and reintegration into the world economy were all intended to produce a new economic model of socialism in keeping with Soviet traditions and experiences, a kind of middle way between old-style Communism and capitalism (see section 1.6).

The GDR leadership under Honecker looked on aghast. Since Honecker's accession to power in 1971, the SED, while committed programmatically to economic intensification, sought to improve the existing system rather than enter into the risky venture of devising a new model. It preferred the highly centralized path and the retention of the party's monopoly on power, a monopoly which would be endangered if it condoned a higher degree of individual and societal freedom in order to release the driving forces necessary for innovation and greater efficiency. But as explained earlier, the GDR's system had inbuilt systemic blocks to innovation and, like the other Eastern European states, fell victim to popular opposition once it became apparent that the Soviet Union would not use coercion to preserve a declining security and economic investment. The attempt during the interregnum of the reformist PDS/SED Prime Minister Hans Modrow to devise a market socialist model to revitalize the economy soon foundered on the rocks of the popular aspiration for convergence with the social market economy and the liberal democracy of West Germany (see sections 3.1 to 3.6). It was difficult to attract support for a new socialist experiment on what was seen to be an economic and political ruin.

Since the collapse of SED rule and the absorption of the GDR into the FRG, east Germany has been undergoing the traumatic shock of the early stage of modernization along the capitalist autobahn. The 'high-speed transplant' of the West German model to the GDR (Poldrack and Okun, 1992, p. 14) led to the collapse, virtually overnight, of the old system: millions of east Germans are either out of work or not in regular employment; few of the reconstructed firms are competitive; the virulence of right-wing political extremism has aroused fears of a Fourth Reich; and east German feelings of inferiority are reinforced by the perception of having been colonized by west German capitalists.

Although east Germany does at least have the advantage of a clearly marked map and the financial support of the FRG and 'Ossis' enjoy the benefits of freedom of association and travel, the convergence is necessarily asymmetrical, with west German influence dominant. After the euphoria surrounding the fall of the Berlin Wall, the frustration of the initial hopes of a short journey to Western levels of prosperity and democracy is engendering disillusionment and alienation in the former GDR, especially as it is now recognized that the transformation from one system to another is a long and difficult road entailing massive changes in social, economic and cultural structures and mentalities. As Offe has argued 'the transplanted tissue from West German institutions may well encounter a socio-cultural incompatibility syndrome, even rejection symptoms' (Offe, 1992, p. 5). After forty years of separation, the internalization of GDR-specific values and attitudes as regards work, social position, gender roles, income, consumption, family patterns, collectivity and social advancement have proved to be far more resistant to change than many had anticipated (Okun, 1992, pp. 30–1).

It is also dawning on the Western mentors that their own system is being reshaped by the incorporation of a 'foreign body'. Thus the whole transformation process is a fundamental challenge to modern society in the West. It has sharpened the basic critique on the principles and pillars of the west German model of industrial or post-industrial society and the financial and social burden incurred by the old *Länder* has aroused much resentment among west Germans. This antipathy is well caught in a television comedy series, *Motzki* (Whinger) launched in early 1993, featuring an Ossi-bashing westerner:

Motzki expresses what many west Germans have been afraid to say in public: reunification is not working, they hate the east Germans, whom they blame for dragging them deeper into recession, and they wish that the Berlin Wall had never come down. [Malcolm-Smith, 1993, p. 8]

This book seeks to chart and to explain the social and economic development of the GDR, beginning with the imposition on the country of the administrative-command mechanism in the immediate post-war period, its evolution in the Ulbricht and Honecker eras and its final collapse at the end of the 1980s. After an examination of the failure to establish a reformed socialist system, a detailed account follows of the introduction and the disruptive impact of the West German market economy on the GDR. The prospects for recovery are analysed in the final section of the book, together with an analysis of the burdens and dangers of reunification. The term 'GDR' is used to denote the separate German republic which existed between 1949 and 1990. The terms 'old *Länder*' and 'west Germany' designate the former FRG, and 'east Germany' and the 'new *Länder*' denote the ex-GDR.

The author is grateful to the British Council, the Nuffield Foundation and the School of Humanities and Social Sciences of the University of Wolverhampton for providing him with the financial assistance to undertake the research for this book.

1 'Perfecting the imperfect'

1.1 Modernization Soviet style

The Soviet zone of occupation, which in 1949 became the German Democratic Republic, contained a major industrial area in the south which had been one of pre-war Germany's most highly industrialized and productive centres. The region accounted for about 30 per cent of German industrial production in 1936, and its firms were well known for high-quality machine tools, textile machinery, precision engineering and optical equipment. Chemicals, shipbuilding and heavy engineering, however, were underdeveloped (Thomas, 1977, pp. 72–3). On the eve of the Second World War, per capita industrial production was 16.5 per cent higher than in the area which later became the Federal Republic (Leptin, 1980, p. 52).

The Soviet zone's economic potential was severely reduced after 1939, over 40 per cent of industrial capacity being lost due to the direct and indirect consequences of war. The situation was exacerbated by Soviet dismantling operations and exaction of heavy reparation payments out of current production. Other serious handicaps included the zone's self-exclusion from the Marshall Aid programme and, after the sealing of the division of Germany, the severing of GDR manufacturing industry from its traditional sources of raw materials and semi-manufactures in the other parts of Germany. Finally, as the GDR became enmeshed in the Soviet and East European protectionist trading bloc during the 1950s, not only was it deprived of unimpeded access to the modern technology of the West but, given the predominance of the barter system in intra-bloc trade, it also lacked powerful stimuli to innovation and competitiveness.

The mechanism with which the GDR was obliged to rebuild and then restructure its damaged economy was the Soviet-type administrative-command economic system. Although originally rejected for Germany by the German Communist Party (KPD) in its programme of June 1945, this system began to take root in the late 1940s and early 1950s, especially after Stalin's break with Tito in

1948. In 1950, a State Planning Commission was created as the supreme planning authority, and the country's first five-year economic plan was introduced. The nationalization of industry and the collectivization of agriculture gathered momentum during the 1950s, particularly after the announcement by the SED General Secretary, Walter Ulbricht, at the Second SED Party Conference in 1952, of the launching of the 'planned construction of socialism'. The collectivization of agriculture was virtually completed by 1960: well over 90 per cent of agricultural land was divided up among agricultural cooperatives (LPGs) and nationalized estates (VEGs). By the mid-1960s, 65 per cent of industry had been nationalized, and whereas private enterprise accounted for 21 per cent of industrial gross production in 1951, its share was squeezed to a mere 5 per cent by the end of the decade (Thalheim, 1990, p. 80).

The main characteristics of the administrative-command economic mechanism, as it evolved with certain national modifications throughout the Soviet bloc, were state ownership of almost all the large factories, mines and banks – the means of production; an extensive central bureaucracy responsible for the elaboration of plans, the determination of allocations and most prices and the regulation of wages and foreign trade; central planning of the economy through detailed short- and medium-term economic plans for production goods; full employment, narrow income differentials and a relatively immobile labour force; administered prices, which performed an administrative function rather than providing signals as in a market economy; a concentration on material balances rather than on financial flows; and intensive investment in heavy industry.

The 'Sovietization' of the GDR entailed far more than the adoption of the Soviet-type economic mechanism; it involved, in a symbiotic relationship, the installation of a political edifice based on the hierarchic Leninist principle of democratic centralism, managed by the leaders and functionaries of the highly disciplined ruling party, the SED, and supervised by the Soviet Union's plenipotentiaries, particularly in the early part of the Ulbricht era. Marxist–Leninist ideology was supposed to provide the ruling party with the keys to the scientific understanding and administration of society. The resultant authoritarian political and social structures were unreceptive to fundamental change and adaptation; they also negated the basic emancipatory core in Marxism.

Soviet-type socialism in one-third of a nation placed the GDR on a different modernization path to that of the FRG's Western-style social market capitalism. The GDR became the laboratory for a major historical experiment: the application to an already relatively advanced industrial region of the centrally planned and highly regulated mechanism which had been developed by Stalin to implement rapid industrialization and urbanization in the Soviet Union during the 1930s. Some of the key indicators of Soviet-style modernization included, as in the Western model, measures of productivity and economic growth; others tended to be characteristic of the Soviet-type system, among them, the expansion of the state sector, the eradication or large-scale reduction of private property, the expansion of agricultural collectivization, the elimination or weakening of large landowners and big business and the enhancement of the working class. As labour productivity and the level of scientific-technological development proved to be lower in the Soviet bloc than among the advanced capitalist states of the West, attempts were made to explain it away as a temporary phenomenon until the socialist forces of production could release their true innovatory potential. And there was always the ideological argument to fall back on that socialist societies, allegedly imbued with a higher level of social justice than capitalist societies, were progressing towards Communism, the highest stage of societal development (see Asputarian, in Gati, 1974, pp. 10–11).

The negative judgement in the West on the social and economic system of the Soviet type is now shared by most social scientists in the former Soviet bloc. An illustration of this change of heart is to be found in the following quotations from two articles: the first by Professor Rolf Reißig, formerly Director of the Academy of Social Sciences in the GDR and the second by Agel Aganbegyan, once an economic adviser to former-President Gorbachev:

Although the economic and social system of the Soviet type may have enabled the compensatory industrialization of the slower growing agro-industrial countries, it was at the same time a model wholly inappropriate for the formation of a modern society with an efficient economy, quality of life, pluralistic openness and democratic civic participation. For eastern Germany and Czechoslovakia, which had previously been economically and culturally developed, it was impossible to regard the imposition of this model as progress. Marxism–Leninism, shorn of Marx's critical analysis of society, became the ideology of the state of this inchoate authoritarian socialism. Its key function lay in providing the ideological legitimation of political practice. [Reißig, in Glaeßner and Wallace, 1992, p. 29]

[The administrative-command mechanism is] good for the barracks, for the military, for wartime or when fire has to be put out, but not appropriate for peacetime, for managing scientific-technical revolutions, or when social and other requirements have grown and a transition is necessary from one set of methods of running the economy to another. [Aganbegyan and Timofeyev, 1988, p. 35]

What are the major deficiencies of the traditional Soviet-type administrative-command economic mechanism? Bureaucratic criteria, exemplified by the emphasis on plan fulfilment and the disinclination to take risks, enjoyed precedence over economic considerations and the wishes of the consumer. Coupled with the political elite's aversion to unrestricted contact with the capitalist world, this resulted in difficulties with innovation and a technological gap with the advanced Western industrial nations. With technical progress impeded by the utilization of prices for the aggregation of physical data rather than the efficient allocation of resources, waste and inefficiency were endemic to the system.

The sheer complexity of the planning process, the inadequacy of data-processing techniques and the inability of planners to attain omniscience led not only to plan instability but also to the proliferation of slack plans. The enterprises, which possessed a better overview of the microstructure, attempted to hide key data from central planners and to negotiate a slack plan in which output targets were held down and inputs minimized. This procedure was inherent within the 'illogic' of the planning process and the 'tonnage' ideology. With fulfilment of the plan as the primary goal, there was no urgent need to rationalize on labour. In fact, labour was frequently hoarded in order to facilitate the achievement of plan goals in a storming process towards the end of the planning period. As not all goals could be realized within the framework of the state sector, a second economy developed in which the demand for certain goods and services was met by a small private sector. And, finally, as the economic mechanism was an integral element in the ruling Marxist–Leninist party's societal strategy, fundamental reform of the economy could only be realized in tandem with broader reforms of the political system, a step which threatened the jealously guarded power monopoly of the party leaders and an army of bureaucrats.

These deficiencies became more palpable with the advent of the scientific–technical revolution when developments in microelectronics demanded greater flexibility, higher rates of innovation and a greater adaptive capacity. Yet throughout the 1950s and even into the 1960s many Western intellectuals gave the Soviet-type system the benefit of the doubt, and in Eastern Europe during the Stalin and Khrushchev eras 'learning from the Soviet Union means learning to be victorious' did not appear to be an empty slogan. For not only had the Soviet Union derived an enormous propaganda boost from its contribution to the defeat of National Socialism, but extensive state intervention in economic planning offered the prospect of overcoming the recurrent crises experienced by capitalist states in the 1920s and 1930s. Moreover, the scientific–technological achievements of the Khrushchev era such as the launching in 1957 of the first earth satellite, Sputnik, lent credibility to the Soviet leader's boast that the socialist camp would outstrip capitalism within two decades. This was underlined in 1961, when the official programme of the Communist Party of the Soviet Union predicted that the Soviet Union would overtake American per capita production by the end of the decade.

As for Moscow's German ally, it has been argued with some justification that the Soviet-type economic mechanism possessed some value in the period of extensive growth and reconstruction in the late 1940s and early 1950s when resources had to be mobilized rapidly in order to develop the basic materials and capital-goods sectors and to tackle the plethora of problems arising from the division of Germany. Although the statistical record was by no means as impressive as West Germany's, the GDR did achieve some respectable results: industry grew at an annual average of 13.7 per cent between 1951 and 1954; wages overtook their pre-war level by 1954; and per capita GDP increased by about 95 per cent during the 1950s (Roesler, 1991, pp. 49, 51; Miegel, 1992, p. 81). Echoing Khrushchev, the SED leader, Walter Ulbricht, set as the main economic task in the 1959–65 Seven-Year Plan the overtaking of West German per capita consumption of all foodstuffs and consumer goods.

1.2 The new economic system of planning and management

Ulbricht's aspirations were soon revealed as unrealistic. With the rate of economic growth starting to fall in the late 1950s and the GDR unable to close the gap in technology and living standards with the FRG, the SED leadership, with Soviet backing, launched an economic experiment in 1963. Known originally as the 'New Economic System of Planning and Management' (NES), it was renamed in 1967 as the 'Economic System of Socialism' (ESS). By transforming the economy into a highly dynamic and more innovative system, it was hoped to demonstrate the superiority of socialism over capitalism and to give the GDR a much needed legitimacy boost in the aftermath of the construction of the Berlin Wall.

The autonomy of the nationalized enterprises (VEBs) was increased by reducing the number of compulsory state indicators and by giving more weight to indirect steering techniques, notably prices, credits and interest. The modification of prices was crucial to the outcome of NES as the price system, which was based on 1944 levels, had become a serious impediment to innovation and efficiency. Price reform was to take place in three stages between 1964 and 1967, and price dynamism measures, introduced between 1968 and 1970, sought to encourage a more flexible response by enterprises to changes in costs resulting from the introduction of new technologies.

Concerned about the difficulty in pushing through economic goals by means of indirect steering methods and about the often mediocre quality of R & D, Ulbricht and his advisers introduced a centrally directed structural policy in 1968. The policy gave priority to so-called 'structure-determining tasks' which were thought to be necessary for the automation and rationalization of production processes. The main beneficiaries of the new state investment policy were electronics, instrument building, machine tools and sections of the motor vehicle industry. Ulbricht, never slow to propagate the advantages of the *Modell DDR*, boasted in October 1968 that the planned acceleration of scientific–technical progress would release driving forces within the GDR which would demonstrate the superiority of its socialist system. In addition, it was envisaged that cybernetics, systems theory and computer science would improve the quality of planning, raise production, benefit the consumer and maintain the GDR's position as the leading socialist industrial power.

But once again, Ulbricht's hopes of catching up with West Germany were to be dashed. The emphasis on structural tasks soon resulted in distortions: the neglect of non-priority sectors led to difficulties in supplies to priority areas, and bottlenecks became acute in energy. The situation was exacerbated by unfavourable weather conditions and a growing though modest hard-currency indebtedness. Local SED organs and the Central Committee's Institute for Public Opinion Research reported widespread dissatisfaction with price increases, shortages of consumer goods, lower bonus payments, stoppages in production and the infringement of internal party democracy (for details, see Naumann and Trümpler, 1990, pp. 20–1, 26, 31–4).

The question facing the SED leadership in 1970 was whether to abandon NES/ESS or to attempt a comprehensive restructuring of the system. If they decided to opt for the latter course, they would have needed to reduce the structural-determining tasks, to revise the price system, to establish greater clarity in the lines of authority between central planning bodies, the VVBs and the enterprises, to achieve a more effective linkage between work norms and earnings and to grant greater enterprise autonomy and flexibility (see Leptin and Melzer, 1978, pp. 81–6; Herbert Wolf, 1991, pp. 26–7).

The eventual abandonment of NES/ESS was the result in the final analysis not of its many operational defects but of political and ideological opposition on the part of key members of the SED elite, notably Erich Honecker, who were concerned lest the GDR's still vulnerable social and political order be threatened by further economic and political experimentation. For although NES did not constitute a fundamental departure from the traditional economic mechanism, by giving the enterprises and the scientific–technical intelligentsia a greater say in economic decision-making it contained an implicit threat to the SED's political monopoly. In the aftermath of the Prague Spring, the SED cadres were allergic to what they perceived as the dangers from a basic reform of the administrative-command system. When strikes broke out in Poland at the about same time as the Central Committee Plenum of the SED in December 1970, it persuaded the SED leaders to terminate their own modest experiment. As the progenitor of NES and the structural policy of the late 1960s, Ulbricht's personal position was undermined by its failings and by the machinations of Erich Honecker and fellow Politburo members such as Stoph, Verner and Sindermann. With Brezhnev's support, Honecker was able to step into Ulbricht's shoes as the First Secretary of the SED Central Committee (for details, see Przybylski, 1992, pp. 22, 241–2). Honecker's GDR soon embedded itself both ideologically and economically within the arch-conservative system associated with the Brezhnev era, the system of 'real existing socialism'.

1.3 Recentralization and the unity of social and economic policy

Without delay, the new SED first Secretary presided over the dismantling of NES/ESS and reinstated the instruments of the administrative-command economic mechanism. Material balances proliferated once more: whereas 500 had been administered by central bodies in 1967, 800 were in operation in 1971–2. The State Planning Commission's role received a boost: for the first time since the introduction of NES it controlled about 300 material balances. Central control was also furthered by an increase in obligatory plan targets covering, among others, commodity production, wages, exports and imports.

The undermining of the limited autonomy of the economic units in the state system was extended into other areas by the nationalization of semi-state and private enterprises, together accounting for 11.5 per cent of industrial production. Industrial artisan enterprises were nationalized, too, and the whole process was completed by June 1972. The concentration process eliminated one of the main advantages associated with the smaller units, that is their flexibility in responding to changes in demand for furniture, clothing and other consumer items. Such an outcome was not readily reconciled with another of the regime's goals, a general improvement in living standards on the basis of higher labour productivity and economic growth.

The goal of a higher living standard was incorporated into the 'Main Task' proclaimed by Honecker in 1971. The interdependence of economic and social policy was enshrined in the SED's new party programme of 1976. The 'Main Task', a leitmotif of the Honecker era, was the foundation of the social contract which Honecker sought to establish between regime and populace. It typified the socio-economic mode of legitimation in communist states whereby in return for an acceptable standard of living the citizens tacitly, if unenthusiastically, were supposed to accept the party's claim to be the leading force in society.

In the early 1970s, the regimes's side of the bargain was to place an urgently needed housing construction programme into the centre of social policy and to uphold the principle of state subsidies for staple foodstuffs, rents and public transport fares. The new policy did not hold out any promise of reaching West German living standards; it offered, instead, as a form of compensation, job security and stable prices (Okun, 1992, p. 37). Material incentives and other rewards were to be used to stimulate higher productivity without widening differentials so far as to undermine a key element of the SED's legitimation strategy, that is the party's claim to be striving for the social equality of the social classes and strata. Underpinning the 'Main Task' was the principle of a close linkage between economic growth and social outcomes. Higher economic growth and greater efficiency were to secure the release of new driving forces for further economic development. Not all experts were convinced that the state would be able to bear the costs of the programme. In 1972, the President of the State Bank, Grete Wittkowski, expressed her fear that such an ambitious programme would exacerbate the GDR's hard-currency indebtedness (Przybylski, 1992, pp. 49–50).

In retrospect, the first quinquennium of the Honecker era can be regarded as 'the best time of Honi': 397,850 new homes were constructed and 70,103 dwellings modernized. Produced national income, according to official figures, rose by 30 per cent, and the stock of consumer durables increased, too. Between 1970 and 1976, ownership per hundred households of motor cars rose from 15.6 to 28.8, television sets from 69.1 to 83.6 and washing machines from 53.6 to 75.7.

1.4 The GDR in the world economic crisis, 1976–84

While the GDR was enjoying modest prosperity, the storm clouds were gathering elsewhere. The explosion of the world market prices of oil and other raw materials, first in 1973–4 and, then, much more seriously for the GDR, in 1979, together with higher charges for Soviet oil and natural gas, caused a sharp deterioration in the terms of trade of the GDR, a country heavily dependent on outside supplies of cheap raw materials. Economic recession destroyed the regime's aspiration to modernize the economy. Modernization was to be boosted with the assistance of technological imports from the West, notably from the Federal Republic, and financed by liberal credits from Western banks. The net indebtedness of the GDR mounted steadily, from $6.7 billion in 1977 to a peak of $11.66 billion in 1981, second only to Poland among COMECON countries. In the latter year, the cumulative trade deficit to the Soviet Union reached 2.3 billion transferable roubles. Furthermore, the Soviet Union cut back supplies of oil from 19 million tonnes in 1981 to 17.7 million tonnes in the following year. In 1982, the situation deteriorated further when in the wake of the rescheduling of the hard-currency debt payments of Poland and Romania the GDR, too, from the middle of the year, was no longer able to rely on new credits from Western banks (Cornelsen, 1987, p. 40, 52).

As part of its short-term crisis management strategy, the SED reduced imports from the West, with the significant exception of the FRG, and launched a vigorous export drive based on an increase in the sale of mineral oil products. With outside supplies of raw materials and energy so costly, the production of the GDR's main domestic source of energy, the highly noxious lignite, was expanded from 258 million tonnes in 1980 to 319 million tonnes in 1988.

Although consumers were obliged to tighten their belts by one or two notches, the SED leadership proceeded with the utmost caution in such a politically sensitive area. The price of basic necessities remained the same, and the state poured massive subsidies into rents, public transport charges and consumer staples. These subsidies escalated from 16.9 billion marks in 1980 to 40.6 billion marks in 1985.

The readjustment of foreign trade with the OECD, excepting the FRG, soon produced positive results: in 1982, at current prices, imports fell by 30 per cent and exports rose by 9.1 per cent. The net hard-currency debt began to fall: from $8.7 billion in 1982 to $6.8 billion in the following year. The West German connection was vital to the whole recovery strategy. Not only did intra-German trade plug some of the gaps left by the drastic reduction in GDR imports from other OECD countries, but two large interest-free loans of DM1 billion in mid-1983 and DM950 million one year later, both backed by the West German government, helped restore the creditworthiness of the GDR. By the end of 1984, the Western credit markets were once more open to the GDR. In addition to the credits, the GDR was able to draw upon a high annual flow of West German transfer payments. At the beginning of the 1980s, about DM3.7 billion per annum were transmitted by the FRG for the use of the roads in the GDR, transit traffic to West Berlin, postal and communication services, receipts in humanitarian causes, visa fees, the minimum currency exchange requirement and the sales carried out through Intershops (a chain of hard-currency shops selling luxury and Western goods to tourists and, from 1974, to GDR citizens (Michel, 1987, pp. 76-82).

A modest political price had to be paid for West German financial aid. In 1984, about 35,000 GDR citizens received official permission to emigrate to the West. The linkage between financial aid and concessions on the humanization of relations disturbed the policy consensus fashioned by Honecker among the SED elites and caused considerable strain between Moscow and East Berlin.

Werner Krolikowski, the colourless Central Committee Secretary for Economic Affairs, from 1973 to 1976, and a Politburo member, urged his Soviet contacts to press the SED leaders for a reduction of the GDR's growing dependence on Bonn as well as in the magnitude of the hard-currency debt. The Minister of Defence, Heinz Hoffmann, and the Chairman of the Council of Ministers, Willy Stoph, seem to have shared some of Krolikowski's reservations, but they put up little more than token resistance to the Honecker line (Przybylski, 1992, pp. 59–60, 126). Günter Schabowski, who joined the Politburo in the mid-1980s, later observed that Politburo members would rather have committed sodomy than be guilty of forming a faction (Schabowski, 1990, p. 25).

The Kremlin was less circumspect. It raised objections to Honecker's attempt to insulate German–German relations from the deep freeze in East–West relations. At a time when Honecker was advocating peaceful relations between states of a divergent social order, the Soviet Union was launching attacks on West German revanchism and on the use of economic aid as a lever to interfere in the GDR's internal affairs. While GDR policy was undoubtedly shaped by the fear of becoming a casualty in a nuclear conflict, a more significant concern for Honecker was the sorry state of the GDR economy. In the opinion of one insider, the GDR diplomat Jens Kaiser, only an extension of West German financial, economic and scientific–technical assistance prevented an economic collapse and thus the political bankruptcy of Honecker's policy (Kaiser, 1991, p. 483). The SED leader was obliged to make one major concession to Soviet pressure: the postponement in September 1984 of his projected visit to West Germany. On the other hand, he managed to limit the damage to the two Germanies' mini-*détente*, an indicator of the skill which Honecker showed in carving out an appreciable political space for the GDR in the early 1980s in its relations with its more powerful neighbours, the FRG and the Soviet Union.

Although the West German connection was invaluable for Honecker's crisis strategy, intra-German trade did not provide the spur to innovation and economic modernization which might have been expected from two such highly industrialized countries. The reason lies in the commodity structure of the trade. Basic materials and semi-manufactures enjoyed a disproportionately high share, whereas capital goods were underrepresented. Despite the attempts to upgrade and modernize its industry, capital goods accounted for only 10 per cent of GDR exports to the FRG in 1982; by contrast, basic materials and producer goods, especially mineral oil products, totalled 55.8 per cent (DIW, 1984, pp. 322, 410). The main demand for GDR technologically advanced goods came from COMECON, the Soviet Union absorbing 70 per cent of the GDR's engineering goods in the mid-1980s. Standards were not so exacting in COMECON, despite efforts by the Soviets to improve the quality of deliveries of machines and equipment by its East European partners. As a result the GDR's foreign trade did not provide an innovation boost commensurate with the country's level of economic development. This created a dilemma for GDR planners: without modernizing and reforming its economy the GDR would continue to lag behind its western neighbour in terms of productivity and the quality and marketability of its products and services. To step up its imports of capital goods, COCOM restrictions permitting, would increase the hard-currency debt and GDR dependence on Western suppliers, which it was reluctant to do for political, security and financial reasons.

In an attempt to boost the efficiency of the economy within the framework of the administrative-command system during the economic crisis, Mittag increased the number of combines in GDR industry and eliminated the middle tier of Associations of Nationalized Enterprises (VVBs). Combine formation was accelerated in 1979–80: whereas only forty-five were in existence in 1975, the number increased to 171 in 1985. The size of a combine varied considerably, from twenty to forty enterprises, and whereas the Robotron combine had a workforce of 70,000 spread over nineteen enterprises, the tiny Konsum-, Druck- and Papierverarbeitung combine employed a mere 600 people in its six enterprises. Other large combines were Carl Zeiss Jena with 58,000 employees and twenty-two enterprises (1986 figure) and Mikroelektronik with a labour force of 65,000 in twenty-four enterprises. The standard organizational type was a series of enterprises linked together by a parent enterprise and presided over by a highly influential general director (Schwarz, 1991, pp. 3–5).

By eliminating the VVBs and by reinforcing the linkage between suppliers and producers, the SED leadership, in particular the czar of the economy, Günter Mittag, envisaged major benefits, among them economies of scale, from the closer linkage within the combines between producers and suppliers. A fundamental disadvantage of the concentration of so much economic power in these large units soon emerged: their monopolistic position inhibited creativity and risk-taking and thereby reinforced an intrinsic defect in the administrative-command system.

In addition to reorganizing industry, the central authorities attempted to 'perfect' the existing system of economic control through the proliferation of material balances and planning indicators such as net production and net profit. According to Gerhard Schürer, head of the State Planning Commission, an army of 25,000 full-time planning personnel at central, regional and district level was responsible for the operation of the planning levers (*Wirtschaftswoche*, 20 July 1990, p. 15).

1.5 A new modernization strategy

As part of their grand strategy, Mittag and his colleagues sought to promote economic growth through a revamped economic modernization programme in which microelectronics was to play the central role. The intensive production of microelectronics commenced in 1977–8 after earlier developments in the 1960s had been allowed to founder. Microelectronics virtually acquired the status of a magic formula and was identified by Honecker at the Eleventh SED Party Congress in 1986 as one of the 'key technologies' which were decisive for the growth of labour productivity. Other 'key technologies' included robotics, electronic data processing, biotechnology, CAD/CAM, flexible automated manufacturing systems, laser technology and nuclear energy (see document 1). The overall modernization strategy was designated 'comprehensive intensification'. The term 'intensification' had been propagated at the Eighth SED Party Congress in 1971 as the main way to higher productivity and efficiency. The term itself denoted the achievement of economic growth not through increased material inputs and an expansion of capital assets but through the more intensive or more efficient utilization of existing productive assets and labour (for an assessment of this strategy, see chapter 2).

A balance sheet for the performance of the GDR economy by the mid-1980s would have on the credit side of the ledger the country's partial recovery from many of its earlier conjunctural troubles. It was once more creditworthy, the net hard-currency debt had been reduced and some savings had been made in the consumption of energy and raw materials. Yet these were essentially 'one-off achievements', the result of what John Garland called 'de-extensification' rather than of 'comprehensive intensification' (Garland, 1987, p. 7). In other words, the SED had demonstrated considerable skill in manipulating the levers of the administrative-command system and the West German connection, but its leaders were reluctant, perhaps psychologically unable, to grasp the nettle of fundamental reform. Such a challenge now beckoned with the advent to power of Mikhail Gorbachev.

1.6 Withstanding Gorbachev

Gorbachev's 'new thinking', which started off as a modest attempt at industrial reorganization through economic acceleration, soon developed into a programme for economic reconstruction (*perestroika*) underpinned by the necessary openness (*glasnost*) and political democratization. In order to realize these domestic goals, Gorbachev and his allies pursued *détente* with the West, so lightening the burdens of empire and enabling the Soviet Union and its East European allies to participate more effectively in the international division of labour.

The top SED leadership was not displeased with the first and cautious stage in the Soviet Union's rethinking of the principles of its economic and security policy. Soviet interest in the GDR's combine organization as a model for Soviet reform (Goldman, 1991, p. 89) was highly flattering to planners in East Berlin, and Gorbachev's warmer relationship with the West seemed to vindicate Honecker's own efforts to keep open channels of communication with the FRG and other Western countries. However, the SED leaders soon became discomforted with the early stages of *glasnost* and *perestroika*; their unease developed into outright hostility when it became apparent in the autumn of 1986, and particularly after the Communist Party of the Soviet Union plena in January and June 1987, that Gorbachev was embarking upon a basic overhaul of the Soviet Union's economic and political structures. Despite many conceptual uncertainties, there was an undeniable movement towards a dualism in the ownership system, a shift of decision-making from the central planning authorities towards the production unit and the utilization of selected market elements. Moreover, Moscow's belief, which had been crystallizing since early 1987, that each socialist country must find a solution to its own problems released ever more radical reform impulses in Eastern Europe, above all in Poland and Hungary. Widespread market reform and partial de-nationalization and privatization of industry emerged as the platform of many reformers. Greater leeway also meant that the East European communist regimes would not be able to call upon the Soviet Union for life support and would thus become more dependent on their own resources for purposes of regime legitimation and survival.

The SED gerentocracy was highly alarmed at what it regarded as a radical, ill-considered and highly risky departure from the fundamentals of the traditional socialist economic system, and it anxiously sought to prevent the spread of the reform virus to the GDR. The spectre of capitalism appeared to be haunting 'real existing' socialists.

At first, the SED leaders sought to discredit the Soviet reforms by belittling them. The classic statement to this effect was contained in Kurt Hager's April 1987 interview with the West German magazine *Stern* when he compared *perestroika* to mere redecoration and queried why anyone should want to redecorate his house simply because his neighbour did so. From the autumn of 1988 onwards, the SED tone grew harsher as several East European states began to deploy market mechanisms and to introduce political pluralism. Dire warnings were issued against the Hungarian and Polish importing of market elements from capitalism. Price rises and rent increases introduced in these two countries were denounced as incompatible with the GDR's own social system. Direct attacks were made on Soviet attempts to implement changes in the cornerstone of the traditional socialist system, the social ownership of the means of production (see Nick and Radtke, 1989, pp. 229–31). And Harry Tisch, a Politburo member and head of the FDGB, inveighed against the deployment of 'capitalist' elements such as job insecurity to raise the efficiency of the socialist economy.

At the December 1988 Plenum of the Central Committee, Otto Reinhold poured cold water on political pluralism – the handmaiden of Gorbachev's *perestroika* – which was being introduced into several socialist countries. The GDR, he insisted, would not reduce the role of the party to a mere debating club, nor would it pursue the transition to a so-called 'market socialism' (*Neues Deutschland*, 3–4 December 1988, p. 5). Reinhold, the Rector of the Central Committee's Academy of Sciences, came to enjoy a high profile as a determined advocate of the unity of economic and social policy, especially of the heavy subsidies on rents and basic foodstuffs. The removal of these subsidies would, in his view, lead to a wage and price spiral; any change in this 'core' of the SED's societal strategy would be dangerous both politically and socially (Reinhold, 1989, p. 3).

The alleged success of the GDR economy was crucial to the SED's Canute-like effort to hold back the tide of reform. At a meeting with party District Secretaries in February 1987, Honecker asserted that the GDR was now reaping rewards in the form of higher labour productivity and greater social security from the decision taken in 1971 to gear the economy towards intensification. Each country, he concluded, had to take heed of its own specific conditions and its own level of development ('Dokumentation', 1987, pp. 440–1). The imposition of a uniform socialist model, it was averred by SED spokespersons, was incompatible with the diversity of social, ethnic and economic developments in the socialist world and would be harmful to the greater efficiency of the more advanced GDR economy. After four decades, 'learning from the Soviet Union' was no longer official party doctrine, but it was the Soviet Union of Gorbachev, not of Brezhnev, to which Honecker took exception.

One of the SED think-tanks, the Institute for Economics and Politics of the SED Central Committee, took up the official line of 'socialism in the colours of the GDR', arguing that the GDR and Czechoslovakia were better equipped than the Soviet Union and its other East European allies to pursue the difficult task of intensification, partly because they had started off at a higher level of economic development and partly because the GDR enjoyed the benefits of an efficient system of management which corresponded to the requirements of intensive reproduction and of the scientific–technical revolution. The transition to intensification, they asserted, required not more democracy through less centralization but the 'complex perfecting' of economic management systems on the basis of democratic centralism (Haupt and Hövelmans, 1988, p. 973; Haupt et al., 1988, pp. 597–8). The hostility of Honecker and his close colleagues to Soviet economic reform was not without some justification for caught in a no-man's land between the traditional system and a market economy the Soviet economy, from 1988 onwards, showed distinct signs of disintegration with adverse effects on output, supplies, the rate of inflation and the budget deficit (for details, see Ellmann and Kontorovitch, in Ellmann and Kontorovitch, 1992, pp. 1–2, 24–5, 30–1).

At the same time as the SED was propagating the virtues of its own version of the traditional socialist system, influential figures within the Soviet political and academic elite were becoming increasingly sceptical of SED claims and were initiating a debate on the existence and nature of the general crisis of the administrative-command economic system of socialism. Oleg Bogomolev, the Director of the Institute for the Economy of World Socialism, contended that the crisis had its roots in the original sin of imposing the flawed Stalinist model on Eastern Europe.

Vyacheslav Daschichev, one of Bogomolev's colleagues, was in no doubt that the GDR, too, was caught up in the general crisis afflicting communism. The GDR's relatively high living standard, he argued, was sustained to a considerable extent by West German transfer payments and by the imports of relatively cheap raw materials and energy from the Soviet Union. He attributed the GDR's poor economic performance to the obsolete administrative-command system; by contrast, West German prosperity derived from its federal political system, its market economy and its full incorporation into the international division of labour. As a way out of the impasse, he advocated a gradual drawing together of the two German states, culminating in a confederation or unification on the basis of guarantees for the security of all European countries (see his memorandum in *Der Spiegel*, 5 February 1990, pp. 148, 152). Daschichev's memorandum, which was submitted to the Soviet leadership in April 1989, was the most advanced reassessment of the Soviet Union's policy towards the two German states, and it expressed his growing conviction that Eastern Europe had become an exceptionally heavy political, economic, military and psychological burden and a drain on the vitality of the Soviet Union (MccGwire, 1991, pp. 357–8).

The notion of a 'common European home stretching from the Atlantic to the Urals', part of Gorbachev's wooing of Western Europe, inevitably led to a rethinking of the bases of Moscow's German policy. By the autumn of 1986, Honecker feared that this reconceptualization of policy might jeopardize the very existence of the GDR (Küchenmeister, 1993, pp. 39–40). Soviet commentators and experts on Germany such as Nikolai Portugalev and Valentin Falin began to drop broad hints of a fundamental rethink, the former implying in early 1987 that 'the citizens of East and West Germany belonged to a single nation' (quoted in Sodaro, 1991, p. 353). During a visit to Moscow in December 1988, an extremely worried Honecker complained to Gorbachev of references in Soviet publications to the unity of the German nation (Oldenburg *et al.*, in Federal Institute for Soviet and International Studies, 1990, p. 245).

It seems, however, that Gorbachev and his advisers still regarded German unification as an undesirable departure from the traditional principles of Soviet policy. What they had in mind was political liberalization and the introduction of market elements in a reform of the economic mechanism, thereby enhancing regime legitimacy and stabilizing the division of Germany (Sodaro, 1991, p. 322). The SED leadership, allergic to the straws in the wind of German unification and disdainful of Gorbachev's attempts to recast socialism, failed to respond to the chance to define their place in the 'common European home'. Instead, Gorbachev was branded in leading SED circles as 'a social democratic revisionist and unprincipled opportunist' whose *perestroika* might be leading to a restoration of capitalist relations in the motherland of the socialist revolution (Kaiser, 1991, p. 490). Determined not to do it Gorbachev's way, Honecker sought allies among Gorbachev's critics in Moscow and tried to establish a 'little-*entente*' with Romania and Czechoslovakia as a conservative bulwark against reform.

In retrospect, the retention of the admininistrative-command economic mechanism, the many technocratic adjustments notwithstanding, and the demarcation (*Abgrenzung*) policy towards the Soviet Union was a fateful decision, for the advent of Gorbachev could just possibly have legitimized a reform process which, if initiated in time, might have arrested the symptoms of socioeconomic decay which became increasingly malignant in the twilight years of the Honecker era, especially after the General Secretary's visit to Bonn in September 1987. The Soviet Foreign Minister Eduard Shevardnaze, an active participant in the dismantling of the Brezhnev doctrine, believed that the GDR – and a reformed socialism – could have been saved. In an interview with *Izvetsia* in February 1990 he argued:

There was a time lag but not on our part. I am convinced that if the leaders of the GDR had embarked on reform say two years ago, the situation today would be different. But they doggedly stuck to their viewpoint. We have built socialism, we do not need any amendments, we are proceeding on the correct path, we have solved the social problems in our country . . . Honecker was not aware of the sentiments of his people. As a result, the time for reform was lost, never to return. [quoted in Brown, 1991, p. 58]

Several top SED functionaries in the Central Committee were covert Gorbachev sympathizers and some, as in the case of Egon Krenz, who succeeded Honecker, were coming to the conclusion in the summer of 1989 that a confederation with the FRG might be necessary in view of the state of the GDR economy and the disintegration of the Soviet bloc (Kaiser, 1991, p. 491). But the public line was more accurately reflected in Otto Reinhold's famous statement in August 1989: 'What right to exist would a capitalist GDR have alongside a capitalist Federal Republic? In other words, what justification would there be for two German states once ideology no longer separated them?' (quoted in Brown, 1991, p. 125). Marketization and democratization threatened to destroy the socialist foundations of the GDR and with it the GDR itself. But could a reformed socialism have saved the GDR? This question will be examined in detail in chapter three, but it seems doubtful whether it commanded sufficient popular support in the GDR. And, secondly, Gorbachev's own notion of a reformed socialism was constantly changing and unleashing forces over which he lost control. Perhaps Lech Walesa's statement best sums up the dilemma for East European reformers:

I wish Gorbachev and his reforms all the best. But we still don't know what communism in its final form will look like. In contrast, we know very well which political and economic models in Europe and the world have passed the test of time, and it is to these models that we must turn as opposed to attempting to 'reform' failed ideologies and concepts. [quoted in Brown, 1991, p. 56]

It might be argued, once again with the advantage of hindsight, that the initiation of a process of reform might have slowed down the speed of the GDR's collapse in 1989 and 1990 and created the platform for a more gradual merger between the economic and political systems of the two Germanies. Honecker, however, remained obdurate to the bitter end. Clinging to outmoded principles, he declared in his last major speech: 'We never turned our economy into one great experiment and made our actions ever more precise while involving ever broader sections of our economy' (*Foreign Affairs Bulletin*, 2 October 1990, p. 211). When Gorbachev, during his short but momentous visit to East Berlin in October 1989, warned his host that whoever comes too late will be punished by life itself, it was in fact already too late not only for Honecker but, as time would soon show, for his party as well.

2 The collapse of the old regime

2.1 The economy in crisis

As the SED's authority crumbled during the autumn of 1989 and
the curtain was at last lifted on the true state of the GDR economy,
it became painfully clear that the GDR economy had been living
not only on borrowed time but also on borrowed money. The facts
could at last be separated from SED rhetoric. The future had been
mortgaged by the SED leaders in a vain attempt to keep the
population quiescent and to preserve the 'Stalin mausoleum'.
Instead of a smooth-running socialist system based on central
planning and democratic centralism, the GDR appeared to be an
antiquated, backward industrial country unable to keep pace with
international trends and fatefully constrained by a system of planning in which the allocation of resources was directed centrally,
not by the more dynamic mechanism of money and markets indispensable for a modern innovative economy.

The GDR economy faced a host of acute short-term problems – a
declining national income, a heavy foreign debt and a budgetary
deficit – as well as the more deep-rooted problems associated with
the structural defects of the traditional economic mechanism. The
situation by the end of the 1980s demanded a radical reassessment
of the whole economic system not just another readjustment of the
myriad of balances, indicators and normatives. The main symptoms of the economic crisis are discussed below

2.2 The decline in produced national income

The major, albeit crude, indicator of the health of the economy,
produced national income, had been in decline since the mid-
1970s. The fall was particularly pronounced in the later 1980s. For
example, whereas the average annual growth was about 4.6 per
cent between 1981 and 1985, it dropped to 3.6 per cent in 1987 and

to 2.0 per cent in 1989 (Kusch *et al.*, 1991, p. 19). The severe dislocation caused by the mass exodus hit the economy hard in the final three months of 1989: on average, the value of production was 40 million fewer marks per day than in the equivalent period in the preceding year. According to the Minister President, Hans Modrow, two-thirds of the fall was due to the mass defection of so many workers (*Neues Deutschland*, 12 January 1990, p. 3).

2.3 The burden of subsidies

The subvention of the 'Main Task' was proving increasingly counterproductive. Rents, public transport and basic foodstuffs (above all, potatoes, bread, milk and milk products, meat, sausages, fish), gas and electricity, many printed materials and some manufactured goods such as children's clothing and shoes received generous state subsidies. Other major beneficiaries were education, sport, house construction, health and social insurance. Basic foodstuffs, rents and public transport were the most heavily supported items, their combined subsidies rocketing from 16.9 billion marks in 1980 to 49.8 billion in 1988. While a kilo of salami cost 10.80 marks in the shops, the subsidy amounted to a further 13.99 marks. It has been estimated by Heinz Vortmann that for every 100 marks spent on foodstuffs, the subsidies amounted to 85 marks. The equivalent subsidy for manufactured goods was considerably smaller: 19 marks (Vortmann, 1990, p. 38). Wastage was encouraged by the ready availability of low-priced energy for domestic users and cheap foodstuffs such as bread. With a kilo of rye bread costing as little as slightly more than half a mark, bread was often squandered as fodder.

It made little sense economically to divert so high a proportion of resources into keeping rents, public transport and domestic energy at these low rates. With an extremely low charge for domestic electricity of eight pfennigs per kilowatt hour, there was no real incentive either for the householder to conserve energy or for the government to introduce energy-saving devices. However, when, in May 1988, the State Planning Commission chief, Gerhard Schürer, suggested to Honecker that living standards be trimmed by raising rents and by increasing the prices of certain consumer durables and energy, the SED leader and Mittag refused to countenance what they saw as a fundamental change to the 'Main Task', the cornerstone of societal policy in the Honecker era (Przybylski, 1992, pp. 68–73).

The heavy subsidies diverted resources from urgently needed investments in industry and infrastructure. Investment in the producing sector as a proportion of national income utilized dropped from 16 per cent in 1970 to 8.1 per cent in 1985, although it did stage a modest recovery thereafter (Cornelsen, 1990, p. 77). Underinvestment, combined with the flow of large sums into consumption, contributed to the economic *malaise* which was expressed in the serious deterioration in the balance of trade. However, in order to reduce the trade deficit, Honecker and Mittag would have had to countenance cuts in domestic consumption (Fleissner and Ludwig, 1992, p. 8).

Another illustration of the imbalance between investment and consumption is provided by the statistics on the distribution of end product between 1971 and 1988 in relation to 1970: while individual and public consumption increased by 41.3 per cent and 68.3 per cent respectively, investment in the non-producing sector rose by 36 per cent (mainly due to the expansion of house construction) and fell sharply, by 94.7 per cent, in the producing sector (Kusch *et al.*, 1991, pp. 22–3).

The leadership's hopes for a performance boost from job security and the subvention of education, health, rents, public transport and staples had not been realized. Many East Germans, while acknowledging the benefits of a high level of social security, came to take them for granted. Furthermore, the lack of high-quality consumer goods, at least outside the Intershop chain, depressed the incentive to improve work performance. The failure to revise the wasteful system of resources, despite much internal criticism, lay primarily at the door of Honecker and the SED gerontocracy who, conditioned by memories of the 1930s, viewed job security and a basic minimum standard of living as proof of socialism's superiority over capitalism.

The housing programme, the core of the SED's social policy since the early 1970s, typified the dilemmas inherent in the 'Main Task'. Vast sums were pumped into the programme which, according to Honecker in 1973, was intended to solve the housing problem as a social question by the end of the 1980s. Soon after Honecker's overthrow, it was revealed that much of the financing of the programme – about 25 per cent – depended upon credits amounting to 55 billion marks (Haase, 1990, p. 31). Although in quantitative terms the achievement was by no means negligible (between 1971 and 1988 1,915,959 new housing units were constructed), investment in repairs and the modernization of the existing stock was far too low. In 1982, whereas 14.3 billion marks were required for this purpose, only 8.2 billion were in fact expended. The government, somewhat belatedly, recognized its error and sought to strike a balance between new construction and the modernization of the existing stock. By 1988, these two elements enjoyed equal weight in the housing programme (Kusch *et al*, 1991, pp. 63–4).

Serious problems remained, however. Rents barely sufficed to cover current repairs. The amount of living space per inhabitant in 1989 was twenty-seven square metres compared to thirty-five square metres in the Federal Republic. The provision of an indoor toilet and a bath or shower improved markedly from 39 per cent in 1971 to 76 per cent and 89 per cent respectively in 1989, but this was still considerably below the West German figures of 94 per cent and 93 per cent respectively (ibid., p. 66). East Berlin's privileged position in the programme reinforced the wide gap between the capital and the rest of the country. In East Berlin 59 per cent of houses in 1971 and 89 per cent in 1989 had a bath/shower and the proportion with an indoor toilet rose from 80 per cent to 95 per cent (Statistisches Amt der DDR, 1990, p. 202). An appreciable difference existed with regard to the condition of buildings in town centres. Whereas East Berlin could point to the impressive restoration of important public buildings and to prestigious avenues such as Unter den Linden, the centres of Leipzig, Meissen, Freiburg, Merseburg and elsewhere were in a serious state of delapidation due to neglect and pollution. The imbalance between East Berlin and the rest of the country was bitterly resented by the provinces and helped to fuel the opposition to SED rule which exploded on the streets of Leipzig in the autumn of 1989.

2.4 The budget in deficit

With subsidies for basic foodstuffs, rents and public transport escalating and with outlays on sport and housing increasing at a disproportionate rate, the state budget went into the red. Between 1971 and 1988, allocations to the population from the state budget as a proportion of total expenditure grew from 33.2 per cent to 41.1 per cent (Kusch *et al*, 1991, p. 126). On 13 November 1989, Finance Minister Höfner revealed to shocked Volkskammer deputies that the public debt amounted to 130 billion marks, including 65 billion marks in liabilities to Western creditors, 55 billion in credits for the housing programme and 10 billion in credits for large-scale projects such as the construction of nuclear-power stations (Herles and Rose, 1990, pp. 170, 173). The debt, though worrying, was not particularly high in comparison to many other countries; much more serious was the level of foreign debt.

2.5 An obsolescent capital stock

A particularly serious consequence of underinvestment and the distorted investment strategy was the failure to replace much obsolescent plant and equipment. Although many of the GDR's economic defects were familiar to outside observers before 1989, the revelation of the high proportion of obsolescent capital stock came as a great surprise. In 1989, 27 per cent of industrial plant was less than five years old, 23 per cent six to ten years, 29 per cent eleven to twenty years and 21 per cent over twenty years. The West German figures were 35 per cent, 30 per cent, 29 per cent and 6 per cent respectively (Kusch *et al.*, 1991, pp. 56–7). At the beginning of the 1980s, the value of machinery and plant in the producing sector which was virtually a total write-off amounted to about 58 billion marks; by the close of the decade this had grown to 133 billion (*Neues Deutschland*, 1 January 1990, p. 3), equivalent to an increase from 14 per cent to 20 per cent of the total value of equipment and plant (Steinitz, 1991, p. 8).

The average working life of capital in industry, expressed as a quotient of gross fixed capital to depreciation, was 40 per cent higher in the GDR than in the FRG. The gap was particularly wide in metal processing and manufacture (65 per cent) and shipbuilding (62 per cent), though less pronounced in steel- and light-metal manufacture (10 per cent), electrical engineering (18 per cent) and the clothing industry (13 per cent) (Görzig and Gornig, 1991, pp. 33, 35).

The GDR emerged unfavourably from a quantitative comparison of the level of equipage with the most modern capital stock (for the details below, see Kusch *et al.*, 1991, pp. 59–60). For example, in 1986 the GDR had 526 electronic data-processing systems with a working memory of 256 kilobytes; the FRG possessed 19,600 systems. Per 100,000 employees this amounted to six and seventy-eight respectively. The stock of personal and/or workplace computers and CAM/CAD systems per 100,000 employees was 393 computers in the GDR and 3,472 in the FRG and 14 and 111 CAD/CAM systems respectively. (All figures refer to 1986 except those for CAD/CAM units in West Germany which are from 1985).

The ageing machinery and plant required frequent servicing and maintenance: 280,000 repair workers were needed in 1988, that is, 75,000 more than in 1975. The proportion was particularly high in energy, chemicals, metallurgy and water supply (Statistisches Amt der DDR, 1990, p. 181). It had, moreover, proved impossible since the beginning of the 1980s to reduce the proportion of manual labour in centrally managed industry (Stinglwagner, 1990, p. 240). Not surprisingly, work stoppages were frequent owing to machine breakdowns, thus lowering worker morale and productivity. Planners were not unaware of the situation, but when, in 1981, the State Planning Commission's secretary of state with responsibility for investments warned Mittag of the negative effects of the increase in ageing and obsolescent stock, he failed to galvanize the economic overlord (Przybylski, 1992, pp. 195–6).

Fixed-asset investment declined between 1982 and 1984 and only reached the 1980 level in 1986. The fall was particularly marked in construction and agriculture which in 1989 had not even attained the volume of investment at the beginning of the decade. In the second half of the 1980s, investments flowed once more, primarily into branches such as electrical engineering and instrument building. However, the main beneficiaries of investment activity – energy and fuel, microelectronics and housing construction – were sectors which were plagued by low productivity or low competitiveness on the world market (Fleissner and Ludwig, 1992, pp. 8, 17).

The high proportion of obsolescent capital stock was a result both of the relatively low level and the structure of investments. The investment quota in the producing sector – in relation to national income – fell from 16 per cent in 1970 to 10 per cent in 1988 (Priewe and Hickel, 1991, p. 63). Within the producing sector, investment was heavily weighted in favour of industry (59.2 per cent in 1970, 71.1 per cent in 1986–8). This resulted in the neglect of important areas such as transport and communications, which accounted for 10.4 per cent of all investments in the producing sector in the late 1980s compared to 24 per cent in the FRG (Kusch *et al.*, 1991, pp. 31–2). Although electric traction and the electrification of railway track had increased throughout the 1980s, the East German railway system, the Deutsche Reichsbahn, was a constant worry for planners. The level of electrification was comparatively low even by East European standards. The poor technical condition of the track necessitated frequent repairs and maintenance work and caused numerous delays to services. The road network was also badly neglected: 18 per cent or 22,000 kilometres belonged to category IV, 'hardly useable'. Equally disturbing was the state of the telephone network: 72 per cent of telephone technology was more than thirty years old, and with 11.2 telephone connections per 100 inhabitants the GDR was a long way behind the average of thirty to sixty-three among leading industrial countries (ibid., pp. 61–2).

Finally, relative to its resource potential, the GDR's production assortment was far too wide. It is estimated that the metalworking industry, for example, produced 65 per cent of the world assortment compared to that of 50 per cent in the United States and of 17

Table 2.1 Labour productivity in the GDR in comparison to that of the Federal Republic, 1970–88

	GDR labour productivity as a percentage of that of the FRG			
	1970	1976	1980	1988
Chemicals, mineral oil, synthetic and rubber goods	34	42	45	50
Metal manufacturing and processing	39	45	44	35
Stones and clays	39	45	41	42
Steel, machine and vehicle building	43	46	46	56
Electronics, precision engineering and optics	41	41	47	63
Textile industry	53	53	56	56
Light industry	54	52	56	57
Food, beverages and tobacco industry	56	51	45	43
Manufacturing industry	45	47	48	53

Source: Görzig and Gornig, 1991, p. 27

per cent in West Germany (ibid., p. 46). The result was not only too high a level of product standardization, a major disadvantage in an age of rapid innovation and customer-specific demand, but also an unnecessary wastage of resources.

2.6 Low labour productivity

Labour productivity in the GDR compared unfavourably with that attained in the Federal Republic. In a comprehensive study two years before the *Wende*, the German Institute for Economic Research, estimated that over the period 1970 to 1983 the East German level was about half West Germany's (Bentley, 1992, p. 42). In a later evaluation, which was based on new data, the Institute calculated that GDR industrial labour productivity in 1988 was 53 per cent of the West German level (see Table 2.1). Although this represented an improvement on the 45 per cent in 1970, the Institute believed that as GDR data inflated the value of production in the key electrotechnics sector, the 1988 figure probably needed to be lowered by 3 per cent (Görzig and Gornig, 1991, p. 26). Other estimates, though less thorough than those of the German Institute for Economic Research, suggest that the gap might have been even wider, perhaps by up to 60 per cent.

Whatever the exact differences in labour productivity between the GDR and the FRG, there could be no doubt that the GDR was a clear loser in what Lenin had once defined as the crucial arena in the struggle between capitalism and socialism. The GDR's failure lay in a combination of factors, notably the low rate of the diffusion of innovation, inadequate investments, obsolescent capital stock, an inflated administrative *apparat*, the inadequacies in the flow of supplies and the deficiencies of labour-rationalization schemes.

2.7 The inadequacy of the socialist performance principle

SED leaders never tired of praising the socialist performance principle 'From each according to his abilities, to each according to his performance' as one of the intrinsic advantages of the system of real socialism over exploitative capitalism. In practice, however, the principle failed to operate as a powerful stimulus to high levels of productivity. This was acknowledged *de facto* in 1976 when a start was made on overhauling the existing wage structure of production workers. The new system, which was completed in 1982, introduced penalties for the underfulfilment of the norms constituting the basic wage (which amounted to between 70 and 80 per cent of earnings). It also sought to give a boost to the 'extra-performance wage' by the payment of bonuses according to 'real' performance. Until then, workers had regarded the extra-performance wage as little more than a reward for the fulfilment of prescribed norms (Jeffries, 1990, p. 114).

Although the reform failed to produce an effective system of performance incentives, the wage structure did allow for some wide differentials. As part of the innovators' movement, successful innovations could earn bonuses of up to 30,000 marks and as high as 200,000 marks if an invention was patented (Pieper, in Gerber, 1989, pp. 49–50). Sectoral differences in earnings were appreciable: the highest wage earners in industry were in coal and energy, machine-tools and the processing industry and the lowest earners in light industry and trade (Winkler, 1990, p. 112). In the latter sector, where women were in the majority, earnings were about 89 per cent of the average of the resident population (Kretzschmar, 1991a, p. 69).

The 10 per cent or so of the adult population who earned over 1,300 marks per month and the 10.6 per cent whose household income was at least 2,600 marks per month can be classified as relatively high earners. They enjoyed an income one-and-a-half times the GDR average. Included within their ranks were a disproportionate number of senior and middle-range managers, members of the intelligentsia, independents and employees in the state *apparat* and the mass organizations (Kretzschmar, 1991a, pp. 53–4).

While acknowledging the existence of these groups of relatively high earners and a degree of income differentiation according to economic sector and qualification, the verdict on the socialist performance principle must be that variables such as qualifications, responsibility and the complexity of work were inadequately reflected in the level of earnings to the detriment of labour motivation and innovation. Considerable overlap and a significant levelling of incomes existed between various occupational and qualification groups: 15.5 per cent of the unskilled and semi-skilled, 11.7 per cent of university and 22.7 per cent of technical college graduates earned 700 to 900 marks per month and 7.4 per cent, 23.1 per cent and 21.9 per cent respectively were on monthly incomes within a band of 900 to 1199 marks (ibid., p. 61).

After Honecker's overthrow, employees vented their anger on the wage system (see *Neues Deutschland*, 23 and 27 October 1989 and *Tribüne*, 2 and 6 November 1989). Complaints were aired against the kind of situation where foremen in highly responsible positions earned no more than skilled production workers. In some cases, managers responsible for work organization, labour productivity and the procurement of materials actually earned 200 to 300 marks less than the workers in their charge. The press abounded with workers' grievances: poor performance went unpenalized; far too high a proportion of the wage packet was unrelated to performance; able workers were leaving skilled employment and earning the same wage for less effort in jobs such as window cleaning; performance was undermined by work stoppages and down time owing to a shortage of supplies and obsolescent machinery; and the inadequate range and poor quality of so many consumer goods dampened work motivation. The newly appointed Minister of Wages and Labour, Hannelore Mensch, admitted that the reform of the wage system had failed to stimulate performance: since 1975, and in particular in 1976, 1987 and 1988, the ratio of average wages to the growth of labour productivity had been 'distorted' ('Sofortmaßnahmen', 1990 p. 3).

A concerted attack was made in the press against the tendency towards a levelling downwards of earnings. It was revealed that in many enterprises and combines the average monthly net wage of master foremen was about 63 marks less than skilled workers in wage group 8 in machine-tools and process-machine building and 50 marks less in heavy-machine and installation building (Kusch *et al.*, 1991, p. 109). A comparison with West Germany sheds further light on the extent of the levelling-down process. In 1988, graduate earnings in the GDR were only about 35 per cent above the national average; in the FRG they were about 50 per cent higher (Geißler, 1991, p. 48). Furthermore, whereas GDR graduates earned on average 57 per cent more than workers without a vocational qualification, the difference in the Federal Republic was 75 per cent (Görzig and Gornig, 1991, p. 66). Soon after the opening of the Berlin Wall, one leading manager, the then general director of the Robotron combine, Friedrich Wokurka, estimated that the ratio of low to high wages in the GDR was 1:3 as against 1:30 in the FRG and that even when teams with high responsibility in R & D and production were taken into account, the GDR ratio was still only 1:5 (*Der Spiegel*, 27 November 1989, p. 120).

The levelling-down process as regards earned income was strongly reinforced by the 'second wage packet', that is, the transfers from the state budget and enterprise funds in the form of subsidies for consumer staples, rents, public transport, factory meals and enterprise holiday camps and so forth. Alfred Kretzschmar, a leading GDR sociologist, has estimated that 75 per cent of people's monetary income was derived from their work and 20 per cent from state funds. In 1988, subsidies for foodstuffs were worth between 132 marks per month for a one-person household and 419 marks for households with five or more members (Kretzschmar, 1991a, pp. 40, 45).

In any event deficiencies and shortages in retail trade meant that it was difficult to translate a higher income into a higher standard of living. The long delays in the delivery of a motor vehicle were symptomatic of the general problem of shortages. One consequence was the growth of savings deposits from 102.9 billion marks in 1981 to 159.6 billion in 1989 (Statistisches Amt der DDR, 1990, p. 115).

Widespread worker indifference to performance indicators had been exposed before the *Wende* by GDR sociologists. On the basis of their research, one West German expert, Fred Klinger (Klinger, 1990, pp. 56–7), estimated that while about one-third of enterprise managers investigated in field surveys were performance-orientated, as many as one-half remained outside this highly motivated circle. A similar picture emerged from studies of specialists with a university or technical-college qualification as well as of industrial workers. Among the latter, in Klinger's view, a non-performance orientation predominated, with only about 10 per cent of industrial workers acknowledging that performance issues affected them in their work collective.

Sociological research carried out in the GDR during the 1980s documented the failure of the existing wage and salary system to motivate workers and well-qualified staff to burden themselves with management responsibilities (ibid., p. 58). Other factors which rendered management an unattractive option were: bureaucratic procedures and the lack of a clear delineation of responsibilities which impeded strategic planning; disruptions to the planning process which caused a high level of psychic stress and made it difficult to achieve plan targets; and the low authority which many managers exercised over their work force. Management authority was undermined by the shortage of labour in many enterprises; and thus even such a crude instrument as the threat of unemployment could not be utilized to enhance work performance (Adler, 1991, pp. 29–30).

The work collective, dubbed 'a place of safe retreat and emotional warmth' (Kretzschmar, 1985, p. 24), was another key factor in depressing performance (for details, see Schmeling, in Assmann *et al.*, 1991, p. 76; and Kasek, 1990, pp. 53–4). In a stable work collective, social relations were vital to the subjective well-being of the individual. Work colleagues acted as sources of information and as contacts for obtaining services which otherwise could only be acquired in exchange for D-marks or by wasting time in queues. Workers took advantage of the recreational facilities which enterprises provided for their workforce during leisure hours or on holiday. In this kind of environment, the social harmony of the work collective often became the highest 'commandment'; productivity and efficiency improvements were regarded as a threat. The operation of the enterprise cultural and social fund reinforced this primacy of the social over the economic. The fund was used, for example, to improve working conditions, to subsidize meals, to promote sport and educational events of all kinds and to support works outings. It was financed on the basis of 400–600 marks per employee per year (considerably less in administrative institutes) and could be left to accumulate. The size and the utilization of the fund bore no relationship to the economic success of the enterprise as it was not linked to enterprise profits or losses.

Levelling downwards and poor work motivation became a political issue of some sensitivity when from the early 1980s leading GDR sociologists such as Manfred Lötsch advocated the promotion of certain social differences as driving forces of economic growth. Sociological research showed that top R & D staff were handicapped by: the lack of appropriate material rewards and social recognition of outstanding achievements; the lack of a critical intellectual atmosphere; the sparcity of contacts with the international scientific community; and the overload of administrative tasks. Many highly qualified personnel had little incentive to improve their performance as they were employed in positions below their level of qualification. For example, about 40 per cent of graduate engineers were employed in positions for which they were overqualified (Geißler, 1992, pp. 137, 139). Lötsch and like-minded colleagues proposed a comprehensive programme for the promotion of a 'creative core' or 'leadership group' among the scientific-technical intelligentsia. Gifted individuals should be developed systematically from childhood onward, creativity and initiative freed from the shackles of routine tasks and top international achievements rewarded by high financial payments. In this way, it was hoped that the heavy investment in the education and training of the intelligentsia, especially in basic and applied research, would be translated into outstanding results and products which could be sold on the world markets and earn the GDR hard currency (Dennis, 1988, p. 53).

Such ideas appeared to be compatible with the SED's strategy for intensifying the factors of economic growth. However, the SED leadership never grasped the nettle of even these modest proposals, partly because they would have entailed a significant overhaul of the price and wage system and partly because they threatened to disturb the ideological commitment to the convergence of the social classes and strata. It was particularly difficult for the SED to reconcile a degree of elitism with the official goal of social equality. Narrow income differentials and/or an overlapping of income and status among the social classes and strata were seen as guarantees of the social peace. As the political system did not possess the mechanisms for the open resolution of social conflict, the ruling group attempted to stabilize existing power relations by defusing potential conflict, especially through the 'social gratification' of the working class (Adler, 1991, p. 26).

2.8 The failure of the economic modernization programme

The economic modernization strategy by means of key technologies proved to be a palpable failure, even if, as Günter Mittag argues in his memoirs, the development of microelectronics – the key technology – was indispensable for the GDR's competitiveness and productivity (Mittag, 1991, pp. 245, 250). However, the over-ambitious programme overstretched the GDR's already limited resources. Planned investments in the microelectronics industry alone accounted for about 15 billion marks in the 1986–90 Five-Year Plan, mainly for developments in the Carl Zeiss Jena, Mikroelektronik Erfurt and Robotron Dresden combines (Herbert Wolf, 1991, p. 50). Given the distorted investment programme, sectors such as transportation and energy conversion suffered relative neglect.

In many enterprises, the new technologies proved to be a false investment as they were not integrated into the production process. Industrial robots and other equipment lay idle because of the lack of technical experts and a compatible production process (Dennis, 1984–5, p. 6). Not surprisingly, the GDR was unable to close the technological gap with leading Western and Japanese firms. The gap can be illustrated in various ways. While 8-byte microprocessors were the standard microprocessors in the GDR, they were replaced in the FRG in 1982 by the 16-byte processor, a type which was first exhibited at the 1986 Leipzig fair. The proto-type of the 1-megabyte chip was unveiled with much ballyhoo in 1988 and serial production was planned for 1990. NEC of Japan, however, was already producing two million of these chips in mid-1988 and four million per month by the end of the year (Dennis, in Gerber, 1991, p. 27). Delays in serial production had serious reper-cussions for profitabilty and competitiveness: the 64-kilobyte memory cost DM150 when it first appeared on Western markets, but it was worth only DM3 six years later (Dennis, 1987–88, p. 66).

The difficulties experienced by GDR firms in integrating new technologies into the manufacturing process are partly attributable to the underdeveloped information infrastructure, the 'lifeline' of a modern economy and a reflection of its technological sophistica-tion. The R & D effort in a key area such as post and telecommuni-cations was appalling: it engaged a mere 1,142 persons in 1987, 8 per cent lower than in 1971 (Bentley, 1992, p. 75).

Further evidence of the GDR's failure to combine what Honecker was fond of referring to as 'the advantages of socialism still more effectively with the achievements of the scientific and technological revolution' (see document 1) can be seen in the permanent short-age of computers and the relatively backward state of electronic data processing. Numerically speaking the GDR economy, ex-cluding private crafts and agricultural production cooperatives, had at the end of 1989 (1987 figures in parenthesis) 71,971 (41,431) 8- and 16-byte personal and workplace computers, including im-ports from the West and COMECON; 41,931 (1988: 23,438) office computers; 13,944 (8,355) computer terminals; 2,054 (1,037) small data-processing systems; 24,863 (3,330) other small and microcom-puter systems and 2,445 (1,532) process computers (Krakat, 1990b, p. 13). The majority – 80 per cent – of the computers came from the Robotron combine which exercised a virtual monopoly in this area as well as occupying a major position in the production of sof-tware. In 1989, Robotron was responsible for over 30 per cent of software production in the GDR; the *Datenverarbeitung* combine followed with about 16 per cent (Krakat, 1990b, pp. 9, 17, 25 and 36).

A recent balance sheet of electronic data processing in the GDR drawn up by the west German expert on GDR science and tech-nology Klaus Krakat puts the technological gap with the West at between five and ten years. Major deficiencies identified by Krakat include the inability of producers like Robotron to satisfy domestic demand for efficient computer hard- and software and a shortage of on-line systems as the basis of an integrated information-processing and computer-aided telecommunications system. In order to overcome some of these problems, GDR enterprises turned to illegal imports and to copying West German software programmes. The hardware products and the software of Western market leaders were used as models for redevelopment in the R & D sections of the GDR. The software products of IBM, Hewlett-Packard and Digital Equipment Corporation aroused great interest (ibid., pp. 5–6, 25).

Bureaucratic procedures made it impossible for GDR producers to react quickly to demand. For example, applications for new software developments had to be submitted to the responsible specialist information and advisory centres. Those responsible were the experts from the leading software producers such as Robotron. Not only did the whole process take a long time, but it also gave well-established firms like Robotron the opportunity to control new developments (ibid., pp. 26–7).

As elsewhere in the economy there was, of course, no market-economy orientated cost structure in electronic data processing, and prices were fixed by the central authorities. Robotron products were inordinately expensive. Its K1840, a 16-byte computer, was available for sale in the GDR at 1.8 million marks, whereas a superior model was available in any West German store for DM10,000 (Schulte-Doinghaus, 1990, p. 219). In 1987, the processing speed of the K1840 of one million instructions per second compared unfavourably with the 6–50 million operations typical of similar machines in West Germany (Bentley, 1992, p. 51). As for sales to Western markets, the low technical quality of its products forced Robotron to sell its typewriters, printers and other products at dumping prices. It is estimated that in order to obtain one Valuta Mark (VM – the special foreign exchange accounting unit), Robotron had to invest 6.24 GDR marks (Krakat, 1990b, pp. 40–1, 58).

2.9 Research and development

The problems associated with the economic modernization strategy and the development of microelectronics and other key technologies were clear signs that the relatively heavy investment in research and development (R & D) was not reaping the anticipated dividends.

If judged by quantitative criteria alone, the GDR's R & D effort was by no means unimpressive. The outlay on R & D increased substantially from 4.9 billion marks in 1971 to 11.8 billion in 1989. In the latter year, according to official GDR statistics, 15.3 per cent was spent on basic research and 29.2 per cent on applied research (Statistiches Amt der DDR, 1990, p. 111). The whole R & D outlay accounted for about 5 per cent of produced national income. In 1989, the official figure of 203,000 R & D personnel undoubtedly inflated the real number, mainly because the GDR's notion of R & D was much broader than the Frascati definition used by the OECD which classified R & D as work containing an appreciable degree of novelty. The more elastic criteria of the GDR stretched so far as to include in the official statistics persons providing an indirect service to R & D, such as maintenance staff and guards. *Bona fide* researchers were obliged to spend between 20 and 50 per cent of their time on routine matters (Bentley, 1992, p. 62–4). Eckard Förtsch of the Institute for Society and Science of the University of Erlangen-Nürnberg (Förtsch, 1990, p. 1689) has estimated that the number of staff involved in R & D did not exceed 140,000, including those engaged in the social sciences and humanities. Even this probably errs on the generous side as investigations carried out after the *Wende* by this same institute concluded that only 50,000–60,000 R & D staff could be integrated without too much difficulty into the new all-German R & D landscape (Brocke, 1990, p. 44).

An examination of the output of GDR output soon reveals serious deficiencies. Too high a proportion – 30 per cent – of GDR industrial products were in the shrinkage phase of the innovation cycle and too low a proportion (23 per cent) in the market entry and growth phase. FRG figures are 9 per cent and 46 per cent respectively (Becker, 1992, p. 472). These figures reflect the well-known fact that the strength of GDR research lay in imitation and redevelopment rather than in innovation. This was partly a consequence of the COCOM embargo list and the isolation of many GDR researchers from developments in the Western industrial states and partly a consequence of the systemic obstacles discussed elsewhere in this book. Much activity labelled as basic research was in fact applied research. The German Science Council's investigation of academic science in the former GDR showed that in 1988 less than 25 per cent of physicists in the Academy of Sciences and in higher education had been involved in basic research or what is defined in the Frascati Manual as experimental or theoretical work for the acqusition of new knowledge without having as its goal any particular application or use (Bentley, 1992, pp. 84–5).

Among the major problems were the slow diffusion of basic research and the translation of quantity into quality. The length of time between an invention and its introduction on the market was on average twice as long as among the GDR's capitalist competitors. One consequence was that innovations made a decreasing contribution to economic growth. As we have already seen, there was a wide technological gap between the GDR and world market leaders, and too many products and services were of a mediocre standard. The reasons for this situation (see in particular Maier, 1987, pp. 122–39) are to be found in a combination of: the obstacles to innovation arising from the existence of large, highly bureaucratized combines; the virtual monopoly enjoyed by certain combines like Robotron in computer hardware; the increasing breadth of the product assortment which fragmented the research programme and dissipated resources; a planning system which discouraged risk taking and an educational system which encouraged conformity rather than creativity; the conservatism of the heads of scientific and university departments, the majority of whom were over fifty years of age; a lack of contact with the international scientific community; and too high a proportion of obsolescent scientific equipment (Mayer, in Knabe, 1989, pp. 229–30, 236).

2.10 Balance-of-payments problems

Foreign trade had long caused economic planners and SED economic functionaries sleepless nights. The limited involvement in the global division of labour was proving increasingly counterproductive. In the mid-1980s, the GDR's share of the world market was a modest 1.3 per cent (Priewe and Hickel, 1991, p. 69), and the GDR's sales to Western consumers faced strong competition from newly industrializing countries like Taiwan, Singapore and Hong Kong. COCOM restrictions and, as ever, the GDR's close trading relations with its COMECON partners deprived the highly industrialized GDR of innovative stimuli from a fully developed and balanced trade with the advanced capitalist states.

The weakening competitiveness of GDR products was not admitted in the GDR press until the fall of Honecker. The SED organ revealed that foreign-trade turnover between 1986 and 1988 grew more slowly than the rate of growth of produced national income, despite the general expansion of world trade (*Neues Deutschland*, 11 January 1990, p. 3). The growth in the volume of foreign trade was less marked between 1981 and 1988 (19.5 per cent) than between 1971 and 1980 (90 per cent) and in 1988 the value of exports was lower than in 1986. At real prices the receipts from exports to the non-socialist area fell from 32,680 million VM in 1986 to 27,519 VM in 1988. A fundamental reason was the failure to raise the crucial metalworking industry's share of exports. By international standards the average kilogramme prices of GDR products and the proportion of research-intensive products were both too low (Luft and Faude, 1989, p, 5).

Data which have been released since the *Wende* shed new light on the deterioration in the GDR's balance of payments. This includes the publication of materials on the shadow exchange rate (*Richtungskoeffizient*) used for internal purposes by planners to estimate the mark-value equivalents of the DM, the dollar and the transferable rouble. (In 1989, DMI = 4.4 marks, \$1 = 8.14 marks and 1 transferable rouble = 4.67 marks: Akerlof *et al.*, 1991, p. 18, f. 15.) On the basis of these data, planners reckoned that between 1980 and the end of 1988 the outlay required by GDR firms to earn DMI in trade with the West had risen from 2.40 marks to 4.40 marks (Haendke-Hoppe, 1990, p. 652). Other new data, which measure the *actual* costs of earning foreign currency, show that in 1989 the highest costs (marks per DM) were incurred in chemicals (4.11), electronics (4.82) and food, drinks and tobacco (4.09) and the lowest in energy (2.08) and metallurgy (3.22). There were, however, appreciable variations across combines and enterprises. Whereas the Carl Zeiss Jena combine needed 3.66 marks to realize DMI, the Mikroelektronik combine's expense ratio was 7.17 marks. It should be noted that subsidies were allocated to firms for costs in excess of the shadow exchange rate and that in the GDR only one enterprise outside the energy sector – the Meissen porcelain works – had costs less than unity! (Akerlof *et al.*, 1991, pp. 18–20).

One consequence of the sharp fall in the GDR's competitiveness was a realignment in the value of the country's foreign trade. Western industrial countries' share of GDR exports, on the basis of the new data, increased from 24.1 per cent in 1990 to 48.5 per cent in 1989, while that of COMECON declined from 65.4 per cent to 43.2 per cent. GDR imports exhibited a similar pattern over this period: whereas in the former year COMECON accounted for 60.2 per cent of the GDR's imports, it fell to 39.4 per cent in 1989, while that of the industrial West increased from 30.4 per cent to 53.1 per cent (Statistisches Amt der DDR, 1990, p. 277). Despite this shift in value terms, the pattern of trade with the West still did not reflect the GDR's relatively high level of industrial development.

The plight of the GDR was expressed in its growing hard-currency debt and the high level of interest paid on credits. The GDR had managed to stabilize its hard-currency debt to the West between 1982 and 1985, mainly owing to the increase in exports of mineral-oil products, but from 1986 onwards the situation deteriorated rapidly. Hard-currency indebtedness continued to rise from

1985, reaching 49 billion VM in 1988 (Hertle, 1992b, p. 1023). The GDR's estimated foreign assets, though not inconsiderable, were of little value in real terms as they were essentially liabilities of states such as Angola, Cuba, Mozambique, Ethiopia, and Nicaragua which were in no position to honour their obligations (Przybylski, 1991, p. 329).

As discussed earlier (see section 1.4), the hard-currency debt caused much animation not only among the SED economic and political leaders but also considerable tension between the GDR and the Kremlin. Moscow feared, as did certain SED Politburo members, that the growing debt was not only a heavy burden on the GDR economy but drew the GDR into an undesirably close relationship with Bonn. The GDR, it was believed, was running the risk of blackmail by its West German neighbour (see Krolikowski's comments in Przybylski, 1991, pp. 121–3, 327, 329, 337, 354). The financial and political fruits of the *mini-détente* of the two Germanies in the late 1970s and early 1980s were, however, a major feature of the policy of Honecker and Mittag, and ones which they were unwilling to surrender. If the GDR were to remain as the technological leader in COMECON, then coop- eration with the Federal Republic was indispensable. Given the documentation available at the moment, it is difficult to delineate clearly the contours of the opposition within the Politburo to Honecker's Western policy. The State Security boss, Erich Mielke, in an interview with *Der Spiegel* identified himself, Krolikowski, Krenz, the Defence Minister Heinz Hoffmann, Werner Jarowinsky, Schürer and 'others' as dissatisfied with the General Secretary's style of leadership; but he acknowledged that many lacked the courage to express their concerns openly and to trigger off a critical discussion (' "Ich sterbe in diesem Kasten" ', 1992, p. 41).

As so many East European states had discovered to their cost in the 1970s, economic cooperation with the West, including the import of investment goods, depended upon the raising of Western credits whose repayment depended upon the ability of the recipient to boost exports. The GDR's strategy was seriously weakened in the 1980s by the Soviet Union's reduction in deliver- ies of raw materials. This meant that the GDR had to pump ever more resources into maintaining exports, a state of affairs which could not be continued. In an interview with *Der Spiegel* (' "Es reißt mir das Herz kaputt" ', 1991, p. 92), Mittag claimed that by the end of 1987 he had reached the conclusion that every chance had been gambled away and that reunification was inevitable. The continu- ation of the GDR as an independent state would, he reasoned, have eventually ended in economic catastrophe as no further assistance could be expected from the Soviet Union, and leading

SED politicians opposed closer economic cooperation with the West (see Mittag, 1991, p. 297). Whether or not Mittag was a genuine convert to reunification – and there is no hard evidence as yet to suggest that he was – it is undeniable that the failure of the economic modernization strategy and the GDR's slackening competitiveness pushed up the hard-currency debt and the interest repayments. Carl-Heinz Janson, from 1976 to 1989 a member of the key economic commission set up by Mittag, believes that the modernization 'deficit' was the main reason for the economic failure of the GDR. It is his contention that Honecker and Mittag should have reduced state subsidies and imports in order to release resources to modernize the economy instead of attempting to keep the economy afloat on credits and protect the consumer (Janson, 1991, p. 63; Mittag, 1991, p. 297).

The plight of the GDR economy at the end of the Honecker era was laid bare in a series of confidential memoranda which are now available to researchers. One such document was submitted in late September 1989 by five economic experts – the Chairman of the State Planning Commission Gerhard Schürer, the Foreign Trade Minister Gerhard Beil, Alexander Schalck-Golodkowski, the Deputy Finance Minister Herta König and the President of the Foreign Trade Bank Werner Polze. All were members of a special working group concerned with the balance of payments and had at various times warned of the problems arising from the debt mountain. For example, in a letter to Honecker in May 1988, Schürer had fired off a salvo against Mittag's inflated expectations of economic modernization through the rapid diffusion of microelectronics. In their September memorandum Schürer and his colleagues were highly critical of the lack of political will in tackling the burden of the heavy social-policy outlays (Christ and Neubauer, 1991, pp. 58–9; Janson, 1991, pp. 104–5), and they held out little hope of an improvement in the period 1989–95. Even if the GDR were able to restrict imports to the existing level of 12.5 billion VM and to double exports to 24 billion VM – which was, as they themselves recognized, an unrealistic target – the hard-currency debt was still expected to soar from 41.5 billion VM in 1989 to 52.6 billion VM in 1995. The main reason for this increase would be the high annual foreign-credit-raising operations of eight billion to ten billion VM. In 1989 alone, the GDR faced the prospect of an outflow of 5.66 billion VM on interest payments and redemptions on its foreign debts, a figure which was expected to rise to 8.7 billion VM in 1995. As the GDR was so heavily dependent on Japanese, West German and other foreign creditors, Schürer and his colleagues were extremely concerned lest the International Monetary Fund became involved in any debt-rescheduling process. Believing that the solvency of the Republic was the decisive prerequisite for political stability and economic development, they advocated a new export drive to the non-socialist area, based on manufactures, and cuts in state subsidies and in private consumption ('DDR schon 1989 "von kapitalistischen Kreditgebern abhängig" ', 1990, p. 4).

In a memorandum which Schürer, Schalck-Golodkowski and colleagues prepared for Krenz one month later (Hertle, 1992b, pp. 1023–5), the tone was even more pessimistic: the estimated hard-currency indebtedness in 1990 was revised upwards to about 57 billion VM; the costs and interest arising from servicing this debt would be between 8 and 10 billion VM; and if the rise in the debt could not be halted, 30 billion marks in domestic product would have to be utilized, that is, a sum equivalent to the planned growth of national income for three years. Although they believed that the situation called for a drastic reduction in consumption by 25 to 30 per cent, they rejected this course of action as it would destabilize the GDR. Since intervention by the IMF was also regarded as undesirable, for political as well as financial reasons, the group suggested various changes in economic policy such as the strengthening of the role of productive accumulation, especially in the export-orientated industries. But in view of the seriousness of the situation, it was recognized that the GDR would have to go cap in hand to Bonn for an additional credit line of DM2 to 3 billion. While the experts ruled out German reunification or a confede-ration as the price for this assistance, they proposed as bait the opening of the Berlin Wall or, as the memorandum put it, the creation of conditions which would make the present border 'superfluous'. The Politbüro discussed the report on 31 October, but it ignored the latter suggestion (see Schürer's comments in ' "Das reale Bild war eben katastrophal!" ' 1992, p. 1036).

Armed with this information, Krenz, in his meeting with Gorbachev on 1 November 1989, was able to acquaint the Soviet leader with the extent of the economic disaster, Gorbachev, deeply perturbed and astonished at the seriousness of the situation, was unable to offer any Soviet assistance given the Soviet Union's own economic malaise (Hertle, 1992b, p. 1027). The GDR was fast running out of options – and time.

In view of the country's hard-currency difficulties, it is perhaps not surprising that Honecker had recourse to extraordinary measures outside the planning process and the state system. The vast KoKo (*Kommerzielle Koordinierung*) empire of Schalck-Golodkowski, who was also a Stasi officer with the rank of colonel, was able to raise hard currency for the state budget (about 1.5 – 3 billion marks per year according to Mittag in his *Spiegel* interview (' "Es reißt mir das Herz kaputt" ', 1991, p. 104). The organization was also responsible for the acquisition of spare parts from the West for hard-pressed enterprises, up-to-date Western technology for the combines and semi-luxury items for sale to GDR citizens. The increasing importance of KoKo during the 1980s was testimony to the failure of the planning system to cope with the exigencies of the economic situation. One example is the special account number 628 opened in 1974 with the Deutsche Handelsbank, which was at Honecker's disposal. The balance at the end of 1988 was 2.3 billion marks. It was available as security to ensure the solvency of the GDR and was also used for the purchase of, for example, fruit and vegetables, maize, electronics from Japan and potato imports for the 1979 Xmas festival (Seiffert and Treutwein, 1992, pp. 91–2).

It is difficult to value the assets of such a shadowy and complex organization as KoKo. The Federal Criminal Office, according to a report in the *Süddeutsche Zeitung* on 24 August 1991, put them at DM5O billion (ibid.). Schalck seems to have been yet another of the pessimists among the SED elite. In the 1980s he claims to have come to the conclusion – partly as a result of discussions with his Western contacts such as Strauß and partly on account of the advent of Gorbachev – that only Bonn, not Moscow, could guarantee the continuation of the GDR as a separate state (ibid., p. 33).

2.10 The ecological nightmare

In stark contradiction to SED claims that only under socialism could environmental problems be resolved, the ecological situation bordered on the catastrophic in parts of the country, notably the upper valley of the Elbe in the Görlitz area, the industrial regions of Leipzig and Halle, the district around the Schwedt petro-chemical combine, the Erfurt–Arnstadt area and the eastern Erzgebirge. Towns like Bitterfeld were so badly polluted that if the criteria devised by the UNO had been applied, they would have been deemed unfit for habitation. Respiratory problems were 20 per cent higher in the southern industrial regions than in the north of the country (Priewe and Hickel, 1991, p. 44). According to some estimates, in the most heavily polluted areas life expectancy would have been increased by four years if the emissions of sulphur dioxide, dust and ashes had been halved (Dennis, 1988, p. 181).

The pollution nightmare was the result of a combination of factors: the GDR's tight resource situation, its geographical location, the primacy of economic growth over environmental protection, outdated production methods, the wasteful consumption of energy and raw materials, the ruthless application of agro-

Table 2.2 Sulphur dioxide and dust emissions, 1980–8 ('000 tonnes/sq. km)

Year	Sulphur dioxide		Dust	
	'000 tonnes	per sq. km	'000 tonnes	per sq. km
1980	4264.3	39	2456.4	23
1985	5339.7	49	2335.1	22
1986	5358.3	50	2322.7	21
1987	5559.5	51	2335.2	22
1988	5208.7	48	2198.5	20

Source: Institut für Umweltschutz, 1990, p. 9

chemicals and the promotion of the lignite and carbo-chemical industries, partly for reasons of economic autarchy.

Taking air pollution as an example of the nature of the ecological nightmare, the GDR had the highest rate of air pollution in Europe on account of emissions of sulphur dioxide and dust. By the later 1980s, over 5.2 million tonnes of sulphur dioxide and 2.1 million tonnes of dust were emitted into the air each year. Sulphur dioxide emissions per inhabitant were on average about six times higher than in the FRG. The situation deteriorated rapidly during the 1980s (see Table 2.2) because of the decision to increase the production of lignite, which contains a high level of sulphur pollutants, and to process it in obsolescent plant. Works such as Buna, Deuben, Espenhain, Leuna 1 and Böhlen were technologically antiquated, absorbing a high proportion of workers on repairs and should have been closed down many years earlier (Paucke, 1990, p. 153). Dust emissions were particularly critical in the vicinity of older power stations, briquette factories, chemical enterprises and cement factories in the Leipzig, Cottbus and Halle regions (Winkler, 1990, pp. 177–8).

Emissions of sulphur dioxide frequently exceeded the legally permitted standards, especially in the Leipzig, Halle, Chemnitz and Cottbus administrative regions (*Bezirke*). In the GDR as a whole, 21 per cent of citizens were exposed to excessive levels of pollution, 12.8 per cent were heavily exposed and 3.6 per cent very heavily exposed. In addition to endangering its own citizens, the GDR was also a net 'exporter' of pollution: 20 per cent of sulphur-dioxide emissions were 'exported' to neighbouring countries such as Norway, Sweden, Poland, Czechoslovakia and the FRG (Institut für Umweltschutz, 1990, pp. 13, 20).

One extremely serious consequence of atmospheric pollution on this scale was widespread damage to the forests. The deterioration was extremely rapid in the later 1980s: the proportion of forests suffering damage increased from 31.7 per cent in 1987 to 54.3 per cent in 1989. The most severely affected *Bezirke* were Leipzig (75.4 per cent), Magdeburg, Berlin (both 62.8 per cent), Dresden (62.1 per cent) and Frankfurt (59 per cent) (ibid., p. 29, figures relate to 1989).

Although investment in environmental protection rose between 1985 and 1988 from 955.1 million marks to 1,657.1 million (Statistisches Amt der DDR, 1990, p. 146), this was totally inadequate to cope with the environmental damage in the final years of the GDR which, according to one estimate, was running at between 28 and 30 billion marks per year (Kusch *et al*, p. 75). It made a mockery of SED claims that socialism was better equipped than capitalism to plan the rational utilization of resources and a gradual reduction in environmental damage. Like neighbouring Czechoslovakia, the GDR effectively borrowed against its own future by neglecting infrastructural and environmental investment (Batt, 1991, p. 19). Environmental degradation and the social malaise in the south of the GDR undoubtedly contributed to the generation of the popular unrest which exploded on the streets of Leipzig, Halle, Dresden, Berlin and Erfurt in the autumn of 1989.

2.11 Denouement

Dissatisfaction with economic, environmental, social and political conditions fed the emigration movement in the 1980s. About 35,000 East Germans had been permitted by the authorities to leave in 1984, and legal emigration fluctuated between 11,459 in 1987 and 27,939 in 1988. Unauthorized flight ranged from 3,614 in 1983 to 11,893 in 1988 (Wendt, 1991, p. 390). The authorities sought to defuse the emigration issue by a sharp increase in the number of short visits to the West. In 1988, 1.3 million East Germans of nonpensionable age, in addition to approximately 1.5 million pensioners, were allowed to pay a short visit to the FRG and West Berlin.

However, this proved to be an inadequate countermeasure once Hungary began to dismantle the Iron Curtain. The trickle of East Germans fleeing to the West after the barbed wire of the Iron Curtain was cut in May 1989 turned into a flood when, on 10 September, the Hungarian government suspended its bilateral visa agreement with the GDR. Within three days of the decision as many as 15,000 East Germans fled to the West. By the time the Berlin Wall came down on 9–10 November, over a quarter of a million East Germans had left their country, either illegally or with official permission. The mass defections catalysed opposition within the GDR, whether as popular demonstrations on the streets of Dresden, Leipzig and Berlin or as organized opposition movements such as New Forum and Democracy Now. This catalyst function of the *émigrés* entitles them in the opinion of erstwhile GDR writers to the title of the 'first children of the revolution' (Maron, 1991, p. 40) and to the claim to be 'the actual motors of all societal change in the GDR' (Schneider, 1990, p. 29).

While this kind of argument understates the contribution of the citizens-rights movements to the undermining of the SED system, it does nevertheless highlight the crucial importance of what Jens Reich called 'the emotional frenzy which gripped the country' (Reich, in Prins, 1990, p. 71), encouraging people like Reich himself to come out into the open.

The mass emigration was a vivid demonstration of the alienation of so many young and skilled workers from state socialism. The internal material of the Central Institute for Youth Research in Leipzig shows that the appeal of socialism was falling rapidly during the later 1980s. Asked to indicate the depth of their commitment to the GDR, 51 per cent of a sample of apprentices indicated in 1985 that this was strong, whereas in October 1988 the percentage had fallen to 18. The 6 per cent who had replied on the earlier occasion that they were hardly committed to the GDR had risen to 28 per cent three years later (Förster and Roski, 1990, p. 39).

The declared motives propelling tens of thousands to leave their country at considerable personal risk were, according to West German researchers, similar to those in 1984, with political considerations such as 'lack of freedom to express one's own opinion' and 'limited opportunities to travel to other countries' narrowly outweighing material factors such as the consumer supply situation (see Hilmer and Köhler, 1989, p. 1385). However, as Peter Schneider has remarked, these *émigrés* were 'not the wretched of the earth' but a 'new type of refugee', a relatively well-off refugee, most of whom had left behind a job and an apartment (Schneider, 1992, p. 14).

The *émigrés* did, of course, have many economic grievances. The files of the Ministry of State Security make this quite clear. In a document dated 9 September 1989, ministry officials listed the major factors behind emigration as: widespread dissatisfaction with the quality, range and quantity of consumer goods; the inadequacies of the service sector; the deficiencies in the health service; limited opportunities for foreign travel; unsatisfactory working conditions and discontinuities in the production process; inadequate material incentives to improve work performance, particularly at a time of rising prices; the bureaucratic obstructionism of managers and functionaries; and the artificiality and sheer monotony of the mass media. Other factors mentioned in the report were people's serious doubts about the future of the socialist system and the desire to rejoin family members in the West. Escaping to the West would, it was hoped, lead to a higher wage, a higher standard of living and greater opportunities to achieve personal goals (Mitter and Wolle, 1990, pp. 141–7). Suggestions by Stasi generals at a meeting with Mielke, at the end of August 1989, that an improvement in the consumer-supply situation and a vigorous propaganda campaign be implemented to combat the mass disaffection was greeted with anger and incomprehension by Mielke, whose ascetic values, at least as far as the masses' needs were concerned, were conditioned by his memories of social deprivation in the 1930s. In his view, real existing socialism satisfied people's basic wants:

Why, so they acknowledge the advantages of socialism and all the advantages that socialism has to offer, but despite this they want out, because they take all this for granted and disregard it all, and put forward all possible reasons for wanting out. [quoted in Popplewell, 1992, p. 57]

Mielke's solution, further coercion and the more active deployment of informers, together with his total insensitivity to popular grievances, was indicative of a loss of touch with reality and the political bankruptcy of Honecker and the older members of the Politburo.

The considerably different weighting given to political factors between the West German investigations and the Stasi materials deserves comment. The preponderance of economic concerns behind emigration in the Stasi documents may well reflect, in view of the sensitivity of a politically-based rejection of the GDR political system, a degree of thought filtering by the Stasi analysts and of a deliberate underplaying of the political aspect by applicants for emigration from the GDR. On the other hand, the responses of GDR *émigrés* to the FRG researchers may have been determined, in part, by the knowledge that FRG legal regulations provided victims of political persecution with a claim for greater assistance than was available for 'economic' refugees (Ulrich, 1990, pp. 16–17). Whatever the fine distinction between economic and political motives and whatever the differences according to age, level of qualification, region and gender (for details, see Torpey, 1992, pp. 25–31), it is quite apparent that while the GDR had managed to provide its citizens with a reasonable standard of living, it could not fulfil expectations raised by comparisons with West Germany and its citizens' aspiration to a life in which they would be subjected to less political control. The pull factors were thus both political and economic.

3 German Economic, Monetary and Social Union

3.1 Economic problems after Honecker's fall

The demographic haemorrhage was not stemmed by the decision of Krenz and his advisers to open the Berlin Wall in a last-ditch attempt to salvage something from the wreck of the old SED regime. By the end of 1989, total emigration amounted to 340,000, including about 225,000 gainfully employed persons. And about 2,000 East Germans were leaving daily in late January and early February 1990, thereby continuing the process of depleting the country of a disproportionate number of young, highly skilled workers and causing disruption to the production process as well as to the health and construction sectors.

Responsibility for stabilizing the economy and reconstructing the GDR after the departure of Honecker fell to his successor as General Secretary, Egon Krenz, and Hans Modrow, the First Secretary of the SED's Dresden regional organization, who replaced Willy Stoph as Minister President on 13 November. Krenz was too tainted by his past as a loyal SED apparatchik in charge of the Central Committee's security, youth and sport department ever to become a credible reformer. Modrow, on the other hand, had been known to be sympathetic to a reform of the socialist system, one of the reasons why a suspicious Honecker and Mittag had kept him at arm's length in the provinces. The moderate and hard-working Modrow was more to the taste of reformers in the Kremlin, and for a short while he was able to shift the orientation of power towards the Council of Ministers.

The chronic state of the economy allowed Modrow little room for manoeuvre and was a crucial factor in the ultimate collapse of his aspirations to restructure the traditional economic mechanism. The official 1989 economic report, which was published in January 1990, revealed the seriousness of the economic situation. National income was 4 billion marks below target, and in December industry was suffering losses of 80 million marks per day. Christa

Luft, the SED politician responsible for economic affairs in the government, added to the gloom by revealing a gross hard-currency debt of $20.6 billion. As January came to a close, strikes and slow-downs were disrupting production, demands for wage and benefit increases of up to 40 billion marks were putting firms in jeopardy, and the true extent of the pollution nightmare was becoming public knowledge.

3.2 The debate on a socialist renewal

For GDR economists the main question before Honecker's political demise was how to make the central-planning system more efficient. As part of the preparations for the Twelfth SED Party Congress scheduled for May 1990, critical questions were raised internally about the role of the combine, the performance principle and the system of balances. Ideas on reform fell on stony political ground (Christa Luft, 1991, pp. 33–6, 40–2, 87–92). It was not until Modrow's appointment as Minister President that the reform discussion became public. The debate ranged over issues such as the creation of greater autonomy for the enterprises, the introduction of a diversity of ownership forms, the encouragement of competition, the linkage between wages and performance, the enhancement of the role of the market and a more flexible response of firms to customer needs (Bryson and Melzer, 1990, pp. 95–9).

Among the active participants in the reform debate were New Forum, Democracy Now (DJ) and the other small citizens' movements which had emerged from the chrysalis of civil society during the autumn of 1989 and had rapidly become a vehicle of popular opposition to SED rule. Their early pronouncements were replete with references to the need for a combination of market and socialist elements within an independent, reformed GDR. Their allergy to the West German economic and political model was determined primarily by their ideological and political roots among the alternative, peace, gay, women's and human-rights groups. Within this countercultural network, criticism had been levelled at the misplaced faith, whether in socialism or capitalism, in the benefits of science and technology and in the prioritization of material needs over spiritual–cultural values. With the SED in its reformed guise as the SED–PDS also propagating the concept of a third way between what Gregor Gysi called administrative–centralistic socialism and the rule of transnational monopolies, it appeared for a few weeks that the GDR might become the testing ground for the development of a socialist market economy.

In its 'Appeal for Intervening in our own Affairs' of 12

September 1989, DJ called for an end to the 'politbureaucratic command economy' and for the replacement of state planning dirigism by state framework planning. It wanted the role of the state to be confined to supervisory and steering functions, and it sought greater economic independence for firms and associations, with supply and prices orientated towards the market. Other proposals included the right of co-determination for trade unions and the authorization of a variety of ownership forms ('Thesen für eine demokratische Umgestaltung in der DDR', in Rein, 1990, pp. 63–4).

Democratic Awakening (DA), which only a few months later, in February 1990, aligned itself with the East German-CDU in Chancellor Kohl's hastily assembled election vehicle, the Alliance for Germany, adopted a pronounced socialist orientation in its public statements in October 1989. In its provisional Basic Declaration, it advocated an economic plan as the general framework for economic activity. While the instruments of the market were to be utilized in order to encourage self-responsibility, the state was expected to protect the vulnerable members of society and to reduce environmental damage. Further demands covered the discarding of the SED's notion of social ownership of the means of production and the restriction of public ownership to large-scale industry with enterprise co-determination and/or forms of self-administration. Finally, small-scale industry and the service sector were to be reorganized on a cooperative or private basis ('Vorläufige Grundsatzerklärung', ibid., p. 44).

The SDP (Social Democratic Party in the GDR), too, wanted a democratization of the economy, for example, by means of co-determination in the enterprises and, like all the other newly emerging groups, insisted upon 'an ecologically responsible policy'. Private ownership was to be recognized alongside state and cooperative forms. One distinguishing feature of the SDP during the early stage of the *Wende* was that it was the first of the new movements to accept the principle of a social market economy, even though its programme was short on specifics (see the documentation in ibid., pp. 86–8, 91).

By contrast, the United Left, which had its origins in a small group called Gegenstimmen founded in East Berlin in 1986 by left-wing and Marxist-orientated members of various Church and autonomous groups, was a determined advocate of a socialist GDR with an anti-fascist, anti-Stalinist and anti-capitalist face. Its 'Appeal' of September 1989 constituted a rich mixture of central planning and grass-roots democracy: the implementation of public ownership of the main means of production through worker co-determination and self-management; the development of cooperative and private ownership on the basis of people's own work; and the implementation of framework plans by means of state orders based on preferential contracts and by the operation of economic levers such as credits, prices and customs duties ('Mindestanforderungen', ibid., pp. 110–11). Whereas the DA and the SDP eventually moved into the orbit of the West German party system and favoured the adoption of the Federal Republic's economic system, the United Left doggedly refused to dilute its socialist principles.

The largest citizens' movement during the autumn of 1989, New Forum, at first made little contribution to the economic-reform debate except to express its sympathy for a system which fostered economic initiative without at the same time degenerating into a West German 'elbow society'. However, in keeping with its grassroots democratic structure, it set up working groups to consider ideas on economic reform and environmental protection. In late November, the New Forum group in Berlin–Pankow convened a major international conference to explore the possibilities for an economic reconstruction of the GDR. At the conference, the Berlin–Pankow working group for economic affairs submitted a plan for the 'creation of a socialist market economy which includes private initiative' (*NEUES FORUM*, 1990, pp. 11–15). The key plank in its socialist proposals was the social ownership of all enterprises with a labour force of over 300, guaranteed by the state's retention of 51 per cent of the shares, which would be made inalienable. Enterprises with fewer than 300 workers would be converted into cooperative or private firms. The working group recommended the gradual convertibilty of the GDR mark and the determination of prices by the enterprises themselves. State planning of the economy was to be curtailed, its areas of activity being restricted to the state budget and to the large concerns and banks. Guarantees of the right to work were demanded, and in the event of temporary, structural unemployment, assistance, instead of unemployment benefit, would be paid to those who were willing to undertake retraining. Rent increases were to be curbed by regulations issued by local representative assemblies and income support was to be provided as compensation for the removal of subsidies for basic consumer goods. The thrust of the proposals of the citizens' groups was towards a combination of selected market mechanisms with 'socialist-type' guarantees for jobs and the dimunition of the state's economic steering functions. However, at such an early stage in the debate the proposals inevitably lacked precision in many key areas, for example in price determination, and the citizens' groups nurtured in the niches of GDR society lacked the political weight and experience to implement their broader goals. Their aspiration to devise a socialist platform for a reformed GDR soon collapsed under the popular pressure for rapid unification and economic union with the FRG.

3.3 The Modrow reform programme

Meanwhile, the task of stabilizing the economy and devising an economic reform package fell on the shoulders of the SED Minister President, Hans Modrow. In his first governmental policy statement on 17 November 1989 Modrow declared:

. . . there is a need for economic reform which must aim at increasing the autonomy of economic entities in order to substantially increase the efficiency of their operations, at reducing central economic management and planning to the required reasonable level and – what is probably the most difficult task – at ensuring that the principle of pay according to performance is increasingly enforced. [*Foreign Affairs Bulletin*, 27 November 1989, p. 251]

Economic reform, Modrow insisted, did not entail the abolition of planning, but he accepted that the market – with its commodity/money relations – must become an organic element of the planned socialist economy. In order to free the economy of the fetters of centralized planning bureaucracy, he proposed that factories be given a new status in the economic system so that they would be able 'to unfold as socialist producers to the fullest reach, to exercise their responsibility on the market without restraint and to implement the principle of cost accounting everywhere' (p. 254). The democratization of planning meant a new character and new role for planning at central level:

Central planning should focus on ensuring well-balanced national economic proportions and interlacings, an effective national economic structure of production based on a growing division of labour, the preparation of long-term strategies for our country's economic and social development in accordance with ecological requirements . . . The system of balances has to be rid of its administrative function and to be given back its original role, viz, finding, preparing and supporting proportionate and rational solutions for the contractual cooperation of our economic units. [ibid., p. 254]

Other changes were to encompass the redefinition of money, finance and credit relations, as well as price fixing. Prices would have to reflect economically rational inputs and encourage cost cutting. There was to be no delay in 'the reduction of the all too large number of plan indicators and the inflated system of reporting, as well as the abolition of the many forms to be filled in by researchers and designers' (p. 255).

While Modrow insisted in his policy statement on the notion of a 'socialist planned economy', he modified his position in his address, in December, to combine directors and other economic leaders when he urged that 'we must break radically with the previous command system of the economy' (*Foreign Affairs Bulletin*, 29 December 1989, p. 270) and that 'the cardinal problem will be to give rise in our economy to an efficient and well-functioning market' (p. 271). Yet he was far from taking the plunge into the deep waters of the market economy: 'cutting the umbilical chord that connects us with the old structures must not be so absolute as to lead to economic chaos' (p. 270). Two months earlier, this would have constituted a dramatic break with the existing socialist system; but with the West German model becoming a feasible alternative, its appeal was considerably diminished.

Ultimately, on the basis of reform ideas submitted by eleven working groups set up by the government, the Council of Ministers produced an overall reform concept in late January. The goal was defined as the radical and rapid transition from the command economy of centralistic directive planning to a social and ecologically orientated market economy whose legal framework would be set by the state. A diversity of ownership forms was envisaged – state, cooperative, communal and private – along with complete freedom of trade. The green light was given to firms to accept foreign investment and it was intended to enhance enterprise autonomy in fields such as research and market strategies, foreign trade and wages. Eight combines, including NARVA and Schwarze Pumpe, were singled out as laboratories for testing the new independence to be granted to the economic units. In addition, 1990 was to witness a 'radical reduction' in state targets, in particular the material, equipment and consumer goods (MAK) balances and the compulsory planning indicators. Other proposals included the adjustment of domestic prices to world prices, the development of an independent state bank, the creation of business banks, the abolition of the state's monopoly over foreign trade and the gradual convertibility of the GDR mark. As the transition to a social market economy was expected to be attended by inflationary risks, appreciable labour rationalization, the removal of subsidies for retail prices and a host of social problems, it was planned to reconstruct the social-security system in order to protect disadvantaged groups. The transition to the social and ecologically orientated market economy within the framework of state regulations was to take place within carefully defined chronological stages and to be completed in 1993 (see Arbeitsgruppe Wirtschaftsreform beim Ministerrat der DDR, 1990).

The reform concept was discussed on 5 February by the Central Round Table, a body formed from the new political movements and the established parties. While the Round Table welcomed the reforms, it was anxious for the inclusion of more comprehensive measures for retraining workers and for social insurance. It also insisted on the rapid introduction of legal regulations concerning joint ventures, freedom of trade and the equality of all ownership forms and it called upon the GDR government to enter into discussions with the FRG on a monetary association between the two states (Herles and Rose, 1990, pp. 107–10).

Some of the ideas floated in the various reform concepts were implemented between January and the Volkskammer election in March 1990. Legislation authorized freedom of trades, private enterprises and joint ventures. An independent central bank was created with the power to establish commercial banks, and a social cushion was introduced in the form of unemployment benefit of up to 500 marks per month (Bryson and Melzer, 1990, pp. 118–20). Although these and other measures marked a start to the difficult transition to a market economy, the Modrow government's underlying reservations about a radical break with the socialist past can be seen in the legislation on joint ventures. West German entrepreneurs were highly critical of the ceiling of 49 per cent ownership imposed on Western investors, unless the GDR's economic interests dictated otherwise.

West German assistance was obviously crucial to the transformation of the GDR economy. Considerable aid was promised by Bonn for the modernization of production and infrastructure, and a DM3 billion fund was created in January as a replacement for the 'welcome money' previously paid to GDR visitors to West Germany. Bonn, however, refused to supply massive direct aid to prop up the socialist-dominated government, even though it broadened its membership by enlisting eight ministers without portfolio from the ranks of New Forum, DJ and other opposition groups. The new groups shared in Modrow's humiliating experience when on the occasion of a GDR delegation's visit to Bonn on 13–14 February Kohl harshly rejected a GDR request for between DM10 and DM15 billion solidarity aid (Christa Luft, 1991, pp. 160–74). By this date, the momentous decision had been taken by Kohl to offer monetary and economic union to the GDR.

If one considers the case for an autonomous GDR government pursuing its own reform course, then in all probability it would have been on the basis of a free-market economy with a variety of ownership forms rather than in the form of a new socialist experiment. It would, however, have undoubtedly been a difficult and perilous road, and West German levels of prosperity might have remained as elusive a goal as ever, as can be seen from the following calculations. In 1989, the GDR's per capita GDP was roughly equivalent to that of the FRG a quarter of a century earlier. Given a doubling of GDP in the Federal Republic and a quadrupling of that of the GDR between 1990 and 2040, the GDR might have been able to raise its per capita GDP from 30 per cent to 58 per cent of West Germany's. Yet even this relatively modest achievement would have entailed enormous sacrifices from the GDR consumer as the investment of about 30 per cent of GNP would have been necessary. Thus for many years, East German citizens would have had to live more modestly than before the *Wende* (Meigel, 1992, pp. 84–5). The political, psychological and socioeconomic preconditions for such a course, never plentiful, were rapidly eroded as the defects of the old system became ever more transparent and prompted East Germans to look for outside solutions.

Economic dislocation, the Modrow government's hesitant steps towards economic reform, the collapse of the SED/PDS in the face of revelations about corruption in high circles and the environmental disaster and bitterness over the unveiling of the extent of the political repression by the Stasi all contributed to a sea-change in the GDR internal debate on political and economic reform. Advocates of economic experiment, including a reformed version of socialism, found little response among broad sections of the GDR population so long accustomed to the FRG as their reference model. Rapid unification was a more appealing route to West German levels of prosperity than a gradual transformation of the socialist system. The proponents of rapid monetary and economic union, notably the East German CDU and its allies the DSU and DA in the Alliance for Germany, seemed to provide a more promising outcome than that offered by the citizens' movements and the PDS, especially as the Alliance could count on the support of its patron, the West German Chancellor.

3.4 The Chancellor's offer

Kohl's offer of a rapid economic and monetary union to the GDR caught most politicians and economists by surprise, although the idea of a monetary union had been outlined in the columns of *Die Zeit* on 19 January by the SPD financial expert Ingrid Matthäus-Maier on the grounds that it would give East Germans a signal of hope for a rapid economic improvement and encourage them to stay at home. The idea encountered widespread criticism, Finance Minister Theo Waigel retorting that it was not possible simply to cover an economy with a monetary overcoat (Christ and Neubauer, 1991, p. 68).

The notion of a gradual transition to the market system with monetary union well along this road had been the consensus among politicians and economists before Kohl's surprising move. In a programme unveiled on 8 February, the then West German Economics Minister, Helmut Haussmann, laid out a three-stage process towards the completion of full monetary union by the end of 1992. Fundamental economic reform, to be implemented in the first stage, was to encompass the introduction of private owner-ship of the means of production, the gradual easing of wage and price controls and the devising of a realistic rate of exchange for the GDR mark. Leading Bundesbank representatives such as the President, Karl Otto Pöhl, and the Deputy President, Helmut Schlesinger, believed that the enormous difficulties inherent in the transition to a market economy made rapid monetary union an unrealistic aim: monetary union, in their view, should be the culmination of the reconstruction of the GDR economy. Proposals for a quick move towards monetary union were dismissed by Pöhl as 'fantastical'.

Much to Pöhl's embarassment the evolutionary path was aban-doned at a Cabinet meeting on 7 February, when Chancellor Kohl, with one eye on stemming the mass influx of East Germans into the FRG and the other on the political kudos to be earned as the architect of unification, offered East Berlin immediate talks on monetary union. With East Germans pouring across the border at over 2,000 per day since the beginning of the year, the citizens of the GDR had literally been following the demand of the demon-strators in Leipzig and many other cities that: 'If the D-Mark comes to us, we will stay; if it does not, we will go to it.' The psychological boost of the offer of the hard D-Mark was Kohl's response to this enormous popular pressure within the GDR. With the GDR's economy continuing to deteriorate and Modrow's political base eroding rapidly, monetary union was justified as the best way to stabilize the GDR, even though it was recognized that vast transfer payments would be required during the transition (Teltschik, 1991, pp. 125–31). Slowing down the flow of *émigrés* had the important advantage of relieving the strain on the West German social secur-ity system and the housing market.

With Gorbachev, at the end of January, having declared his willingness to accept gradual unification 'in principle' and with Modrow having crossed the national Rubicon soon after, Kohl's offer of rapid monetary union was determined by his wish to take immediate advantage of the open window of political opportunity. He could perhaps reason that the coolness among some Western governments to the prospect of German unification (see section 7.5) and a less receptive successor to Gorbachev might lead to delays and procrastination, even to a closing of the window. And perhaps Kohl recalled Gorbachev's words: 'He who comes too late is punished by life itself.'

The embattled GDR premier had little option but to accept, on 13 February, the invitation to start discussions; a joint commission responsible for drafting the legislative framework for rapid economic and monetary union started work one week later. Events were moving too fast for implementing Christa Luft's idea of a referendum on monetary union (Christa Luft, 1991, p. 55). The countdown had begun not only for the socialist economy but also, with the impending loss of control over fiscal policy, for the end of an independent GDR.

3.5 Monetary union: for and against

The advocates of rapid monetary union, while not oblivious to the numerous transitional problems, believed that a shock therapy had many advantages: no procrastination by the GDR government over such vital issues as freedom of trade and privatization; the surrender by the old SED political cadres and managers of their control over the enterprises; and an encouragement for West German companies to participate in the restructuring of the GDR economy. Furthermore, the introduction of the D-Mark was expected to prevent the development of a flourishing black market and give the East Germans the incentive to remain at home. In short, it was hoped to minimize 'time-consuming administrative controversies over minor details of reform proposals and to avoid half-baked measures and politically counterproductive compromises' (OECD, 1990, p. 48).

On the other hand, without underestimating the need for urgent action, critics of rapid monetary union warned that a sudden confrontation with the pressures of competition on the world markets would lead to the precipitous collapse of the many uncompetitive GDR enterprises and consequently a high level of unemployment and a corresponding burden on the social-security network. One of the most authoritative critiques was delivered by the Council of Economic Experts (Sachverständigenrat), the 'five wise men' who since 1963 have advised the Federal government on macroeconomic developments. In a letter to Kohl on 9 February, they argued that rapid monetary union was the wrong method for stemming the stream of *émigrés*. The way ahead lay in comprehensive reform, including rapid price reform, the full convertibility of the GDR mark in the not-too-distant future, freedom of trade and the adaptation of the GDR banking and credit system to the conditions of the market economy. While monetary union was not regarded as necessarily the culmination of this process, the experts advised strongly against placing it at the beginning (*Jahresgutachten 1990–1*, 1990, pp. 306–8).

The Council anticipated a host of problems from the quick route. As a common currency would not rapidly close the gap in incomes and productivity, pressure would arise for a swift equalization of West and East German wages. Nominal wages were likely to rise more quickly than productivity, to the disadvantage of production in the GDR. East German consumers, equipped with D-Marks, would turn to West German goods, thus precipitating a fall in production and productivity. The pressure on the West German government to close the gap in wages and pensions would lead to vast financial flows from West to East, primarily for consumption rather than for structural investment. The consequence would be tax increases and an immense drain on the public sector budgets (ibid., pp. 306–7).

The Council's pessimism was shared by authoritative figures. The President of the German Institute for Economic Research in West Berlin, Lutz Hoffman, feared that rapid economic and monetary union would complicate economic recovery and be extremely costly; not only would billions of D-Marks be required for the payment of benefit to between 2.5 and 3.0 million unemployed but also subsidies would be essential for propping up non-competitive firms (Christ and Neubauer, 1991, pp. 72–3).

Within the GDR itself, warnings against overhaste came from many quarters. At the Central Round Table session on 5 February, Christa Luft predicted widespread bankruptcies in industry and agriculture, high unemployment and social conflict (Christa Luft, 1991, p. 189). Her worry about social dislocation was shared by the political parties and citizens' groups represented on the Central Round Table. A Social Charter, approved at the Round Table's fifteenth session on 5 March, was intended to codify the GDR's fundamental interests and to be used as a lever by the GDR government in the negotiations on economic, monetary and social union. The Charter spelled out a list of key principles: the right to work, the right to a decent dwelling, the right of co-determination in all firms, equality of the sexes at work and in the family and the right to social insurance. It appealed for as high a level of employment as possible, the retention of the GDR's extensive network of pre-school institutions, state control over rents and a health-care system independent of income and social status (Herles and Rose, 1990, pp. 238–47). One basic flaw lay in the failure to show how the Charter's recommendations, many of them emanating from the social system of 'real existing socialism', could be financed and sustained under a fundamentally different political and economic order.

A powerful argument against the gradual approach was advanced by the eminent CDU politician and later premier of Saxony, Professor Kurt Biedenkopf. Believing that a GDR government would lack the experience and the popular support to implement the necessary legal, financial, administrative and economic arrangements for the introduction of a social market economy, he advocated the rapid introduction of the D-Mark as the prerequisite of socio-economic restructuring, not as the culmination of a reform programme (Biedenkopf, 1990, p. 11). Biedenkopf emphasized that the GDR, unlike Poland, Czechoslovakia and Hungary, had an open border with the FRG, a country which so many GDR citizens had adopted as their frame of reference. The German–German border could not be closed whenever it became necessary to protect the reform process in the GDR; and in the meantime the mass emigration was seriously destabilizing the GDR economy. The D-Mark had virtually become the GDR's second currency, a fact which was creating a two-class society with all the attendant social and political tensions.

The way out of this impasse, though not without considerable risk, was the introduction of the hard D-Mark. Biedenkopf (ibid., pp. 20–2) sketched the advantages of such a course as:

— better economic prospects would encourage East Germans to remain at home;
— work and performance would become more rewarding and motivation would be enhanced;
— investments would not be impeded by currency barriers and firms could participate in the all-German division of labour;
— the establishment of a capital market would be followed by flows of private capital for the modernization of the GDR capital stock;
— and the productivity of GDR firms would receive a powerful boost from the infusion of relatively modest capital investment.

Biedenkopf was sufficently realistic as to anticipate serious adjustment problems, in particular relatively high unemployment and the collapse of the many firms which would be unable to cope with the transition from the highly protected trading relations in COMECON to the competitive conditions prevailing on the open world markets. Nevertheless, he was optimistic that a high rate of economic growth, of between 8 and 10 per cent, would be triggered off by the emergence of a new *Mittelstand* of small and medium-sized firms, by the rapid increase in productivity through higher outside investment and by the improvement of consumer supply. The GDR economy, he concluded, could be restored to its existing level within two to three years.

The great discrepancy between West and East German wages and salaries was particularly worrying as Biedenkopf doubted whether GDR citizens would tolerate for long an average gap in living standards of 100:40. As West German experience suggested that a gap in living standards of 100:66 did not lead to emigration, Biedenkopf advocated narrowing the gap to this kind of level by such measures as relief from direct taxes on business income and by social contributions. Biedenkopf envisaged that this support, as well as assistance for regional infrastructure programmes, would constitute West Germany's main contribution to the reconstruction of the GDR. Although no accurate forecast of the total unification bill could be made, Biedenkopf anticipated that it would not exceed the average growth in West German GNP in recent years. In the belief that these rates of growth would be achieved in East and West Germany, Biedenkopf expected that reconstruction would cease to be a burden within a few years (ibid., pp. 30–1). While the West German public authorities would necessarily be heavily engaged in the transformation process, Biedenkopf predicted that most of the investment capital would come from private sources.

In general, the advocates of rapid monetary union were located among the economic policy experts rather than among the academic economists. At first very much in the minority, they were essentially what Otto Singer dubbed those of 'an institutionalist orientation'. They included in their ranks the economic research institute of the West German Confederation of Business, the Institute of the German Economy, and the former Economics Minister Karl Schiller. One day after the introduction of monetary union, the latter argued, in the pages of the *Financial Times*, that the GDR '. . . must throw off centralised planning to make way for the market economy, involving a shift to economic specialisation and the entry of modern technology. Many people will inevitably be put out of work. But they will be re-employed as new jobs are created' (quoted by Singer, 1992, p. 92). Another leading economist who was converted to the need for rapid GEMSU was Professor Hans Willgerodt. His views led to his departure from the influential Kronberger Kreis, which, like the Council of Experts, opposed rapid monetary union (Willgerodt's arguments are reproduced in document 2).

Ranged against Schiller, Willgerodt and other proponents of monetary union as an initial step towards convergence was a broad coalition which included the Bundesbank, the Council of Economic Experts and the loose coalition of left-orientated economists in the Alternative Economic Policy Working Group. However, Kohl's decision on monetary and economic union defused the criticism of many West German economists and bankers and cut short the debate on a viable alternative. The Confederations of Business and Labour fell into line, and Bundesbank President Pöhl signalled his bank's acquiescence when he remarked at a press conference on 9 February that though surprised by the Chancellor's offer, the Bundesbank would cooperate with the government in the negotiations on monetary union and give its advice on how to minimize the risks. The Bundesbank had bowed to the primacy of politics (Priewe and Hickel, 1991, p. 85).

While the proponents of gradual economic and monetary union undoubtedly possessed a strong economic case, the majority of GDR citizens, though not unaware of the risks for jobs and prices, wanted to take the fast lane with Chancellor Kohl. In a survey conducted shortly before the momentous Volkskammer election in March 1990, 91.1 per cent of respondents were in favour and only 7.6 per cent were opposed to rapid monetary union (Gibowski, 1990, p. 19). Most GDR political parties adjusted to the prevailing political wind. Not only did they quickly surrender their aspiration for a reformed independent GDR but in the case of the parties in the Alliance for Germany preached the virtues of the D-Mark and the rapid implementation of the market economy. Democratic Awakening undertook a rapid journey across the political spectrum; after a sharp internal battle from which the proponents of unification emerged victorious, it swallowed its scruples against association with a former bloc party and on 5 February joined the CDU and the newly formed DSU in the Alliance for Germany. One day later, the party leadership announced 'Never again socialism in Germany' and soon afterwards the then party chairman, Wolfgang Schnur, called for unification via Article 23 of the Basic Law of the Federal Republic (Süß, 1990, p. 17 and Süß, in taz, 1990, p. 144). The DSU, which established itself as a political party in January, with its main base in Saxony and Thuringia, was a fierce adversary of socialism and an enthusiastic supporter of the social-market economy and rapid unification via Article 23 (Hesse, 1990, p. 503). The major force within the Alliance, the East German CDU, had taken the plunge as early as its Special Party Congress on 15–16 December 1989 and opted for German unification, albeit via a confederation as a transitional form, and for the market economy with a social and ecological stamp (Lapp, 1990, p. 65).

The SDP, which had drawn close to its Western counterpart as signalled by its change of name to SPD at its delegates' conference in mid-January, committed itself not only to a united and federal Germany but also to an ecologically responsible and socially orientated market economy little different from that of the FRG. The creation of an economic and monetary association was identified as a task of high priority (Fink, 1990b, p. 185). The East-SPD chairman, Ibrahim Böhme, pleaded, at the party congress at the end of February, for the introduction of the D-Mark by July at the latest. However, Oskar Lafontaine, the prospective West-SPD candidate for Chancellor, was much cooler. He criticized Kohl's 'rush to unity' and warned that the introduction of a social-market economy needed a relatively long period of time before it could come into full effect (Suskind, 1990, p. 3).

New Forum went through a period of intense and agonizing debate as it struggled to adjust to the rapidly changing political and economic climate. Matters came to a head at its founding conference on 27 and 28 January when the left-wing group around the 'Berliners' Bohley, Köppe and Schult found themselves pitted against a right-wing group of delegates, recruited primarily from the south and in favour of the West German economic model (Fink, 1990a, p. 516). The growing influence of the latter group was illustrated by conference rejection of a proposal for factory councils to exercise the right of veto over enterprise management; even the right to employment only narrowly escaped deletion (*Der Fischer Weltalmanach*, 1990, p. 302).

Although New Forum was obliged to abandon some of its earlier idealism and although it was plagued by internal disputes over strategy, it was still able to establish a clear line of demarcation from the Alliance for Germany and to present itself as the defender of what it regarded as the basic interests of the GDR in the unification process. Its acceptance of German unity was qualified by its rejection of rapid unification as well as of an overhasty economic, monetary and social union. It feared that the consequences would be high unemployment, prosperity for a privileged minority, rent racketeering and the legalization of extreme right-wing and neo-fascist organizations. Instead, New Forum supported the gradual drawing together of the two Germanies on the basis of a democratization of the GDR and the stabilization and reform of the GDR economy. That meant guarantees of the right to work, democratic co-determination at work, the legalization of different forms of ownership, freedom of trade and restrictions on the operation of the market mechanism in such vital areas as education, health, the environment, the mass media, science and culture. This policy was encapsulated in the slogan: 'As much market as necessary, as much social security as possible' (Krüger, 1990, p. 8). Equipped with this programme, New Forum formed an electoral pact – Bündnis 90 – with two other citizens' movements, Democracy Now and the IFM on 7 February. Bündnis 90's acceptance of German unification meant that during the election campaign the United Left was the only group to insist on the preservation of the GDR as a separate state and as a socialist alternative to the FRG

3.6 The East German electorate supports Kohl

The campaign of the Alliance for Germany was better fitted to the mood of the East German electorate. Its star campaigner, West German Chancellor Helmut Kohl, sought to allay East German fears of the negative repercussions of German Economic, Monetary and Social Union (GEMSU) by holding out the prospect of rapid economic recovery and prosperity and, five days before the Volkskammer election, by openly backing a one-to-one conversion rate for wages and small savers (Bark and Gress, 1993, p. 724). These were facile promises but they did have the effect of discrediting those who advised caution and also created illusions among East Germans of a relatively smooth transformation from a planned economy to a market system.

The overwhelming victory of the Alliance in the Volkskammer election on 18 March (it scored 48.1 per cent of the vote to the SPD's 21.8 per cent, 16.3 per cent for the PDS and 2.9 per cent for Bündnis 90) was a clear vote for rapid unification and economic union. The citizens' movements clustered together in Bündnis 90 were decisively rejected by the electorate, together with their platform based on gradual assimilation. What was particularly galling for these groups was the relative success of the SED successor party, the PDS, in garnering so many votes among that section of the electorate which harboured fundamental doubts and fears about unification. Voters preferred to put their trust in the Chancellor to bring the GDR out of crisis and to transplant the economic prosperity, political pluralism and social system of the Federal Republic into the GDR. As the holder of the purse strings, Kohl appeared to be a better bet than the SPD, whose campaign gave out too many mixed messages for the voters' comfort.

The SPD appeared to be trying to get the best of both worlds by catering for those who wanted rapid unification and those who wanted to keep some of the positive aspects of the old system, especially the system of social welfare (Donovan, 1990, p. 15). The West German SPD's designated candidate for chancellor in the FRG elections scheduled for later in the year, Oskar Lafontaine, preached the virtues of restraint and moderation to the East Germans. And he warned of five million unemployed in both parts of Germany and vast public transfers from West to East if unification occurred before economic reforms in the GDR came to fruition (see his speech to the Saarland Landtag on 14 March in Schui, 1991, pp. 14–15). Although Lafontaine's prediction proved to be accurate, a vote for Kohl's East German proxies was regarded by the GDR electorate as a vote for a known quantity in a situation of instability. Hence the resonance of the Alliance slogan of 'No more experiments' which proved to be highly ironic in view of what would shortly descend on the GDR. But in the spring it had the advantage of promising an end to socialism, in whatever guise.

Was the decision to introduce rapid economic and monetary union inherently flawed and the root cause of the subsequent collapse of the East German economy? Did a step-by-step process offer a less painful alternative? No definitive answer can be given to these questions. There was no easy solution; both the swift and the gradual roads were attended by risks, uncertainties and pain for all those involved. But against the slower road one can argue that the political preconditions were highly unfavourable as most East Germans, increasingly so after the opening of the Berlin Wall, were manifestly against the survival of a separate GDR state and the old currency. They tended to associate their own mark with the old regime which they wished to remove. The March election results demonstrated clearly that a market-socialist hybrid, even under the reformist Hans Modrow, commanded only minority support. Without the backbone of political legitimacy, it is difficult to see how a separate GDR government could have steered the country through the formidable task of economic, political and social modernization. It could not have been managed, anyway, without vast aid from the FRG, and Bonn was now committed to rapid union. And it should be remembered that the gradual route as part of an autonomous economic–political process would have been beset by enterprise closures, high unemployment, social dislocation, the removal of price subsidies, ownership problems and political controversies over the influence exercised by former state and party functionaries. This would have been extremely difficult for any GDR government to manage and might well have led to the whole reform process losing momentum.

Although the rapid disintegration of the old political structures undermined the whole notion of gradual change under a separate

GDR government, the economic preconditions were also unpropitious for such a course. The open borders would have made it virtually impossible to protect the GDR economy from international competition by means of a fixed exchange rate between the GDR Mark and the D-Mark. There would undoubtedly have been a flight from the GDR mark to the D-Mark, requiring intervention by the Bundesbank and at considerable cost to the FRG. A flexible exchange rate of say 1:5 would have had dire social consequences if West Germans had been able to obtain goods and East German assets at a very low price, while it would have been extremely difficult for GDR enterprises to have obtained Western consumer and investment goods and services. And the location of Berlin would have made it impossible to seal off the GDR other than by some physical barrier (see von Dohnanyi, 1990, p. 148 and Priewe and Hickel, 1991, pp. 88–90).

Under the circumstances, Bonn's decision to opt for rapid monetary and economic union was defensible, at that time, although the political case was more clear-cut than the economic argument. But where Kohl and his government can be criticized is in their underplaying of the scale and magnitude of the problems inherent in the transformation process and in the steamrolling of their policy critics. Kohl should have refrained from inflating East German expectations by promising them a landscape in bloom within five years, especially in the light of the palpable economic plight of the GDR (Bark and Gress, 1993, p. 718). One dilemma for Kohl, anxious to take his place in history as the Chancellor of Unity and to revive the flagging political fortunes of his Christian Democrats in the West, was that an intensive and searching public debate might cost the CDU votes, delay the unification process and introduce elements into the final all-German state which might jeopardize the functioning of what was regarded as a successful West German model. But the most fundamental criticism is that the West German government – and many economists – tended to regard the mechanism of the market as some kind of magic formula which when applied would quickly work a miracle in the GDR. When it soon became apparent that this was not the case and that private investment in the rebuilding of the GDR was sluggish, the Federal government was far too slow in reshaping the original design of GEMSU (see chapters 4 and 6).

3.7 The State Treaty

With the electorate having opted for the fast lane, Kohl had received his mandate for the speedy implementation of economic and monetary union in association with the East German CDU-led coalition government under Lothar de Maizière. The new government wasted little time in pledging itself to rapid monetary union, thus enabling GDR citizens, in de Maizière's words, to go ahead with their summer holidays with D-Marks in their pockets. In late April, the two governments started negotiations on GEMSU. The first State Treaty was signed on 18 May to come into operation on 1 July. Although much of the groundwork had already been prepared before official negotiations began, this was an unusually short time for negotiations and unconducive to a careful assessment of the procedures, complexities and risks inherent in the merger of two such divergent systems. Under these circumstances a merger of equals was out of the question.

While the negotiations on GEMSU were proceeding, analysts attempted to predict the speed with which the benefits of the West German social-market economy would come into operation in the GDR and thus narrow the disparity between the two countries in labour productivity, living standards and output. According to one model, given a GDR labour productivity 40 per cent below that of the Federal Republic, it would take the GDR fifteen, twenty or thirty years to catch up with West Germany if GDR labour productivity grew on average at 8.5 per cent, 6.75 per cent or 5.25 per cent respectively while that of the Federal Republic increased by 2 per cent per annum. These high rates of increase in the GDR would depend upon removing impediments to growth such as overmanning and low motivation and upon the GDR attracting a high level of outside investment (Götz-Coenenberg, 1990, pp. 38–40). Predictions of the impact of GEMSU on employment varied wildly. Some forecast unemployment accelerating rapidly to 3.8 million in 1992 and 1993; by contrast, others anticipated a growth in demand for labour as early as 1991 and a labour shortage of about 3 per cent by the end of the century.

An animated debate centred around the conversion rate of the GDR mark. To a great extent, economists and financial experts were working in the dark as the GDR price system was internally fixed without any reference to international prices, and key data on the true state of the GDR economy were only just coming to light. Various possibilities were discussed on the basis of existing practices: the official 1:1 exchange rate in intra-German trade; the shadow exchange rate used by planners to calculate the profitability of GDR exports; and the exchange rate after the opening of the Wall, which fluctuated between 1:20 and 1:2. But the problem with these rates was that they were unsuitable as a market rate. A conversion rate had thus to be devised which took account of the many conflicting economic, political, monetary and economic interests (see Hesse, in Ghaussy and Schäfer, 1993, pp. 26–40).

Anxious to dampen inflationary tendencies and to reduce the liquidity problems of firms having to pay a burdensome interest in D-Marks on the high level of existing debt of 260 billion marks gross, the Bundesbank proposed two GDR marks to one D-Mark, except for small savings. The Bank also suggested that there should be a wage equalization for the removal of subsidies and for higher social-security contributions. The West German Finance Minister, Theo Waigel, too, favoured a two-to-one conversion rate. The response in the GDR to these proposals was immediate: tens of thousands of demonstrators took to the streets in East Berlin, Leipzig and Halle in protest against what Helga Mausch, chairperson of the FDGB, described as a threat to reduce East German wages to below those of Taiwan.

A simple conversion rate of two-to-one would indeed have decimated wages in the GDR. In 1988, average monthly pay was 1,000 GDR marks gross and 925 GDR marks net, compared to DM3,300 gross and DM2,200 net in the FRG. The advocates of parity argued that a halving of wages would depress motivation and stimulate emigration, especially when price increases started to bite after the removal of consumer price subsidies. It was, of course, recognized that the wage bill would not be the sole determinant of a firm's survival and competitiveness; the quality of products and the productivity of the workforce would have a crucial bearing, too. There was, however, a certain degree of artificiality to the whole debate in that it would ultimately be impossible to maintain such wide disparities in wages and salaries in an open economy.

The savings accounts of East Germans was yet another highly sensitive issue. Between 1980 and 1989, total savings had risen from 99,730 million to 159,671 million GDR marks. Most of the savings were small, 70 per cent being below 5,000 marks. Whereas popular feeling was strongly in favour of parity for all accounts, the main argument advanced against such a proposal was that parity might stimulate an extra purchasing power with inflationary effect, particularly if the East German consumers went on a spending spree.

The final agreement on GEMSU (see document 3), which went into effect on 1 July, represented a compromise between the many diverse interests. Wages, salaries, rents and pensions were converted at one-to-one. The basis for the conversion of wages and salaries was the level of payments as of 1 May 1990. Pensions were raised to 70 per cent of West German levels. As for savings, a conversion rate of one-to-one was allowed for up to 4,000 GDR marks per capita for GDR citizens aged fifteen to fifty-nine and up to 2,000 marks for young people under fifteen years of age. Citizens aged sixty and over were allowed this rate for accounts of up to 6,000 marks.

Financial assets and liabilities were generally converted at a rate of two GDR marks to one D-Mark. This put a heavy debt-service burden on the state-owned enterprise sector. The high level of debt of 260 billion GDR Marks arose primarily from practices in the planning system which made it difficult for enterprises to generate funds for investment on plant and equipment. It was argued, in vain, that the cancellation of this debt or its assumption by the GDR government would improve the liquidity and in some cases ensure the solvency of GDR enterprises (Burda, 1990, p. 8). The situation was compounded by a reduction in the value of assets from the original optimistic estimate to below DM230 billion once it was established that GDR fixed assets did not measure up to West German technical standards. The net indebtedness quota of the enterprises subsequently rose sharply from 18 per cent before GEMSU to 37 per cent afterwards; this burden should have been another reason for devising a way to cancel inherited debt (Alt-vater, in Schulz and Volmer, 1992, pp. 14–16).

As the conversion rate for flows was fixed at parity, the D-Mark became the basis of GDR prices and costs. In consequence, East German products were overpriced literally overnight in relation to West German goods. GDR planners, it should be recalled, had fixed the shadow exchange rate at DM1 to 4.4 GDR marks.

No less important than the monetary aspects of union was the GDR government's agreement to adopt the principles and practices of a social-market economy. In the early stages of negotiations, the de Maizière government sought legislation to protect the weakest branches of industry but was ultimately obliged to accept the West German market-economy package virtually in its entirety: private ownership of the means of production, freedom to choose a profession and to exercise economic activity, the liberalization of trade and capital movements, the introduction of well-defined property rights and the encouragement of a wide variety of small and medium-sized businesses. The GDR was obliged to undertake the rapid implementation of West German environmental standards and regulations. The Bundesbank was empowered to act as the bank of issue of the common currency area. GDR agriculture was enjoined to adopt EC standards, including the introduction of market regulations and adjustment to West German producer prices. However, provision was made for transitional arrangements in sensitive areas, and agricultural subsidies of DM5.3 billion and DM9.1 billion were approved for the second half of 1990 and for 1991 respectively. Finally, the GDR agreed to honour its contractual obligations to the COMECON countries (for details, see document 3).

In the Unification Treaty (document 4), which came into force in October 1990, arrangements were made for the financial provision of the *Länder* and communes. The Federal Republic has a complex financial system according to which tax revenues are distributed among the various levels of government (vertical financial equalization), and the richer *Länder* are obliged to contribute to the revenue of the poorer *Länder* (horizontal financial equalization). In addition, the Federal government pays grants-in-aid to the financially weaker *Länder*. As the addition of the financially impecunious East German *Länder* threatened to disturb this highly complex and politically sensitive mechanism, it was decided to exclude the new *Länder* from the system for a transitional period. The East German communes were granted an annual share of at least 20 per cent of the Land share of total revenue from joint taxes and 40 per cent of the Land share of the German Unity Fund. Furthermore, the new *Länder* were granted an average share of turnover tax per inhabitant and a fixed proportion of the average share per inhabitant in the old *Länder*, rising from 55 per cent in 1991 to 70 per cent in 1994 (see document 4). It soon became apparent that these arrangements for the financial provision of the regional and local authorities left them seriously underresourced.

The economic and monetary aspects of union were buttressed by a third component – stipulations concerning a social union. The GDR was expected to adopt, though with some modifications, the West German labour, trade-union, welfare and tax legislation. Many of the laws relating, for example, to pensions and unemployment were to be introduced gradually.

The unemployment insurance system in the GDR was required from 1 July to conform to the Employment Act of the FRG. This entailed not only the payment of unemployment benefit and assistance but also an active labour-market policy, including vocational training and retraining as well as a more generous application than in the FRG, until mid-1991, of the regulations governing short-time work. The State Treaty stipulated that in the transitional phase the special labour-market situation in the GDR would be taken into account. Social assistance was provided in accordance with the West German Social Assistance Act. The cost, most of which was to be met by the GDR local authorities, was expected to be low at first since most of the unemployed were to be covered for some time under the unemployment system and most pensions were expected to be above the level provided by social assistance. GDR pension law was adapted to the pension insurance law schemes of the FRG. Initial pension levels and future adjustments were to be determined by trends in net wages and salaries in the GDR.

The State Treaty (document 3) made provision to meet some of the anticipated costs of unification. The West German government agreed to contribute DM22 billion for the remainder of 1990 and a further DM35 billion in 1991 to cover the GDR budget deficits. Furthermore, it agreed to payments of DM750 million towards the new pension-insurance scheme and DM2 billion towards unemployment insurance during the second half of 1990. A German Unity Fund of DM115 billion was to be created by the Federal and the *Länder* governments to help finance restructuring until the end of 1993. Savings in the Federal budget were to release DM20 billion, while the remainder would be raised by bonds and other means. Finally, provision was made for DM7 billion for the remainder of 1990 and DM10 billion in 1991 to help enterprises facing closure during the transitional stage.

One of the most contentious issues concerned the privatization of state property. Although private-property rights were identified in the State Treaty as one of the principles on which GEMSU was based, the treaty failed to lay down detailed privatization guidelines. Subsequently, agreement was reached by the two governments on the principles of privatization and the Volkskammer passed the Treuhand Law regulating the privatization and reorganization of state-owned property. The inter-governmental agreement stipulated that expropriations between 1945 and 1949 would not be reversed, but compensation rights would be determined by an all-German government. Second, expropriated or state-administered land and real estate would in principle be returned to the previous owners or their heirs. Compensation, however, was allowed in the event of the land or real estate having been used for other than its original purpose and could not be retained. Third, companies or participations expropriated after 1949 would, in principle, be returned to their previous owners. For companies expropriated between 1949 and 1972, compensation might be paid instead of restoration of property rights. Finally, the GDR was empowered to set up an extrabudgetary fund to finance compensation payments. In view of the problems associated with unresolved ownership questions, it is of interest to note that the de Maizière government favoured the principle of compensation for previous owners in order to speed up investments. This was rejected by Bonn as the Federal government preferred restitution (Sinn and Sinn, 1992, p. 17).

Although the technical aspects of monetary union were admirably managed by the Bundesbank, those responsible for financial policy failed to develop an adequate medium-term concept and to devise effective counter-measures to alleviate the impact of the transformation process. Policy was characterized by a mixture of ignorance of the situation in the GDR, restrictions on public debate, muddling through, market-political dogmatism and a general optimism (Priewe and Hickel, 1991, pp. 97, 117).

Much of the optimism was based on a belief that the situation in the GDR was not too dissimilar from that of West Germany in the immediate post-war period. After all, the western parts of Germany had once, under the Third Reich, been subjected, like the GDR, to a planned economy, and at the end of the Second World War much of West Germany's capital stock had been run down and its infrastructure badly neglected.

Once market forces and monetary union had taken effect, the ex-GDR might, it was reasoned, be blessed by an economic miracle similar to that experienced by the FRG after the currency reform of 1948 (Knop, 1990, pp. 344–5). Unfortunately for East Germany, the situation proved to be different in certain crucial respects. Forty years of socialism had created a completely different social, political, economic and administrative order, whereas under the Third Reich the entrepreneurial spirit had managed to survive, as had many of the old property rights and enterprise structures. Another important difference was that post-1948 West Germany possessed the enormous advantage of a low exchange rate, which enabled it to boost exports while restricting imports; and its level of productivity and prosperity was not significantly different from that of its main trading partners (Flassbeck and Scheremet, in Jesse and Mitter, 1992, p. 287). Furthermore, West German wage increases lagged for a long time behind the high increase in productivity, thereby facilitating economic modernization. With business profits at a high level, the post-war FRG had the capacity to generate an endogenous modernization of its capital stock. East Germany, on the other hand, soon discovered that the conversion rate of the GDR mark denied the economy a protective umbrella, and the peculiar conditions of the labour market pushed wage increases above productivity gains (Gornig, 1992, pp. 2–5; Kröger, in Heisenberg, 1991, pp. 200–1; Schui, 1991, pp. 36–7).

4 *Länder* in gloom

4.1 Overview

The 'big bang' approach to German unification precipitated the collapse of GDR industry and agriculture and triggered off a massive upsurge in unemployment and short-time work. The pessimistic predictions both of the Sachverständigenrat and of GDR citizens' groups such as New Forum were thus realized. So deep was the crisis that a team of American economists deemed it to be 'one of the worst and sharpest economic depressions in European history' (Akerlof *et al.*, 1991, p. 1).

A selection of key data (see Table 4.1 and documents 5 to 8) reveals just how widespread and precipitous the collapse was. On the basis of 1991 prices, it is estimated by the Federal Statistical Office that GDP fell by 28.4 per cent and 34.9 per cent in the third and fourth quarters of 1990 respectively and by a further 31.4 per cent in 1991 (Müller-Krumholz, 1993, p. 71). Within the first two months of monetary union, industrial commodity production dropped by almost 43 per cent, with metallurgy, textiles and the foodstuffs industry experiencing the sharpest fall (Schui, 1991, p. 84). Foreign trade was badly hit: in 1990 imports declined by 44.5 per cent and exports by 7.4 per cent (see Table 4.2). With the economy in free fall, East German workers were confronted with a new problem, structural unemployment. Between May and December 1990, unemployment escalated from 142,098 to 642,182. One year after GEMSU, unemployment stood at 1,068,639 and was only held in check by the deployment of a variety of labour-market policy instruments. Between the autumn of 1989 and the spring of 1992, the number of gainfully employed persons had fallen from about 9.9 million to 6.25 million (Blaschke *et al.*, 1992, p. 121). A further drop to 5.5 million in 1993 cannot be ruled out ('IWH-Gutachten vom Dezember 1992' 1993, p. 2).

The sheer speed of the collapse, though foreseen by some observers, came as a surprise to many others and has generated a heated debate on the relative weight to be assigned to what are regarded as the two main determinants, the meteorite of monetary union and the imperfections inherent in the administrative-

Table 4.1 Creation of gross value in east Germany 1990 to the third quarter of 1992 (in billions of DM at prices in 1991)

	1990				1991				1992*		
	1	2	3	4	1	2	3	4	1	2	3
Agriculture and forestry	1.0	1.0	2.5	−0.4	−0.2	−0.0	2.0	0.7	−0.3	−0.7	1.2
Producing sector	35.1	34.5	23.6	21.2	17.2	16.7	17.5	18.4	16.9	17.5	18.5
Energy and mining	7.1	6.5	5.9	6.5	6.1	4.9	4.9	5.4	4.5	4.2	4.7
Manufacturing	22.3	20.7	10.8	8.3	6.4	6.3	7.0	7.9	7.6	7.6	7.8
Construction	5.7	7.3	7.0	6.4	4.7	5.5	5.6	5.2	4.8	5.7	6.0
Trade and transportation	17.2	15.9	11.3	10.7	7.7	8.4	8.5	9.5	8.0	8.1	8.5
Trade	10.8	10.3	7.6	7.9	5.5	5.7	5.8	6.9	5.3	5.3	5.6
Transportation	6.4	5.6	3.7	2.8	2.2	2.7	2.7	2.6	2.7	2.8	2.9
Services and state	25.9	25.4	21.2	22.9	20.7	23.1	23.9	24.3	24.5	24.9	25.5
Services	11.4	11.1	8.6	9.0	10.2	11.2	11.9	12.1	12.6	12.9	13.7
State (including job creation measures)	14.4	14.3	12.6	13.9	10.5	11.9	12.0	12.2	11.9	12.0	11.8
Private non-profit organizations	0.9	0.9	0.8	0.6	0.6	0.6	0.7	0.8	0.9	0.9	0.9
All economic sectors (not seasonally adjusted)	79.2	76.7	58.6	54.4	45.4	48.2	51.9	52.9	49.9	49.8	53.7

Source: DIW and IfW, 1992c, p. 710

* = 1992 figures provisional

command mechanism. Whereas many governmental agencies and economic institutes emphasize the latter, the so-called 'original sin', there is a tendency to understate the harm caused the patient by Dr Kohl's social-market medicine. To these two main determinants should be added the unexpectedly swift disintegration of COMECON and the consequent loss of so many traditional Soviet and East European customers and, second, the sheer complexity and scale of the unprecedented transition from an administrative-command system to a social-market economy. The interpretation of the Board of Academic Advisors to the Federal Economics Ministry, which includes many of Germany's leading economists, is reproduced in document 9. The Board sees the collapse essentially as the result of the inefficiencies and distortions of the socialist system combined with the problems arising from the changes in the former COMECON.

Table 4.2 East German foreign trade, 1985–91

Year	Imports	Exports	Balance of trade	Change against previous qtr		Change against previous year	
	DMm.			imp.	exp.	imp.	exp.
						%	
1985	41,249	45,693	+4,444				
1986	42,617	42,961	+344			+3.3	−6.0
1987	42,978	41,694	−1284			+0.8	−2.9
1988	41,828	40,152	−1676			−2.7	−3.7
1989	41,142	41,105	−37			−1.6	+2.4
1990	22,852	38,072	+15,221			−44.5	−7.4
1991	11,275	17,961	+6,686			−50.7	−52.8
1991							
1st qtr	3,211	5,038	+1,827	+6.8	49.5	−58.0	−40.3
2nd qtr	2,627	3,430	+802	−18.2	−31.9	−71.4	−66.9
3rd qtr	3,076	4,288	+1,212	+17.1	+25.0	+1.5	−53.8
4th qtr	2,361	5,206	+2,845	−23.2	+21.4	−21.5	−47.8

Source: Greulich, 1992, p. 97

Popular opinion is also divided over the issue of responsibility for the collapse, with 'Wessis' inclining towards the Board's line of argument. An opinion poll in late 1992 found east and west Germans differing significantly in the allocation of blame. Among the 1,000 east German respondents, the responsibility was placed primarily on west German attempts to eliminate competition (63 per cent), the government's failure to save more workplaces (49 per cent), mistakes committed by the Treuhand (47 per cent), decades of economic mismanagement by the SED (37 per cent) and the backwardness of most enterprises (26 per cent). Among the 2,000 west German interviewees, these factors attracted a support level of 24 per cent, 15 per cent, 21 per cent, 63 per cent and 58 per cent respectively ('Erst vereint, nun entzweit', 1993, p. 53).

As had been predicted by the Sachverständigenrat, the introduction of monetary union at the beginning of the transformation process caused economic turmoil. Monetary union ended overnight the forty-year separation of the GDR from developments on the world market, but, unlike the East European countries, the East German economy could not use the shield, however thin, of protectionist measures or of the manipulation of the exchange rate (Herr, 1992, p. 3). The introduction into the GDR of the D-Mark on 1 July 1990 at a rate of about one-to-one exposed the grave deficiencies of the GDR economy – obsolete capital, a run-down infrastructure, low productivity and millions of uncompetitive workplaces – in a merciless manner. Given the resultant inflation of costs, with the GDR mark appreciating by about 300 per cent (Sakowsky, 1992, p. 1255), most East German firms were no longer viable, particularly as higher-quality West German consumer and investment goods were readily available at reasonable prices (Matthes, 1991, pp. 602, 612).

In the new economic environment, GDR firms were caught in a vicious price-cost squeeze. Producer prices plummeted by about 36 per cent in the month after GEMSU and hovered around this level until the end of 1991. In the summer of 1990, the fall was particularly marked in chemicals, metallurgy, electronics, light industry and textiles. The drop in producer prices was complemented by a fall in output. It had been hoped that the relatively low East German wages and salaries would provide firms with some protection, but despite a contracting output and the appreciable shedding of labour, nominal wages in industry climbed by about 42 per cent between the first quarter of 1990 and the month of formal unification. This translated into a threefold increase in product wages (wages in relation to product prices) and a 45 per cent increase in consumption wages (wages related to the cost of living) (Akerlof *et al.*, 1991, pp. 9, 13, 32). In other words, wages were simply too high for East German firms to operate profitably in what was in any event a desperate situation; recourse to Treuhand credits was therefore necessary in order to keep firms afloat.

With the opening of the border and the introduction of the D-Mark, the East German consumer's pent-up demand for free access to West German goods – especially cars and electrical appliances – could at last be satisfied. The Federal Statistical Office estimated that in September 1990 alone DM2.4 billion worth of goods were transferred from the FRG to the GDR, a sum which did not even include purchases by East Germans in the West (ibid., pp. 34–5). In consequence, demand for the lower-quality and less attractively marketed East German products contracted sharply. The psychological aversion to GDR products even led to a rejection of high-quality GDR goods. The West German foodstuffs and semi-luxuries industry, retail trade and the consumer-goods industry reaped enormous benefits, with the first increasing production in the winter half-year period 1990–1 by 20 per cent in comparison to the corresponding period in 1989–90 (Flassbeck and Scheremet, in Jesse and Mitter, 1992, p. 290).

Another factor in the economic disintegration of the GDR (foreign trade is discussed later) was the ignorance among many members of West Germany's economic and political elites of the real condition and the *modus operandi* of the GDR economy. This partly explains why these elites so seriously underestimated, at least initially, the difficulties in the transformation of the GDR economic system by the deployment of the instruments of West Germany's market economy. Economists and politicians later indulged in bouts of recrimination. For example, shortly after his retirement as Secretary of State in the Federal Ministry of Economics Otto Schlecht complained:

We were wrongly advised by the economic scientists. In the autumn memorandum of the Council of Economic Experts as well as in the memorandum of the research institutes you will find the forecast that the economy in the new federal Länder will be emerging from the bottom of the depression by the middle of 1991. At that time, we had no idea of the extent of the malaise. [quoted in Maier, 1991, p. 3]

Schlecht's criticism was not without substance: in their autumn 1990 report, the five leading West German economic institutes had indeed predicted, albeit cautiously, a stabilization of production and employment and a turning point in economic recovery in the summer of 1991 ('Die Lage der Weltwirtschaft und der deutschen Wirtschaft im Herbst 1990', 1990, p. 615). On the other hand, as Bundesbank President Pöhl reminded Bonn, it was the Federal government which had opted for rapid monetary union against the advice of many economic advisers. And within only a few months of GEMSU, it had become apparent that the market mechanism was no magic formula for restoring the GDR economy to health and that selling off the assets of a whole economic system was not equivalent to the sale of an individual firm. Nor were the conditions similar, as many claimed, to those in existence before West Germany's 'economic miracle' after the currency reforms of 1948.

The vertiginous fall of the GDR economy underlined another deficiency: the lack of an adequate theoretical framework. Ironically, while there was an an abundance of theoretical work on the transition from capitalism to socialism, the changeover from state socialism to a social-market economy had been sorely neglected. Some theoretical guidelines on the establishment of the latter were provided in the corpus of literature produced by Eucken, Müller-Armanack, Erhardt and other pioneers of the West German economic system. This did not, however, constitute an integrated theory on the management of the inevitably painful transition from 'real socialism' to capitalism. The eminent German political scientist Kurt von Beyme elaborates on this problem:

One could not expect the emergence of a theory of transition to capitalism after socialism when the socialist countries withered away in 1989. In such a situation the German government was doomed to schizophrenia. It preached the victory of Ludwig Erhard over Karl Marx and the triumph of a market society, but it was forced to expel the 'devil' of a 'planned economy' with the 'Beelzebub' of a new provisional planning bureaucracy. The 'Trusteeship Society' (Treuhandgesellschaft), a para-statal organization, which was created already under DDR law in spring 1990 became the new 'Leviathan' which an unholy coalition of market ideologues and left-wing critics of the transformation process in Germany started to hunt with all their means. [von Beyme, 1992, pp. 162–3]

One question which will long be debated is whether, on balance, the incorporation of the GDR into the FRG should be described as a benign takeover rather than a rapacious exploitation of the GDR's assets and the ruthless de-industrialization of a once advanced industrial state. At an early stage in the unification process, there were few doubts in the minds of many East and West German intellectuals, engaged in an emotional debate on the implications of unification. The veteran GDR socialist dissident Stefan Heym inveighed against the 'cannibalistic lust' of East German consumers (Heym, 1991, p. 31); Habermas feared the regressive effects of 'chubby-faced DM-nationalism' (Habermas, 1991, p. 84); and Günter Grass warned of the danger of 'new colonial lords' moving into the GDR and predicted widespread bankruptcy and high unemployment in East Germany (Grass, 1991, pp. 69–70).

Critics of the unification process are perfectly justified in censuring the often callous dismantling of old structures – whether in the economy, education or public administration – and the dissipation of much creative potential (for details, see van der Meer and Kruss, 1991). Hard-nosed west German businessmen have been reluctant to invest more heavily in the establishment of an indigenous east German production structure and the taxpayers in the old *Länder* are distinctly unenthusiastic about any solidarity pact which entails major material sacrifices. Moreover, in the new *Länder* resentment is widespread against western know-it alls. Yet even if the pessimistic scenario of the citizens' movements and many left-wing intellectuals has come about, it is undeniable that the disparity between the two German states was so great that the enfeebled GDR would be heavily dependent upon the FRG for its restructuring and revival. Its chronic economic weakness is apparent in its low contribution of about 7 per cent to the all-German GDP as against its 20 per cent share of the population. And it should not be overlooked that west Germany, mainly the public authorities, is currently transferring vast resources – over DM150 billion per annum – into the new *Länder*, thus persuading Gerald Livingston, the director of the Institute for Contemporary German Studies at the Johns Hopkins University to describe the process as a 'friendly takeover' (Livingston, 1992, pp. 160–1). Friends, however, can sometimes be misguided, even neglectful. The most pertinent criticism of Bonn is not so much its initial underestimation of the magnitude of the reconstruction task – although it can be objected that if it did not have a clear picture, it should not have made so many reassuring noises – but rather that it delayed far too long in making the essential readjustments to its economic strategy, thus failing to utilize the favourable political climate during 1990 to mobilize popular support, especially in West Germany, behind a policy of retrenchment and redistribution of resources (see Section 6.1).

4.2 The development of east German industry, construction and services 1990 to 1992: a statistical review

It is generally agreed that the economic nosedive was halted in the spring of 1991 but, despite a few green shoots in construction and services and a modest growth in total production in the following year, by late 1992 there was still no real sign of a general economic upswing. One extremely worrying development was that the weakening economic performance in the old *Länder*, together with a slackening of growth in other Western countries, would seriously delay east Germany's prospects of recovery. Manufacturing output and foreign-trade turnover were still well below pre-1989 levels and no improvement was anticipated for 1993.

The chronic condition of the east German economy can be illustrated by the data on GDP: in the first half of 1992, it was still significantly lower than in the corresponding period in 1990 (DM93.2 billion as against DM111.5 billion) (Müller-Krumholz, 1993, p. 70). Furthermore, the economic chasm between the two parts of Germany was reflected in the low eastern contribution of DM231.5 billion to the all-German GDP of DM3,003.5 billion in 1992. Had productivity been equivalent to west Germany's, then this 7.7 per cent share of GDP would have been three times higher (Strohm, 1993, p. 13). Some gains in productivity were recorded: labour productivity increased by 4.6 per cent in 1991 and by 5.3 per cent in 1992. Yet even this modest improvement was partly the result of the size of the labour force falling more rapidly than GDP. Moreover, in comparison to west Germany, productivity per hour worked was lower than before the collapse of the GDR. In 1992, the gap between east and west German hourly productivity per gainfully employed person remained constant, with the east German level being 39 per cent that of west Germany (Müller-Krumholz, 1992a, pp. 264, 266, 270, 271; Müller-Krumholz, 1993, p. 62; Strohm, 1993, p. 23).

In order to delineate the contours of economic development and to identify likely sources of recovery, an examination follows of the performance of the various branches of the economy. Most of the data cover the period from 1990 to late 1992.

By the summer of 1992, manufacturing industry had still not emerged from the depths of the depression. Production was still two-thirds lower than before 1989 (DIW and IfW, 1992b, p. 468). A survey of 2,500 Treuhand and privatized firms in manufacturing conducted by the German Institute for Economic Research between May and October 1992 identified the main obstacles to the commercial viability of east German firms as: the rapid growth in wages and salaries (74 per cent of all firms mentioned this factor), lack of investment capital (64 per cent), out-of-date plant and buildings (54 per cent), the tardiness of local administration in processing applications for commercial development and in resolving property disputes (53 per cent), the inadequate distribution and marketing system (51 per cent), infrastructure deficiencies (46 per cent) and a shortage of appropriately qualified workers in many economic branches (40 per cent) (ibid., p. 474).

Two years after the introduction of GEMSU, severe adjustment problems were being experienced in such crucial areas of the economy as iron and steel production, foundries, precision engineering, optics, electronic data-processing, instrument-making and textiles. Costs were too high and new production lines were urgently required to meet the higher-quality demands of Western customers. Predictions of a relatively rapid recovery in investment goods had proved false: firms had been battered by the collapse of COMECON and by their inability to attain Western quality standards. Progress in the chemical industry was handicapped by its inherited ecological burden. World-wide overproduction inhibited investment in the steel industry. Machine building, comprising one-fifth of the industrial labour force and 15 per cent of industrial production, remained the most important branch of industry, but it had suffered serious disruption since the beginning of 1991 when transactions with the ex-COMECON countries changed over to hard currencies. Within a short period of time, turnover fell by two-thirds and then stagnated at this level. Privatization was slow to make an impact: by mid-1992, only one-fifth of units within the former machine-building combines had been privatized, mainly because of the shortage of capital for modernization and deficiencies in marketing operations.

The colossal transformational problems in shipbuilding, chemicals and textiles are reflected in the massive destruction of workplaces: at the beginning of 1992, only one-third of the pre-1989 workforce of over 300,000 remained in textiles and clothing (Boden and Zimmermann, 1992, p. 30). Where the textile industry had been a major source of employment in regions like Lusatia, the outlook is bleak. Over 20,000 people had once been employed in the textile industry around Cottbus, Gulben, Forst, Löbau and Zittau. After GEMSU the industry was no longer profitable and even technological innovation offered no prospect of recovery. Little more than 10 to 20 per cent of the old labour force can expect to remain in the region's textile industry (Loke, 1992, p. 29). Sales opportunities on Western markets are limited because of the competition from cheap imports from Asian dragons, and traditional customers in the former Soviet Union can no longer afford to pay for the products. Where the destruction of the textile industry is combined with cutbacks in the lignite industry, the consequences for employment in the region can be devastating. In areas like Zittau and Kamenatz, the unemployment rate in July 1992 was around 21 per cent, far above the east German average (*Sächsische Zeitung*, 6 August 1992, p. 1). As for the shipbuilding industry in Mecklenburg-West Pomerania, the agreement in 1992 between the Treuhand, the EC and the regional government to save the industry was expected to preserve only 10,000 of a labour force which had once numbered 54,000.

Although the privatization of the chemical industry has made some headway, over 50,000 of a total of 74,000 work places can be expected to disappear in the major centres of Leuna, Buna, Bitterfeld and Wolfen (Boden and Zimmermann, 1992, p. 30). In the summer of 1992, the Treuhand was extremely active in negotiations with west German, Italian, French and other foreign investors for selling-off the large chemical companies in the Leuna–Böhlen–Buna region. The centrepiece of the restructuring process was the contract signed in July 1992 with the German–French consortium TED, which comprises Elf-Aquitaine, the Thyssen Handelsunion and the German SO Kauf (DSBK). The consortium agreed to purchase the refineries in Leuna and Zeitz as well as the Minol chain of petrol stations. Although full details were not released when the contract was signed, it is known that the consortium agreed to invest DM4.3 billion in the new refinery at Leuna. The capacity of the refinery was expected to reach 10 million tonnes per annum by the time of its completion in 1996. TED's total investment in the reconstruction of the petro-chemical industry and the petrol station network was expected to reach DM6 billion and to provide 6,700 jobs and in the long term perhaps 10,000 (Baumann, 1992, p. 23).

Negotiations were also underway in the summer of 1992 with a consortium headed by the Italian state power conglomerate Ente Nazionale Idrocarburi for the investment of DM2.9 billion in the east German chemical industry. The main target was the purchase of polyol production outlets in Buna, Böhlen and Leuna. It was hoped that these and other projects, for example, with Shell and the Iranian National Petroleum Corporation, would lead to a total investment of DM10 billion in the east German chemical industry (*Berliner Zeitung*, 27 July 1992, p. 29). The badly polluted sites in Bitterfeld and Wolfen, however, aroused less interest among prospective buyers and only when the Treuhand's plan for the chemical industry in Saxony-Anhalt comes to fruition can some modest progress in privatization be anticipated. According to Joachim Kaiser, the head of the Treuhand's chemicals section, only 18,000–20,000 workplaces would remain in the business core of the chemical firms and a further 10,000 in related branches (*Mitteldeutsche Zeitung*, 25 July 1992, p. 1). Given its DM2 billion loss in 1992 and no real prospect of an improvement in sales, the general outlook for the east German chemical industry is so bleak that the President of the Association of the Chemical Industry, Wolfgang Hilger, has speculated whether even the core branches should be retained (*Neue Zeit*, 22 January 1993, p. 9).

The heavy production losses suffered by the high-tech and intelligence-based branches of industry is very disturbing as the speed of general economic recovery depends very much upon machine-building, electrical engineering, electronics and the precision engineering and optics industry, which together accounted for 45 per cent of production in the former GDR. If they do not recover, the new *Länder* face the real danger of becoming an economic backwater (Arbeitsgruppe Alternative Wirtschaftspolitik, 1992, pp. 115–16). After GEMSU about 30 per cent of the 2,000 enterprises in microelectronics and computing registered as collapsed businesses; a further 20 per cent came under Treuhand control; and the chances of survival were rated as negligible among most of the remaining 1,000 with fewer than five employees. Only the larger privatized enterprises appear to have any chance of survival (Flug, 1992, p. 144). Despite the considerable reduction in staff among the Treuhand firms in this sector, the growth in per capita turnover in 1992 was expected to be only 11 per cent, well below the international norm. The transformation process has claimed some notable scalps, in particular the manufacturer of personal computers in Sömmerda. The Sömmerda firm had enjoyed a high reputation before the Second World War as a centre for office machinery. At the beginning of 1991, the last computer rolled off the conveyor belt (ibid.). Another example comes from Frankfurt on the Oder where the semi-conductors firm with about 8,000 employees in 1989 was the largest source of employment in the town. Under obligation to reduce its labour force to 1,300, 3,900 had already been given notice of dismissal by the end of June 1991 (Institut für Angewandte Wirtschaftsforschung, 1992, p. 232).

Not all branches in manufacturing industry are in such a parlous state. A more favourable climate is observable in building materials, printing and the foodstuffs, beverages and tobacco industry where west German firms have managed to penetrate the east German market. The extraction and processing of stones and clays has been a notable exception to the general depression. Stones and clays, like timber processing and light-metal construction, has received a boost from its close links with the construction industry, and the level of privatization is second only to that in motor-vehicle construction. However, development has been slow among firms still under Treuhand control because of obsolescent plant, high labour costs, overstaffing and limited resources for investment (DIW and IfW, 1992a, p. 141).

Despite progress in the modernization of infrastructure and despite the expansion of the service sector, the collapse of traditional east German industry is, as Brandenburg's Minister President Manfred Stolpe has warned, like a time bomb ticking away in the new *Länder*. A situation could well arise where the modernization process produces a superstructure without an adequate industrial base. Then if the reconstruction of eastern Germany fails to become self-sustaining but reliant upon vast financial flows from the old *Länder*, this could, according to some prophets of doom, spell the end of the economic miracle in the western *Länder* (see Rudolph, 1992, p. 1).

It had been widely predicted that the construction industry would revive rapidly and give a powerful boost to general economic recovery in view of the urgent need for modernizing the housing stock, for urban renewal and for the development of commercial and industrial property. Over the next few years, about DM100 billion per annum are likely to be required for construction work. An upturn in the construction industry has in fact been apparent since the spring of 1991, stimulated by infrastructure programmes in the public sector and by the emergence of private firms ('Die Lage der Weltwirtschaft', 1992, pp. 210–11). During 1991, orders in construction rose by over 100 per cent, albeit from an extremely low take-off point. In the second quarter of 1992, production was one-third higher than in the preceding quarter. This improvement has not created extra jobs. In July and August 1992, total employment was 297,000 or about 46,000 lower than at the start of the year (DIW and IfW, 1992c, p. 730). Another disappointing trend has been the inadequate flow of investment capital, a mere DM10 billion in 1991. Among the major obstacles to expansion are increasing labour costs, the lack of large public programmes, the shortage of well-qualified workers and overmanning. And as elsewhere in the economy, unresolved ownership questions have delayed planning approval for new projects (DIW and IfW, 1992a, pp. 143–4 and 1992b, pp. 468, 484).

Like the construction industry, the service sector had been expected to make an important contribution to reconstruction and general recovery. As the east German economy drew closer to west Germany's, it was believed that growth in relatively underdeveloped areas such as banking, insurance, business consultancy, advertising, hotels and restaurants would partly compensate for job losses in manufacturing and agriculture. The structural differences between the old and the new *Länder* seemed to support this expectation. In 1987, services, including government, constituted 25 per cent of the GDR labour force but 36 per cent of employment in the FRG. The respective percentages for manufacturing were 47 per cent and 40 per cent. The proportion of the workforce engaged in agriculture was about twice as large in the GDR as in the FRG (see Mayer and Krakowski, in Ghaussy and Schäfer, 1993, pp. 177–82).

Some growth has been recorded in the service sector, especially of private firms. State firms, on the other hand, have suffered a contraction. Sections of the service sector have adjusted more rapidly to the market economy than manufacturing industry. A highly diversified business landscape has taken shape consisting of a myriad of new and reprivatized small and medium-sized businesses. As early as the end of 1990, 150,000 independents had sprung up in the service sector and the free professions, and this number may well have doubled over the following twelve months. The contribution of services to east German net value-added in 1991 was two-fifths, that is, more than the share of agriculture, power and construction combined (DIW and IfW, 1992a, pp. 145–6).

As firms in the service sector at first remained closely linked to local markets, they suffered severe losses with the disappearance of traditional customers. Demand was also dampened by higher prices and unemployment. Some improvement was registered during 1992 as market structures evolved and demand was stimulated by the high level of financial transfers from west to east Germany. Although the average east German household income is two-fifths lower than in west Germany, a similar proportion of the household budget is absorbed by services.

In the retail branch of the service sector, the outlook is much brighter than in transport and among hotels and restaurants. The privatization of retail trade was completed relatively quickly: in the course of 1991 virtually all of the former 30,000 state trading organizations (HOs) were sold to private investors (*Jahresgutachten 1991/92*, 1991, p. 68), and many establishments underwent extensive refurbishment. The pace of redevelopment has been largely determined by big west German chains, whose outlets offer fierce competition for east German retailers. One hopeful sign for the latter was the favourable response by many east German consumers to an improvement in the quality and the packaging of foodstuffs. In August 1992, according to a high-ranking official of the Central Marketing Association of German Agriculture, a survey had revealed that about 60 per cent of east Germans expressed a preference for foodstuffs from the new *Länder* as against only 21 per cent two years earlier (*Berliner Zeitung*, 6 August 1992, p. 30). The penetration of the east German market has been essentially limited to foodstuffs, cigarettes, detergents and a variety of everyday household goods. West German suppliers continue to dominate the consumer-goods branch, especially in technical appliances and clothing. A survey of 1,000 east German households in the summer of 1992 ascertained that east German goods' share of household expenditure was on average 32 per cent for foodstuffs but only 6 per cent for non-foodstuffs (DIW and IfW, 1992c, p. 727).

A new departure for east Germany has been the rapid expansion of mail-order firms and mobile sales operators. The general situation in retail is, however, by no means uniformly positive: many of the newly privatized units are miniscule; high rents in the urban centres have forced some firms out of business or into outlying districts; unemployment and rising prices restrict demand; and unresolved ownership questions inhibit expansion. Employment has fallen as a result of the expansion of the larger stores and of the less labour-intensive sales operators. In the twelve months since the end of 1989, the labour force dropped to 480,000, an overall reduction of about one-third (DIW and IfW, 1992a, p. 149).

The hotel and restaurant trade has not weathered the economic storm well. Many restaurants have been trapped between stagnating demand and rising costs for labour, energy and rents. Rents often absorb as much as 10 per cent of turnover and energy up to 20 per cent. Investment is urgently required, but the estimated requirement of DM10,000 per restaurant place is out of the reach of most landlords. Moreover, many are heavily in debt to the Treuhand. Hotels are in a much better position. In 1991, 35 per cent more guests were accommodated than in the preceding year, and the hotel trade is a lucrative business in the cities. Nearly all of the former thirty-three, prestigious Interhotels have been privatized and room prices are very high. This is partly the result of a serious shortage of accommodation: 200,000–280,000 extra beds are needed, a reflection of the low provision in east Germany, which has twenty-seven hotel beds per 10,000 inhabitants compared to 175 in the west (ibid., pp. 149–50).

The transport sector is encumbered with problems typical of the whole transition phase: overstaffing, delays in privatization, west German competition and a fall in orders. After experiencing a sharp decline in the volume of passengers and freight, the east German railway – the Deutsche Reichsbahn – has managed to stabilize its position since the autumn of 1991. It is hoped to maintain the present level of passengers now that track modernization has commenced. The freight trade, however, faces serious competition from goods carriers on the roads. In order to attract more freight business, labour costs must be reduced as the labour force of 200,000 in early 1992 was about 50 per cent higher than in west Germany, relative to the size of the railway network (ibid., pp. 152, 154).

The public road transport system has suffered from the shift towards the ownership of private vehicles. In early 1992, per capita car ownership had climbed to three-quarters of the west German level. However, increasing congestion and other traffic problems in urban areas have slowed down the shift from public to private transport. In the second half of 1991, the decline in the number of passengers on public transport in the inner-city areas came to a halt, and since the beginning of 1991 the increase in passenger charges has provided some financial relief for many firms. Nevertheless, the general picture remains gloomy: all firms are in the red; much of the rolling stock is worn out; the condition of many roads and track is poor; and maintenance and administrative departments still have surplus staff (ibid., p. 152).

Despite the prolonged depression in the new *Länder*, there has been a veritable flood of applications for establishing a business. In 1990 281,096 businesses were registered and a further 291,385 in the following year. On the other hand, at a time of economic uncertainty deregistrations have been common, rising from 26,694 to 99,069 during the same period. Activity was still lively in 1992: 197,286 were registered and 108,953 deregistered by the end of November (Statistisches Bundesamt, *Mitteilung für die Presse*, 14 January 1993, n.p.). This kind of feverish activity is not unusual during periods of rapid change. Most of the activity is located in the trade sector where 90 per cent of registrations and 80 per cent of deregistrations have occurred (DIW and IfW, 1992a, p. 160). A registration does not necessarily imply that a new business has been founded as the term also covers the relocation of an existing firm. Impressive though the level of business activity is, the new firms have not given a major boost to employment as many of them are small units of the 'mamma and papa' kind, small fastfood stalls, video shops, second-hand car dealers. Many businesses were born out of sheer necessity and, lacking both capital and know-how, it is estimated that less than half are capable of survival (Geißler, 1992, p. 107).

4.3 Agriculture

Under the SED regime the agricultural sector was heavily subsidized by the state, and the workforce, comprising about 11 per cent of the economically active population, was unusually high for such an industrialized society. The basic organizational unit was large, the average size of the 4,500 agricultural production cooperatives being 1,180 hectares. Private plots accounted for slightly less than 4 per cent of useful agricultural land. One key feature was the high level of specialization with a widespread separation of animal husbandry and crop farming. The material situation of the farming community corresponded roughly to that of the GDR average, helped considerably by a higher level of subsidization of producer pricers than in the EC. The subsidies for foodstuffs rose from 7.8 billion marks in 1980 to 31.9 billion in 1988 (Mittelbach, 1992, p. 28).

After the introduction of the D-Mark and the agrarian union with the EC on 1 August 1990, GDR agriculture experienced a dramatic collapse as it struggled to adapt to the European Common Agricultural Policy (CAP), privatization, a lower degree of specialization, obligatory cutbacks in production and a change in the pattern of subsidies for production. Although the initial plummeting of producer prices levelled out during the first year of monetary union, it gave little comfort to the hard-pressed producer (*Agrarbericht*, 1992, p. 22). As part of the adjustment to CAP quotas and the demands of the embryonic market economy, agricultural production had to be cut back. This was problematic as production per inhabitant of, for example, potatoes, poultry-farming and cattle-farming was 7.2 and 1.5 times as high respectively as in west Germany. Output, especially of crop production, fell to DM12.4 billion in the economic year 1990–1, an appreciably lower figure than before 1989. By early December 1990, butter production had fallen by over 30 per cent and cheese production by 80 per cent compared with 1989 (Schilling, in Heisenberg, 1991, pp. 250, 252). A particularly sharp decline – by 59 per cent – occurred in livestock between 1989 and the end of 1991 (Mittelbach, 1992, p. 36).

Expenditure in 1990–1 reached DM13,173 billion, including DM3.5 billion on animal feed. This meant that gross-value creation was minus DM818 million. However, thanks to west German subsidies of DM5.182 billion for the agricultural enterprises, net-value creation was about DM2.189 billion. The most significant of these subsidies was the DM3.7 billion bridging and financial aid to enable enterprises to cope with adjustment problems. As the transfers for social policy and investment projects have to be added to this figure, the final bill was considerably higher (*Agrarbericht*, 1992, p. 22).

The overblown agricultural labour force shrank rapidly, from about 850,000 in 1989 to an estimated 300,000 at the end of 1991. Even this latter figure understated the true fall as it included 150,000 on short-time work. Out of the original labour force 130,000 had taken advantage of early retirement schemes, 105,000 were engaged in job creation or further training programmes, 40,000 older workers had retired, 120,000 had obtained alternative employment and 150,000 were unemployed (ibid., p. 19). The slashing of the labour force continued throughout 1992, dropping to 160,000 by the end of the year (Statistisches Bundesamt, *Mitteilung für die Presse*, 22 January 1993, n.p.).

The economies of the new Federal states of Mecklenburg–West Pomerania and Brandenburg have been hit extremely hard by the disintegration of the old agrarian system, particularly as there are few alternative sources of employment within these regions. Shortly before the *Wende* 20.2 per cent of employed persons in Mecklenburg–West Pomerania were engaged in agriculture compared to 15.3 per cent in Brandenburg, while industry accounted for 23.3 per cent and 33.4 per cent respectively (Braun and Obenau, 1992, p. 27; Institut für Angewandte Wirtschaftsforschung, 1992, p. 16). These percentages were much higher than the GDR average.

Mecklenburg-West Pomerania accounted for 27.2 per cent of the total agricultural land in the former GDR. A comparison with its western neighbour, Schleswig-Holstein, illustrates the difficulties confronting this new east German *Land*: on average, the number of employees per 100 hectares of useful agricultural land in Mecklenburg-West Pomerania was twelve as opposed to four in Schleswig-Holstein, and the average crop yield was 45.7 and 61.5 decitonnes per hectare respectively (ibid., 1992, p. 29). The region's agricultural sector is faced with many fundamental adjustment problems: changes in the balance between animal husbandry and crop production; a less intensive use of chemicals; a reduction in the stock of cows, pigs and sheep; and the restructuring and privatization of the maintenance and repairs sections. The situation was critical in those districts where alternative employment was scarce and productivity was well below average. These areas were the western and southern administrative districts of

Hagenow, Ludwigslust, Schwerin-Land, Parchim and Lübe as well as those of Neustrelitz, Waren, Röbel, Ueckermünde and Wolgast (ibid., 1992, pp. 63–5). Emigration and commuting to the west provide a solution for some workers. According to the Mecklenburg-West Pomeranian Ministry of Social Affairs in Schwerin, thousands of workers have emigrated to the old *Länder* and 66,000 commute daily to Hamburg, Lübeck and other West German cities ('Im blauen Dunst', 1992, p. 78)

The reconstruction of the agricultural sector is based on the privatization principle, with the west German family farm as the ideal type. An Agricultural Adjustment Act, which was passed by the Volkskammer on 1 July 1990, defined the procedure for the conversion of existing agricultural cooperatives into registered co-operatives (Lambrecht, 1990, p. 471). An important amendment to this Act was approved by the Bundestag and Bundesrat one year later; it aimed to complete the transformation of the agricultural cooperatives into new legal entities and to accelerate the pace of privatization. However, few east German agricultural experts and associations were called upon for advice (Gräf, 1993, p. 12), thus giving rise to the feeling in the rural community of once more being under tutelage (Kurjo, 1992, p. 63). A leading west German expert on GDR agriculture, Andreas Kurjo, has argued convincingly that the speed at which GDR agriculture was expected to adapt to West German and EC regulations and the unsuitability of some of these regulations demonstrated a high level of ignorance in Bonn and Brussels about GDR agriculture. Overhasty privatization precipi-tated a series of bankruptcies at an early stage in the reconstruction process, and Bonn's own privatization ardour was not matched by the banks, who proved reluctant to grant credits (ibid., p. 58).

Economic realities soon undermined the Federal government's goal of a rapid reconstruction of east German agriculture on the basis of private family units. By the end of 1990, about 0.5 per cent of persons formerly engaged in agriculture had opted for indi-vidual farming (Schilling, in Heisenberg, 1991, p. 256). Bonn was obliged to encourage diversification through the promotion of leasing, limited liability companies, registered cooperatives and other forms (Kurjo, 1992, p. 58). In August 1991, the number of private units was still only 12,100, working 11.5 per cent of the useful agricultural land (*Agrarbericht*, 1992, p. 19). This rose to 26 per cent by the end of 1992 (Statistisches Bundesamt, *Mitteilung für die Presse*, 22 January 1993, n.p.). Despite the initial slow pace of the privatization process, by late 1991 many changes had taken place in the legal status of the LPGs: three-quarters had acquired a different legal form and the remainder had gone into liquidation or were awaiting foreclosure. The most popular new legal entities are the registered cooperative and the joint-stock company. By the end of August 1991, 830 registered cooperatives had been established with an average size of 1,710 hectares. In addition, there were 744 joint-stock companies averaging 1,020 hectares (*Agrarbericht*, 1992, p. 200). Registered cooperatives enable farmers to enjoy certain tax advantages but deprive them of the benefits of limited liability. Although the new farms are much smaller than their LPG predecessors, they tend to be several times larger than most west German farms. This is not unwelcome to many east German farm managers as they believe that larger units improve the chances of survival (Mittelbach, 1992, p. 39).

Although assistance in the form of liquidity grants and other equalization aid to farmers in accordance with the State and Unification Treaties has helped some farms to become commercially viable and has eased the transition process, the subsidies have often failed in many cases to cover the wages bill, interest payments and the cost of leases. For example, transitional arrangements in 1990 and 1991 allowed for set-aside subsidies of DM500 to DM750 per hectare on condition that land was withdrawn from cultivation for one year. As these subsidies turned out to be higher than the profit which many enterprises derived from farming, the demand for the premia proved excessive (*Jahresgutachten 1991/92*, 1991, p. 244).

The entire sector is beset by a plethora of problems: a chronic lack of investment capital; an inadequate administrative system; unresolved ownership claims; difficulties in raising credit; and inherited liabilities. A severe drought in the summer of 1992 exacerbated the situation and brought many farmers close to ruin. As a result of the drought, farmers harvested 21.2 per cent less than in 1991; the fall was particularly steep in the *Land* Brandenburg – 34.6 per cent (Mittelbach, 1992, p. 49).

At the time of GEMSU, the total debt of agriculture, forestry and the foodstuffs sector was about DM8 billion and the average debt burden DM1.9 million per LPG (Kurjo, 1992, p. 63). Although the Treuhand has assumed responsibility for DM2.8 billion of debt, repayments on the interest and redemption of inherited debt are another unwelcome handicap (Mittelbach, 1992, pp. 47–8). Given this accumulation of problems, it is not surprising that many enterprises have been forced into liquidation and that privatization has been so unpopular among many members of the rural community. An early survey conducted by the GDR Ministry of Agriculture revealed that only 5 per cent of the GDR's cooperative farmers were prepared to assume the risks inherent in the privatization process (Lambrecht, 1990, p. 471).

Kurt Krambach, one of the GDR's leading researchers on agriculture, released, in the PDS journal *Utopie kreativ*, some interesting findings from a representative survey conducted at the end of 1990 into the attitudes of collective farmers towards the changes in their work environment. The survey included interviews and group discussions with 728 workers on fourteen LPGs. One striking conclusion was that out of the 62 per cent of the whole sample who wished to remain in agriculture 77.6 per cent preferred collective farms and a further 17 per cent wished to start off in this way before considering the possibility of transferring to another type of ownership. Only 3.3 per cent of the respondents were keen to establish their own family enterprise. The strong preference for cooperative forms of production was rooted in a combination of uncertainty about the general socio-economic situation and a positive appreciation of aspects of the old system of cooperative farming. All respondents indicated that the lack of job security was their main worry. About half the sample had already been affected by unemployment (8.1 per cent), short-time work and early retirement (Krambach, 1991, pp. 25–7). Many were also confused: even at this early stage only 18 per cent knew exactly what was required to keep their jobs; 37.2 per cent had some notion but were uncertain as to its feasibility; and 44.8 per cent had no idea (Müller and Vogel, 1991, p. 41).

The desire to continue farming on a cooperative basis was strongly influenced by fond memories of the security and the range of social contacts within the LPGs. Even among the half of the respondents who had already become or wished to become private farmers, their decision was not conditioned by an aversion to their former LPG. They were appreciative of the social provision and services – such as enterprise canteens and kindergarten places – which were expected to disappear under market conditions (Krambach, 1991, pp. 28–9). By contrast, private family enterprises were seen to entail a high risk of personal indebtedness. However, whatever the legal form adopted, east German farmers cannot avoid the traumatic change-over from a socialist system to the new conditions associated with a social-market economy and the EC agricultural markets. And that, as we have seen, entails heavy production and job losses.

4.4 Foreign trade

Many east German enterprises initially pinned many of their hopes of survival during the transition phase on foreign trade, notably on retaining their links with traditional COMECON partners. Many of these hopes have proved to be pure illusion. Calculations by the

Federal Statistical Office bear this out: total exports fell by 44.5 per cent in 1990 in comparison to the previous year, and although the decline in imports was only 7.4 per cent, the two combined declined by over 50 per cent in 1991 (Greulich, 1992, p. 97; see Table 4.2). In 1991, the share of the new *Länder* in total German trade was extremely modest, underlining the dominance of the old *Länder*: 1.7 per cent of imports and 2.7 per cent of exports (ibid., p. 100). Until the end of 1990, exports to the COMECON countries remained close to their earlier level, thanks to various arrangements in the Unification Treaty. It had been agreed that existing contracts with the COMECON countries would be honoured and that exports would be based on the transferable rouble at a favourable conversion rate of DM2.4. The conditions changed abruptly when from 1 January 1991 trade with the former Soviet Union and other East European countries was based on transactions in convertible currencies and freely negotiated prices. The result was a dramatic fall of 60 per cent in the annual value of east German exports to those countries, from DM29.8 billion in 1990 to DM11.9 billion in 1991. Imports fell by 56 per cent during this period (ibid., p. 101). Hard-currency shortages and economic dislocation in the former Soviet Union and its former client states as well as the failure of east German goods to match the quality of those now more easily available on the world market were the key factors in this plunge in the volume and value of trade (*Jahresgutachten 1991/ 92*, 1991, p. 77).

With approximately 600,000 jobs in east Germany originally dependent upon trade with the former Soviet Union, the provision of Hermes credits of DM9.7 billion in 1991 was crucial for the survival of many firms. These credits enabled Soviet enterprises to obtain goods from their east German partners without recourse to hard currencies. According to the terms of the Hermes programme, framework deposits and interim payments may be waived and the period of credit repayment extended to a maximum of ten years (ibid., p. 77). Virtually all of the credits in 1991 were used for deliveries to Soviet/CIS firms and about four-fifths were claimed by Treuhand firms. This heavy demand for Hermes credits reflected the uncompetitiveness of vast swathes of east German industry and the failure to find new markets. In 1991, 59 per cent of east German imports and 67 per cent of exports were still with the former COMECON states (Greulich, 1992, p. 103). However, the outlook was bleak as new regulations governing Hermes credits in 1992 threatened a further reduction in this level of trade. The uncertain political and economic situation in the former Soviet Union caused the Federal government to restrict credits only to those countries which were prepared to accept responsibility for old liabilities; Georgia, Ukraine, Azerbaijan and Uzbekhistan were unwilling to do so. Another constraint was the decision to release securities only to business contracts with a ceiling of DM100 million. This was most disturbing as almost half of east German exports involved contracts worth more than DM100 million (DIW and IfW, 1992a, pp. 139–40).

Another cause for concern lay in the fact that the commodity structure of east German trade has not undergone any fundamental change. As in the GDR era, the pattern of trade does not not reflect the relatively high level of industrial development. In 1991, the main category of imports was mineral fuels, lubricants and related products (37 per cent) followed by machine-building products, electro-technical products (29 per cent) and vehicles; finished products accounted for only 14 per cent. The main exports were machine-building and vehicle-construction products (50 per cent). The uneven east German trading profile is thrown into sharp relief by a comparison with west German imports in 1991 when the share of machine building and vehicles (36.2 per cent) was much higher than in the new *Länder* and the share of mineral fuels and related products (7.8 per cent) much lower (Greulich, 1992, p. 108). This imbalance simply pinpoints the urgent need for the modernization of east German industry; Hermes credits can ease but not cure the transitional problems.

4.4 Labour market policy and unemployment

Predictions in the spring of 1990 of the likely level of unemployment after GEMSU ranged from the pessimistic forecast of 3 to 3.5 million by West and East German economists such as the President of the West Berlin German Institute for Economic Research, Lutz Hoffmann, and the Rector of East Berlin's Hochschule für Ökonomic, R. Streich, to the Institute of the German Economy's forecast of virtually no unemployment, with the proviso that the GDR achieved the expected rapid growth in productivity (Götz-Coenenberg, 1990, pp. 32–3).

With registered unemployment at 1,188,234 in mid-1992 and an unemployment rate of 15.1 per cent the pessimists have been vindicated, particularly as these figures are an imperfect reflection of the true state of the labour market (see document 6). Labour-market policy instruments such as short-time work, job creation schemes and further training courses absorbed a further 1,837,469 persons. In addition, 833,718 workers had taken early retirement, and commuting and emigration to the old *Länder* accounted for an additional several hundred thousand. It is estimated that out of an original labour force of about 9.95 million only about 6 million were engaged in some form of employment in the autumn of 1992 (Gröbner, 1992, p. 6; DIW, and IfW, 1992c, p. 711).

The prediction of the Institute für Economic Research, Halle, was for employment to fall to 5.5 million (not including job creation schemes, retraining and so forth) in 1993. Converted to full-time equivalents, this would mean that in 1993 about 34 per cent of the potential labour force would be out of work or not incorporated into the 'normal' labour market ('IWH-Gutachten vom Dezember 1992', 1993, p. 2).

In order to provide a safety net for the transformation process, the government's recourse to labour-market instruments such as short-time work has constituted a level of intervention in labour-market policy which is at odds with the 'supply-side' reforms of the early 1980s. However, typical of its policy in other areas, the Federal government has tended to react to developments rather than be proactive. For example, Bonn's failure to anticipate the magnitude of the problem may be gauged by the Federal Labour Office's original projection of 130,000 job-creation places (Flockton and Esser, in Smith *et al.*, 1992, pp. 282, 296).

Documents 6–8 trace the rise of unemployment in a society which had long been accustomed to job security, a feature frequently lauded by Honecker as one of the achievements of socialism; he preferred, however, to maintain a discreet silence on the endemic underutilization of labour. Unemployment increased in a linear fashion from the summer of 1990 until August 1991. The jump in unemployment in July 1991 was caused by the expiry of agreements protecting workers against dismissal, as in metalworking and the electrical industry (*Jahresgutachten 1991/92*, 1991, p. 108). Then at the start of 1992 the termination of special short-time regulations for east German workers produced a sharp increase of 305,740. At the end of July 1992, unemployment surged once more, to 1,188,200, an increase of 65,914 in one month. This was mainly due to the removal by the Federal Agency for Labour of its health-insurance subsidy for short-time workers. With short-time labour becoming more expensive, many firms decided to shed many of their workers on short time.

While unemployment has affected all the new *Länder* and east Berlin, Mecklenburg-West Pomerania, where the labour force is heavily concentrated in the ailing shipbuilding industry and agriculture, has been hit the hardest (see documents 7 and 8). Yet even in the *Land* Saxony, which has tended to have the lowest unemployment rate, the job situation is extremely gloomy: by the autumn of 1991, the workforce had dropped by 1.9 million from 2.6

million in 1989, and in October Minister President Biedenkopf predicted that structural change would eventually destroy a further 25 per cent of the state's workplaces (Lapp, 1992, p. 246).

Unemployment is high in all branches of the economy. In manufacturing industry and mining the fall in employment in 1991 was 35.9 per cent but this figure, as indicated earlier, underestimates the true extent of the transformation as it does not include commuters and various categories of labour-market policy. In branches such as machine building, clothing, chemicals, electrical engineering and motor-vehicle engineering the job losses were slightly above the average; in non-ferrous metal production the rate was almost 50 per cent (Statistisches Bundesamt, *Wirtschaft und Statistik*, no. 4, 1992, p. 225).

Women's unemployment has been running at a consistently higher level than that of men. Whereas in the second half of 1991 the male unemployment rate ranged from 8.9 per cent to 9.8 per cent, that of women was about four points higher. In January 1992, the female rate surged to 21.8 per cent and men's to 12.6 per cent (see document 6). The main reason for the higher unemployment rate of women is to be found not in a differential shedding of labour – this was roughly equal between men and women in 1991 – but in the fewer alternative sources of employment available to women. For example, in late 1991 men were about four times more likely to be commuting to west Germany than women. And at a time of surplus labour, male job applicants have tended to be given preference over women (Müller, in Kieselbach and Voigt, 1992, p. 162).

Women's employment opportunities have been appreciably reduced by the fall in the number of part-time jobs from one million to 600,000 in the twelve months after GEMSU. In the GDR, part-time work was an important way of enabling women to cope with the multiple burdens of family, career and housework and of preparing older women for eventual retirement (Holst and Schupp, 1992, pp. 236–7). Women over fifty years of age, single parents and younger women have been especially vulnerable. Women's unemployment rate is high in traditional 'female' branches of the economy such as textiles, chemicals, light industry, foodstuffs and electrical engineering (Meyer, 1991, p. 1331). Finally, not only are women much more likely to be unemployed than men but also they are less likely to retain a management post, a highly qualified white-collar position or a skilled worker's job. For example, less than 20 per cent of women in management have held on to their job compared to 30 per cent of male managers (Holst and Schupp, 1992, p. 236).

All these changes challenge well-established perceptions of gender roles. In the GDR, about 90 per cent of women between sixteen and sixty had a job or were engaged in some form of training (63.4 per cent in the FRG). Although the prevalence of sex-specific values and attitudes was partly responsible for the persistence of an unequal division of labour within the family and for discrimination against employed women with respect to pay and promotion, work was regarded as intrinsic to a woman's life. This is clear from investigations undertaken in the GDR both before and after the collapse of the old regime. In a representative investigation organized by the west German polling group Infas in the month of unification, women identified their reasons for going out to work as (in ranking order): the need for money, enjoyment of work, the company of other people, the desire to apply what they had learned and financial independence. About two-thirds of the women desired to continue working, even if their personal circumstances meant that they did not require an income from work (Meyer, 1991, p. 1332).

In the GDR, women made a significant contribution to household income: about 44 per cent compared to 38 per cent in the FRG. As the equalization of east and west German wages and salaries has not yet been achieved and as so many men are unemployed, women's earnings continue to be crucial to a household's standard of living (Holst, 1991, p. 422). However, as the rate of women's unemployment is higher than men's, and continuing to grow, the significance of women's contribution is likely to decline. Another most disturbing development is that unemployment constitutes a source of immense psychological stress as well as of material deprivation for single mothers (see Section 4.7). Women's share of unemployment among single parents is 95 per cent (*Amtliche Nachrichten der Bundesanstalt für Arbeit*, vol. 40, no. 11, 1992, p. 1657). In short, after several decades of full employment, women now find themselves seriously disadvantaged in competing with men for jobs and promotion and are under increasing pressure to adjust to traditional west German gender-specific roles (Schenk, in Kieselbach and Voigt, 1992, p. 295).

East German women have not so far offered much resistance to the upheaval. Irene Dölling, a leading east German researcher in women's studies, describes their reaction pattern as:

Helpless outrage or resigned acceptance of the brutal forms of discrimination and exclusion with which primarily men are now beginning to practice competition are 'normal' responses; organized forms of resistance are unfortunately the great exception. [Dölling, 1991, p. 5]

Her explanation is that forty years of patriarchal paternalism in the

GDR repressed emancipatory demands; women basically adjusted to the preordained double burden of career and family.

Short-time work has been a crucial element in easing some of the pain of the transformation. It was introduced in June 1990 and incorporated into the Unification Treaty. The regulations provided for allowances not only for a temporary loss of work, as in west Germany, but also where unemployment was anticipated. The majority of short-time workers were entitled to claim 90 per cent of their wages, most of the cost being covered by contributions from the Federal government. All the social-security contributions of the short-time workers were to be paid by the unemployment fund in east Germany for the hours not worked. In the old *Länder*, employers have to pay part of these contributions.

For many east Germans, short-time work is no more than a thinly veiled form of unemployment. In 1991, for each short-time worker more than half the working time was cut and for almost a quarter working time was reduced to zero (see document 6). The government's goal of combining short-time work with further training has not been fulfilled: in 1990 and 1991, on average less than 5 per cent of all short-time workers made use of unworked hours to do so. This was partly the result of the lack of financial incentives as payments barely exceeded short-time work without training and partly because few companies provided their own training facilities ('Short-time work' 1992, p. 6).

Although short-time work is found in all branches of the economy, the heaviest concentration has been in manufacturing industry, with 60 per cent of all such workers in 1991. The 14 per cent in agriculture and forestry represented an above-average proportion (*Jahresgutachten 1991/92*, 1991, p. 108). Non-privatized Treuhand firms accounted for a half of the total of all short-time workers in October 1991. The numbers on short-time work rocketed from 656,277 in June 1990 to a peak of 2,018,907 in April 1991 and then dropped gradually until another sharp fall in January 1992 took the number to 520,591. During the period mid-December 1991 to mid-January 1992, the contraction was especially pronounced in electrical engineering (a fall of 55,600 to 74,500), the textile and clothing industry (minus 40,000 to 26,200) mining (-33,400 to 16,700) and chemical/synthetic materials (-27,000 to 20,800) (*Amtliche Nachrichten der Bundesanstalt für Arbeit*, vol. 40, no. 2, 1992, p. 135). The contraction, which has continued throughout 1992 (see document 6), has largely been the result of the application to the new *Länder* of the less generous west German regulations.

Some relief for the labour market in east Germany has been provided by the flow of commuters from the new to the old *Länder*:

numbers rose from about 200,000 in November 1990 to 540,000 one year later and then fell to 450,000 in May 1992 (*Handelsblatt*, 20 January 1993, p. 4). Commuters are overwhelmingly male (83 per cent – all data refer to late 1991), two-thirds are thirty-five and younger, and though skilled workers predominate (43 per cent), the semi- and unskilled constitute the next largest group (22 per cent) (Scheremet and Schupp, 1992, pp. 23–4). By far the most important motives for commuting are higher wages and jobs. On average, commuters' wages are 100 per cent higher than in east Germany (Schupp, 1992, p. 32). In addition to commuters, the west has absorbed a substantial flow of *émigrés* from the new *Länder*: 388,700 in 1990 and 243,600 in 1991. In the latter year, Saxony lost 70,800 of its residents, Saxon-Anhalt 46,800 and Thuringia 40,900. Emigration is not a one-way street, however: the west to east flow doubled to 75,700 in 1991 (*Berliner Zeitung*, 10–11 October 1992, p. 1).

Many older workers have taken advantage of the provision for early retirement, about 400,000 doing so between 8 February and 2 October 1990. Subsequently, in accordance with the Unification Treaty, transitional payment for early retirement became available for men aged 57 and over and women from 55 years of age. The minimum age was lowered to a uniform 55 on 1 July 1991 (*Jahresgutachten 1991/92*, 1991, p. 108). The transitional benefit, which represents 65 per cent of the last average net wage, is paid until the earliest date on which a pension becomes due. The recipient must assure the local Labour Exchange that she/he has left gainful employment ('Vorgezogenes Altersübergangsgeld', 1991, p. 2). In December 1992, 578,090 persons were in receipt of the transitional benefit. The scheme, which was due to terminate at the end of 1991, was extended to the end of June 1992 in view of the numerous economic and social problems (*Amtliche Nachrichten der Bundesanstalt für Arbeit*, vol. 40, no. 2, 1992, p. 136). The outcome for the generation which was born during the Second World War and grew up in the difficult years immediately after the war is that it has now been doubly disadvantaged by unemployment and relative poverty in old age.

Job-creation schemes have been another prominent instrument of labour-market policy. Expansion was modest until DM990 million were released in March 1991 from the Upswing East programme as supplementary aid for job-creation places (*Jahresgutachten 1991/92*, 1991, p. 108). Numbers then rose rapidly, reaching 404,853 in May 1992 (see document 6). The job-creation programme absorbs considerable resources: DM5.2 billion in 1991. This sum, which was expected to increase to DM10 billion in 1992, included DM3 billion from the Upswing East programme

(Gröbner, 1992, p. 6). Several large-scale projects were launched in 1991, each with over 150 people. By October 1991 120 had been approved, most of them for eighteen months to two years and involving *in toto* about 40,500 persons. The most ambitious projects, each with 2,200 employees, were organized by the Vereinigten Mitteldeutschen Braunkohlenwerk and the Lausitzer Braunkohlenwerk for the recultivation of land severely damaged by lignite mining (*Jahresgutachten 1991/92*, 1991, pp. 108–10). Fifty per cent of job-creation schemes are located in agriculture and forestry, coastal protection, land development and building construction, a reflection of the urgency of the environmental clean-up in these areas. Office work, administration and social services account for 27 per cent of places. Women's share of the scheme is only 36 per cent (Arbeitsgruppe Alternative Wirtschaftspolitik, 1992, pp. 60–1).

Further training and qualification schemes have been introduced to equip workers with the skills and experience required in new jobs. As with other labour-market schemes, the numbers have increased appreciably. During 1991 the number of workers participating in some form of further training rose from 38,154 to 435,200 and reached a peak of 494,600 in November 1992 (see document 6). As participation in a training course was made a precondition of the receipt of short-time pay, the proportion of short-time workers in further training increased from a relatively low level to 37 per cent in 1991. Most further training activities have been for short-to-medium periods. About 47 per cent of the measures which commenced in the first half of 1991 lasted only three months; a further 38 per cent ranged from three to twelve months (*Jahresgutachten 1991/92*, 1991, p. 110). Most of the subsidies are provided by the Federal Labour Agency: in 1992 DM11 billion will be released for financing further training courses, an increase of about 3.1 billion on the 1991 figure (Gröbner, 1992, p. 6).

The creation of employment and training companies (*Beschäftigungs- und Qualifizierungsgesellschaften*) has marked a new departure in labour-market policy. A few companies were established in the summer of 1990, and in February 1991 Brandenburg became the first of the new *Länder* governments to launch a programme in this policy area. Further progress was delayed until, in September 1991, the Treuhand abandoned its opposition to its firms becoming heavily involved in the scheme. By early 1992, there were 333 companies with about 130,000 participants. The full range of labour-market instruments is utilized. Although in many of the employment and training companies job-creation measures are combined with training, the emphasis is on publicly financed job-creation places. The companies absorb about 52,000 workers on job-creation schemes or 13 per cent of all job-creation posts

(Arbeitsgruppe Alternative Wirtschaftspolitik, 1992, pp. 66–70).
The companies are usually formed from Treuhand firms which have been unable to establish a foothold in the market. In early 1992, the companies attracted about 13 per cent of total employment creation funds. Most companies are small, with an average of five to six employees (OECD, 1992b, p. 83). They provide limited though by no means insignificant relief for the labour market situation in the new *Länder*. They have not developed into serious competitors for private concerns, partly due to the fact that, relying on the Federal Labour Office for financial support the competitive incentive is less than among private firms (ibid., p. 84). It had been feared that the new companies would tie up public funds and make little practical contribution to the economic growth potential of the new *Länder*. The Board of Advisers to the Federal Ministry of Economics, for example, was most anxious lest they developed into 'a new type of public service throughout eastern Germany' engaged in 'unrealistic and non-applicable labour-market activism' instead of 'advanced on-the-job training' (Bundesministerium für Wirtschaft, 1992, pp. 40–1).

The concern that the training companies would divert public funds from the creation of competitive workplaces was underpinned by the fact that whereas an unemployed person first obtains 68 per cent and then 63 per cent of his/her previous wage, the employment and training companies pay the full wage. And when employment terminates in this type of company after the guaranteed two years, the worker is able to obtain unemployment benefit and social assistance for up to a further two years. This is not, it is argued, conducive to the creation of a competitive business climate. Other objections are that training in what is often run-down firms produces workers whose newly acquired skills are unlikely to be needed and, finally, that one of the main justifications for the companies, the utilization of workers for clearing up polluted land, could just as easily be done by other firms (Krumrey, 1992, pp. 99–107). These criticisms are not without substance, and even advocates of the companies concede that they cannot replace the Labour Exchanges and the worker's own efforts as a way into a new job (Arbeitsgruppe Alternative Wirtschaftspolitik, 1992, p. 73). On the other hand, given the economic and social circumstances prevailing in the *Länder*, they represent a useful though limited instrument for preventing a labour-market catastrophe.

Labour-market policy instruments have entailed the transfer of vast sums from west to east Germany: DM30 billion in 1991 and an anticipated DM40 billion in 1992 (Gröbner, 1992, p. 5). This burden on public funds has aroused much controversy. In an interview in *Die Zeit*, Norbert Blüm, whose Federal Ministry for Labour is at the centre of the transfers, expressed anxiety lest a job-creation society emerges from the old socialist planned economy. While not denying the need for restructuring and job-creation schemes, he insisted that labour-market policy could only perform a bridging function. In his view, every bridge requires a river bank; in the present context, investments are analogous to a bank in that they create the 'normal' competitive workplaces. In the reconstruction of the new *Länder*, business leaders, he insisted, should take the lead, though with the requisite support from the federal finance and economic authorities (*Die Zeit*, 22 May 1992, p. 24).

4.5 Wages

The new *Länder* basically adopted the west German system of collective wage bargaining organized on a regional and sectoral basis between unions and employers' organizations. The wage contracts, embracing the vast majority of the west German labour force, cover not only basic wages but also holidays and working time. The principle of the autonomy of the wage negotiators underpins the bargaining process and rules out direct government intervention except under certain clearly specified conditions.

In 1988, average monthly pay in the GDR was 1,100 GDR marks gross and 925 GDR marks net as against DM3,300 gross and DM2,200 net in the FRG. In the run-up to unification, West German politicians raised East Germans' expectations of a sharp increase in their wages during what was expected to be a relatively short transitional period of convergence in living standards. Wages were already climbing as unification day approached: between the first and second quarters of 1990 the average industrial wage of full-time workers increased by 15 per cent (Akerlof *et al.*, 1991, p. 56).

Since GEMSU, when wages and salaries were converted at one-to-one on the basis of the level of payments on 1 May 1990, the trend in wage settlements has been towards parity with west German levels. For example, during the first half of 1991 wage and salary agreements were concluded which benefited about 5.5 million east German employees and workers. Most of these agreements raised wages and salaries to between 60 and 65 per cent of the western level. In the second half of the year further agreements were signed which brought east German contractual wages and salaries in retail trade and the roofing trade to within 30 per cent of west Germany's (*Jahresgutachten 1991/92*, 1991, pp. 110–11). By the summer of 1992, east German wages and salaries were on average

Table 4.3 Wages and productivity in east Germany, 1990–2

	1990		1991		1992
	Jan–June	July–Dec	Jan–June	July–Dec	Jan–June
Wages[1]	10.86	12.22	16.04	22.72	21.11
Productivity[2]	19.16	18.66	17.81	20.39	19.18
Unit labour costs	1991=100				
east Germany	56.2	64.9	89.3	110.7	109.3
west Germany	91.8	99.7	94.6	105.2	99.1

Source: DIW and IfW, 1992b, p. 470
[1] Gross income per hour of work
[2] GDP at constant prices per hour of work

between 70 and 75 per cent of the western level (Sakowsky, 1992, p. 1256).

The first significant wage agreement which specifically incorporated a stage-by-stage equalization of east–west German wages was concluded in the metal-working and processing industry, normally a pace-setter in the old *Länder*: from 1 April 1991 wages and salaries, which were then 52.5 per cent and 58.5 per cent respectively of west German levels, were to rise until they reached the western level exactly three years later. Similar agreements were reached in the steel industry, ceramics, glass, skilled roofing and the rubber industry. By the end of 1991, numerous wage and salary negotiations were being settled within a band ranging from 50 per cent of west German levels in the power industry to 83.5 per cent in the construction industry in east Berlin (Clasen, 1992, p. 8).

The increase in gross earnings has not been matched by similar gains in labour productivity, thus imposing enormous cost pressures on firms. Data collected by the German Institute for Economic Research showed that unit labour costs were about one-quarter higher in the first half of 1992 than in the corresponding six months in 1991 (see Table 4.3). A survey of 2,500 Treuhand and privatized firms between May and August 1992 established that the wage burden was regarded as the most important problem facing firms in manufacturing. Two-thirds of the firms considered that the increase in wages and salaries was a 'very great' or 'important' problem. Mounting labour costs were depriving firms of resources for restructuring the production process (DIW and IfW, 1992b, p. 473). Throughout 1992, the gap in labour productivity remained constant, but as wage unit costs rose in the new *Länder* by 13.5 per cent as against 4.5 per cent in west Germany, this meant that they were 72.5 per cent higher in the former and a serious impediment to competitiveness (Müller-Krumholz, 1993, p. 62).

Effective earnings sometimes deviate appreciably from the level fixed in basic wage and salary contracts for a variety of reasons. First, fewer east German firms are bound by basic wage and salary settlements than are their western counterparts. Second, in west Germany effective wages tend to be slightly higher than the contractual wages and salaries in all sectors except the public service, whereas in east Germany the two rates are similar. It is estimated that in west Germany effective wages, although not uniform across all sectors, are often 20 per cent above the basic rate (Herr, 1992, p. 4). Finally, additional payments such as the thirteenth-month bonus and holiday pay are lower than in the west, and employed persons in the new *Länder* work on average one hour longer per day than their western counterparts (Clasen, 1992, p. 8). If this difference in basic and effective wages survives, then an appreciable divergence between east and west German earnings will continue even when basic wages have converged. For example, it has been estimated that by 1994 the effective wages of engineering workers will be 20 per cent lower than in the west (Flockton and Esser, in Smith *et al.*, 1992, p. 293).

Further insight into the impact on earnings of the different regulations was provided by an investigation conducted by the DGB's Economic and Social Institute in June 1991. The basic earnings of metal workers in Saxony corresponded to 62.6 per cent of that of their colleagues in Bavaria. But a calculation of hourly earnings produced the lower figure of 57.9 per cent on account of the longer working week of the Saxon workers. Other factors such as the longer holidays of the Bavarians and an effective wage 10 per cent above basic rate reduced the east German hourly earnings to 39.9 per cent below the west German level (*Handelsblatt*, 29 July 1991, p. 3).

The phenomenon of an escalation of wages at a time of contracting output, rising unemployment and low productivity gains has given rise to a long and animated debate in governmental and business circles. The Institute for Economic Research Halle, in a statement to the CDU/CSU Bundestag party grouping in autumn 1992, estimated that at least one million east German workplaces had become uncompetitive in one year as a result of the convergence of wages and salaries (*Berliner Zeitung*, 10–11 October 1992, p. 9). The failure to establish a clear linkage between wage increases and productivity gains has been a bone of contention between labour and capital. The Federal Economics Ministry, on the basis of calculations of a rise in per capita wages in east Germany to almost 45 per cent of west German levels but an output per worker of barely 30 per cent of that in west Germany, warned:

This substantial gap between wage levels and productivity must have considerably increased the number of jobs lost and appreciably hindered the creation of new ones. If 1992 were to see a further sharp rise in unit wage costs, the existing difficulties would continue to mount and the need for financial support from the west of Germany would rise again – thus placing further burdens on the shoulders of the western German economy.

There are chances for a rapid recovery in economic activity in both the east and west of Germany, but they can be utilised only if it is borne in mind that high wages cannot be coped with in view of the slackening of the economic situation in western Germany and the unsettled economic situation in eastern Germany. [Bundesministerium für Wirtschaft, *Monthly Review. The Economic Situation in the Federal Republic of Germany*, no. 1, 1992, p. 11]

Nor could the Ministry take much comfort from the trend in unit wage costs: in 1992, the 14 per cent increase in unit-wage costs outstripped prices and were considerably higher than in the old *Länder* (Arbeitskreis Konjunktur im DIW, 1993, pp. 9–10). Unit wage costs are, however, not the only significant determinant of competitiveness and profit. For example, while hourly wages increased by about 50 per cent in precision engineering and stones and clays, the latter, though shedding less labour, managed to increase production by 200 per cent in contrast to a decline of about two-thirds in precision engineering. The explanation for the discrepancy lies in the much greater success of stones and clays in finding customers in local markets; precision engineering, more orientated towards international markets, encountered much fiercer competition and greater pressure to cut costs. High wage increases thus add to the cost burden and create a need for massive subsidies (DIW and lfW, 1992a, pp. 136–7).

Given the drawbacks of wage increases for the competitiveness and survival of east German firms, why has wage equalization gathered such momentum? First, it is very difficult to justify to east German workers why pay levels should be so different for the same or similar work in both parts of the country when the labour market is in the process of uniting. This sense of social equity is reflected in the statement by the former managing director of the Treuhand, Rainer Gohlke: 'It is unfair that an engine driver should receive three times the pay to make a roundtrip from Hamburg to Leipzig as to make the same journey in the opposite direction' (quoted in Akerlof *et al.*, 1991, p. 59). Higher wages, it has also been argued, should represent a form of compensation for the damage and distress caused by an overhasty monetary union (Schui, 1991, pp. 54–5). Second, wage increases cushion the removal of price subsidies. While this argument is valid for some groups, it should be noted that wages have generally managed to stay ahead of the rise in the cost of living. Third, it is frequently contended that the prospect of higher incomes may persuade skilled workers to remain in east Germany and contribute to the reconstruction of its economy. Although the attraction of a higher income in the old *Länder* undoubtedly persuades many to migrate, it is only one of a series of factors; and it should be remembered that at a time of high unemployment job opportunities are limited, even for well-qualified labour.

Union pressure has undoubtedly helped to push up wages. The western trade union organizations, which soon came to dominate their counterparts in the east and took over negotiating rights in autumn 1990, rejected a long period of transition. Their policy was influenced by their concern to combat the threat of cheap east German labour and products. In addition, the trade unions reasoned that efforts to increase wages would enable them to recruit new members from among the east German labour force. East German managers, inexperienced in wage negotiations, did not at first offer much resistance to union demands. In fact, many had no incentive to keep wages down and the Treuhand, apparently unwilling to violate the principle of autonomy of the wage negotiators, refrained from intervention. Although the unions have been criticized for their insistence on parity, the policy has had at least one significant benefit: the reduction of social tensions in the east. And it should be recalled that some west German businesses have had an interest in suppressing wages in east Germany as it was felt that the existing capital stock in west Germany would not be put at risk by higher wages in the new *Länder*. If anything, the competition from a low-wage region represented a greater threat. Finally, as pensions and other benefits are related to previous earnings, this has been an incentive for workers to improve their earnings before joining the dole queue. Wage negotiators could also take into account the fact that higher wages and benefits might in the final analysis be picked up either by the Treuhand or by the Federal government anxious to keep the social peace (see Bundesministerium für Wirtschaft, 1992, pp. 15–20, 25; Akerlof *et al.*, 1991, pp. 56–64; Sinn and Sinn, 1992, pp. 170–9).

The central dilemma of wage policy is addressed in a memorandum drawn up by the Board of Economic Advisers to the Federal Economics Ministry:

A prevalent view is that the wages in the east should be oriented towards productivity or, rather, towards the value that the market attaches to the output of workers in the East. The wage level in the West should be based on the corresponding value in the West. Another view is that in a re-unified economy, where regional labour markets are linked through a high level of mobility, wages for the same work should become equal throughout the respective market.

There are grounds for both views, which taken together promote a middle position. However, there are no reasons for the incompatible view that wages in the West should be oriented towards the (high) productivity there and that wages in the East should also be oriented towards western levels. But this is precisely what is being recommended. Whoever recommends a rapid wage equalization according to the principle of equal pay for equal work must take into account that labour productivity in Germany as a whole is on average clearly lower than in the old Federal Republic. Therefore, the above argument would only make sense if a policy of rapid wage alignment in the East were linked to a policy of wage restraint in the West. The pressure to migrate which would emerge from accelerated wage increases and the resulting unemployment in the East would then at least correspond to a greater demand for labour in the West due to a decline in unit-wage costs there. Further, a policy of increased income taxes, together with high transfer payments for intensifying infrastructure development in the East, would make sense. But nothing which might burden their clientele, neither in the East nor in the West, corresponds with the unions' position. This endangers prospects for a consensus on a generally consistent economic and wages policy. [Bundesministerium für Wirtschaft, 1992, pp. 30–1]

The OECD, too, has expressed anxiety over developments:

If wage levels do not reflect the surplus of labour in eastern Germany, prospective levels of profitability for new investment will be lower, reducing the incentives to invest; the viability of existing plant is also affected, reducing output and employment, with consequent burdens on the social security budget, and diminishing the ability of the eastern German economy to generate domestically some of the funds needed for investment. [OECD, 1992b, pp. 73–4]

Furthermore, the OECD, while accepting that many job losses have been 'the inevitable result of economic restructuring', insists that rapid wage convergence has been a serious obstacle to recovery. It underlines its case by pointing to the Czech and Slovak economies where wage rises are only ten per cent of west German levels, yet productivity is roughly the same as in east Germany (OECD, 1992a, p. 74). Although these arguments carry much weight, the CDU politician and Minister President of Saxony, Kurt Biedenkopf, speaks for many east Germans in rejecting the idea of the new *Länder* as a low-wage region. Contending that this is simply not feasible in a single labour market, he has proposed that west German wage and salary earners renounce real wage increases for two years. The firms, who would thereby enjoy lower operating costs, should either invest the money saved in east Germany or pay an equivalent sum in taxes (*Berliner Zeitung*, 28 July 1992, p. 21).

In the deteriorating economic climate in Germany as a whole, the notion of wage parity came under increasing pressure. The engineering employers' association Gesamtmetall flagged, in February 1993, its intention to renegotiate the agreement with the metalworkers' union IG Metall for a 26 per cent wage increase in April 1993 as part of the realignment of eastern and western wages by April 1994. Arbitration talks broke down in early March when the employers tabled a 9 per cent offer. The unions accused the employers of having reneged on the collective agreements and underplaying the fact that east Germans are having to pay west German prices. The steel employers' federation followed the example of Gesamtmetall, both arguing that most of their members simply could not afford to adhere to the original timetable for increasing east German wages. This prompted a two-week strike in May by thousands of metal and steel workers throughout the new *Länder*. The dispute was eventually settled by the employers agreeing to pay, at the start of December, most of the wage hike promised for April and to implement wage parity in mid-1996, two years later than originally agreed. Eastern companies may, however, pay their workers less if they take advantage of a special 'hardship clause' and persuade IG Metall to cooperate. Whether this agreement will stick depends very much on the Chancellor's ability to keep the solidarity pact alive (see Section 7.2) and on the health of the German economy.

4.6 The cost of living

Immediately after GEMSU prices were slow to rise, partly because the price of manufactured goods such as household utensils and furniture fell with the removal of product taxes. In fact, despite the removal of state subsidies for certain foodstuffs at the time of formal unification, the cost of living index in October 1990 was only 96.8. In the months immediately after GEMSU, with wages rising faster than prices, net real wages by February 1991 were at least 15 per cent higher than before the introduction of monetary union (Akerlof *et al.*, 1991, p. 59). The first time the cost of living exceeded the 1989 level occurred in January 1991 (102.5) when the cost of energy rose sharply and public transport subsidies were reduced.

Table 4.4 The cost of living index in east Germany, 1990–2 (All employee households)
Second half of 1990/First half of 1991 = 100

	Total	Foodstuffs, beverages, tobacco	Clothing, shoes	House rents	Energy excluding fuels	Furniture, household goods	Transport and communications
1990							
Sept	95.3	97.1	96.5	97.1	63.8	98.1	97.6
Oct	96.8	97.4	100.0	97.1	63.8	98.3	100.1
Nov	96.6	97.3	101.8	97.1	· 63.8	98.8	98.1
Dec	97.3	98.8	103.7	97.1	64.4	99.7	97.3
1991							
Jan	102.5	99.9	102.8	99.6	130.3	101.2	100.7
Feb	102.9	100.5	103.5	103.3	130.5	101.8	99.9
Mar	104.1	101.8	104.1	103.6	130.6	102.1	102.1
Apr	105.1	102.6	104.7	103.6	131.9	102.4	104.3
May	105.6	102.4	104.1	103.6	146.9	102.8	104.5
Jun	105.9	103.2	103.6	103.6	146.7	102.7	104.7
Jul	106.7	103.8	103.0	103.8	146.5	102.6	107.4
Aug	106.8	103.3	103.4	103.9	147.0	102.9	107.9
Sep	107.1	103.0	104.2	103.9	149.8	103.3	108.0
Oct	117.3	103.1	104.9	396.7	216.5	103.7	108.2
Nov	118.0	104.3	105.4	396.8	216.6	104.2	108.3
Dec	118.0	104.2	105.9	396.8	216.5	104.4	108.1
1992							
Jan	118.8	104.9	105.4	397.9	215.9	104.8	109.3
Feb	119.2	105.4	105.0	397.7	216.4	105.0	109.7
Mar	119.8	105.9	105.1	399.6	215.9	105.0	114.4
Apr	120.0	106.2	105.2	400.4	214.1	105.3	118.8
May	120.6	106.4	105.4	400.1	213.5	105.5	112.4
Jun	120.8	106.7	105.3	400.0	212.4	105.5	112.8
Jul	120.7	106.1	105.2	400.1	212.1	105.7	113.0
Aug	120.6	105.6	105.2	400.3	213.5	105.8	112.8
Sep	120.7	105.3	105.7	400.3	215.5	105.8	112.7
Oct	120.8	105.3	106.1	401.2	214.2	106.1	112.7
Nov	121.1	105.1	106.3	401.3	214.2	106.3	113.2

Source: Statistisches Bundesamt (ed.), *Wirtschaft und Statistik*, no. 4, 1992, p. 252; no. 1, 1993, Appendix, p. 60

The most dramatic change took place in October 1991 when a reduction in rent subsidies led to a sudden spurt of 292.6 per cent in rents (see Table 4.4).

The Federal Statistical Office has carried out several studies of the cost of living in east Germany. A survey of consumption in the second half of 1990 and the first half of 1991 revealed that the cost of living in November 1991 was about 21.5 per cent higher than in the corresponding month in 1990. An earlier comparison between these two months had put the increase at 26.5 per cent. The discrepancy between the two studies is due to the use of a new basket of goods to reflect the adjustment of consumers to changes in relative prices and to the wider range of goods available since GEMSU (*Monthly Report of the Deutsche Bundesbank*, vol. 44, no. 3, 1992, p. 12).

In another study, the Federal Statistical Office assessed the impact of price increases on the cost of living and on the consumption behaviour of four-person households in east Germany in 1991. The reduction of subsidies for virtually all foodstuffs and canteen meals and the removal of high taxes on many semi-luxuries significantly affected household expenditure on foodstuffs, drinks and tobacco products as a group. Considerably less was spent on drinks, 165 marks in 1989 as against DM122 in 1991. Although the price increases of foodstuffs, drinks and tobacco products rose by 25 per cent in 1991 compared to 1989, households spent only slightly more on these items than before GEMSU. However, since the middle of 1990, outlays were reduced on meals and snacks at work. In 1991, DM32 per month were spent on this group of commodities, which – despite appreciable price increases – was still DM11 less than had been spent in GDR marks in 1989. While many households had obviously decided to make savings on their regular warm mid-day meal, parents did not economize on the meals of their children in day-care institutions and at school. There was an increase here from DM38 per month in 1989 to DM104 in 1991 ('3154 DM Einnahmen im Monat', 1992, pp. 2–3).

The purchase of a new or second-hand car as well as outlays on petrol, car taxes and insurance figured more highly in household budgets. In 1991, household expenditure on these items was DM587 per month, a threefold increase since 1989. This was also a major reason for the increase in loans: 1.5 per cent of the households took out a loan (ibid., p. 4).

From the second half of 1991, far more was spent on household goods than before the *Wende*, in particular on new washing machines, electrical heating appliances and general household maintenance goods. An average of DM104 were spent each month on the last group of items, that is DM60 more than in 1989. The increase in rents in October 1991 and in the cost of electricity, gas, briquettes and the removal of refuse at the beginning of the year resulted in 11 per cent of the budget being absorbed by these items in October 1991 as against only 4 per cent in 1989. The Federal Statistical Office concluded that the real increase in private consumption in 1991 – given an average price rise of about 25 per cent since before GEMSU – was only about DM300 (ibid., pp. 3–4).

General living standards have therefore not undergone a severe erosion, but this is only because of the vast public transfers from the old *Länder*. Averages, however, conceal serious instances of social deprivation.

4.7 A new poverty

The rapidity of the exit from the planned economy and the growing significance of monetary income have created new risks of poverty as well as reinforcing some old ones. Although it is difficult to devise satisfactory criteria for defining poverty, one method utilized in west Germany is to assess poverty according to average income. Thus 50 per cent of average income constitutes a medium poverty value. If average household income is taken as the benchmark in the GDR/east Germany, only three per cent of households in 1990 and five per cent in 1991 were living in poverty. However, the incidence of poverty was much higher among single parents – 16 per cent in 1990 and 19 per cent in the following year. Households with five or more members were the next group most seriously affected (Statistisches Bundesamt, 1992, p. 492).

Different levels of unemployment widen the social gap between eastern and western parts of Germany, and the size and quality of dwelling, medical care, educational opportunities for children and so forth are now more closely related to earned income than in the old socialist system. New sources of inequality are therefore generated and a cleavage is opening up between the 'have-jobs' and the 'have-no-jobs' (Peel, 1992b, p. 12).

At the end of 1991, an estimated 200,000 east Germans were receiving social-security benefits. This figure undoubtedly understates the real level of need as many do not claim assistance for a variety of reasons: embarrassment, ignorance of their rights and a long-standing antipathy to bureaucracy (Helwig, 1992a, p. 229). Lothar Stock, the chairman of the Bundesarbeitsgemeinschaft der Sozialhilfeinitiativen, believes that as few as one in ten of those eligible actually apply for assistance.

A sharp increase of east German recipients of social security is predicted for 1993 as many workers were expected to lose the cushion of short-time work and earnings-related unemployment benefit at a time when rents and the cost of living would also be on the rise (*Berliner Zeitung*, 25–26 July 1992, p. 4). The Minister of Labour and Social Affairs in the *Land* Brandenburg, Regine Hildebrandt, depicts the situation in even gloomier terms. She reckons that about half of the inhabitants in the new *Länder* are living on the poverty line, including three-quarters of all pensioners. Women pensioners are especially threatened as their average GDR earnings had been about 25 per cent lower than those of men and in consequence were on a lower pension. The unemployed and recipients of transitional payment for early retirement might also find themselves in a precarious position. As the wage compensation payments amount at most to two-thirds of their previous income, many fall below the basic level of subsistence defined by Regine Hildebrandt as DM600 and DM700 (Helwig, 1992a, pp. 228–9).

Rita Süßmuth, the President of the Bundestag, has sought to draw attention to the plight of single parents. The vast majority of the 350,000 single or divorced parents are women (Flockton and Esser in Smith *et al.*, 1992, p. 287), many of whom are dependent on unemployment benefit or social welfare, housing subsidies and child allowance. The seriousness of the situation can be judged by the fact that out of 192,000 families in east Berlin, there are 60,000 single parents. Whereas in the GDR single parents could rely on having a job and relatively generous work-time arrangements as well as *Horten*, crèche and kindergarten facilities for their children, this provision has deteriorated since unification. Mothers find it difficult to find the time to attend retraining and further training courses as these often require an absence from home of about a week. Many employers require flexibility from their workforce and, as some of the old GDR labour provisions still apply, shrink away from employing women who can claim paid time for looking after sick children. Women face grave difficulties if the father is unable or unwilling to pay child maintenance, a problem which has been compounded by the application of regulations from GDR family law to divorces before unification in October 1990. According to GDR law, the economic dependence of former partners ceased after divorce, although about 10 per cent of divorced women were entitled to claim a period of grace during which their ex-husband had to make maintenance contributions. The law of the old FRG, which aims to maintain the marital standard of living for both parties after divorce, applies only to east Germans who divorced after unification (Piepgas, 1992, p. 3).

The situation in housing is critical despite the aspiration of the Honecker regime to solve the housing question as a social problem by the year 1990. An estimated one million new housing units are required and much of the existing stock needs to be renovated. For example, in the city of Potsdam about 20,000 people were hunting for suitable housing in early 1992. Although at the end of April over 11,000 had an authorized right to a dwelling, the shortage was so acute that only a few had a realistic chance of obtaining accommodation. With the local authorities strapped for cash – the annual budget in 1992 was only DM589 million – they were in no position to meet the estimated DM2 billion required for a construction programme encompassing public buildings, housing, environmental improvement and other projects. Property disputes, which have caused so much hostility between occupants and claimants, also delay progress in the housing programme. In Leipzig, the 48,000 claims will take about twenty years to clear up at the present rate of progress. Discussions on a further increase in rents in the new *Länder* caused so much unrest that the Federal government had to postpone the increase until the start of 1993 and to lower it to between DM0.75 and DM2.10 per sq.m. But with so many unemployed in relatively low-paid job-creation and retraining schemes or on early retirement payments, even this level of increase will constitute a significant erosion of living standards for those who are unable to claim a housing subsidy (Helwig, 1992b, pp. 789–90).

5 East Germany in trust

The Federal government in Bonn, while initially putting much of its trust in the power of the market to revive the GDR economy, also devised a two-pronged policy to reconstruct and modernize the old socialist system. First, it reshaped Modrow's Treuhand and utilized the agency as the main instrument for breaking up the old state-owned enterprises and combines and then through privatization to make them into competitive and commercially viable firms. Second, in order to encourage the investment essential for the rebuilding of the GDR economy, Bonn made available a wide range of direct and indirect incentives. One year after GEMSU, the Federal Economics Ministry calculated that about 80 per cent of total investment in the new *Länder* was financed through public funds, the majority being spent on the massive infrastructure requirements.

5.1 State assistance for investment in east Germany

The major forms of direct investment are tax allowances, credits at favourable interest rates and loan guarantees (for full details, see Federal Ministry of Economics 1991a and 1991b). Taking tax incentives first, investment grants are available for the purchase and production of new, depreciable and movable assets. The level of tax allowance is 12 per cent of purchase and production costs before 1 July 1992 and 8 per cent incurrred between 30 June 1992 and the end of 1994. This form of allowance is regarded by the German Institute for Economic Research and the Kiel Institute of World Economics as the most important of the various types of aid. Special depreciation allowances are available until the end of 1994 for up to 50 per cent of the costs for the purchase or the production of fixed assets and for the modernization or expansion of buildings.

Second, a number of grants are available under various regional policy programmes. As part of the Unification Treaty, the Law for the Improvement of the Regional Economic Structure was extended to the former GDR. For a period of at least five years, east Germany is treated as a special investment zone under the act. The

Federal government and the five new *Länder* are obliged each to provide 50 per cent of an annual sum of DM3 billion over the five-year period. Investment grants can be made from the programme's funds which reduce the costs of investment and commercial projects of business start-ups by a maximum of 23 per cent, the expansion of an existing enterprise by up to 20 per cent and the conversion and modernization of an enterprise by up to 15 per cent. The acquisition of a closed-down plant or one which is threatened with closure may also receive grants of up to the maximum support rate of 23 per cent. Surveys of east German businesses have shown that this differentiation between expansion, modernization and start-ups as well as the distinction between new and existing enterprises is very difficult to operate and that a uniform grant would probably be preferable (Heimpold, 1991, p. 3).

Small and medium-sized businesses are eligible for assistance from a wide range of programmes. For example, equity capital can be provided towards the establishment of private business, the acquisition of a company and follow-up investment. Loans from the European Recovery Programme (ERP) are a second and popular form of assistance. ERP loans are granted to small and medium-sized businesses with annual sales of up to DM50 million (DM500 million in the case of loans for investment in environmental protection). They should not exceed DM1 million and should finance at most 50 per cent of investment costs. Loans are granted at favourable rates: for example, long repayment periods of up to twenty years and no amortization during the first year. The demand for ERP credits has been very lively: by May 1991, 93,000 applications had been made, representing DM12 billion or 90 per cent of the total credit line. Eight thousand applications worth DM8.4 billion had been approved and DM3.9 billion actually paid out (DIW and IfW, 1991a, p. 345).

Investment loans are given by the Kreditanstalt für Wiederaufbau (Reconstruction Loan Corporation), based in Frankfurt on Main, for the establishment and expansion of small and medium-sized enterprises and for the improvement of the environment. The loans can be used to supplement ERP loans and equity capital assistance and are available to companies with a turnover not usually exceeding DM500 million per year. Investment loans from the Deutsche Ausgleichsbank (German Equalization Bank) are available for establishing a company, moving its location and for innovation. The maximum loan is DM1.5 million per project and the minimum is DM10,000. Fixed interest rates apply to the entire loan period, usually up to ten years with two years' grace.

Table 5.1 Investment plan of a large business

Total investment DM100.0 mn		
of which:		
Equipment (operating life of 10 years)		DM70.0 mn
Buildings		DM30.0 mn
Incentives and tax allowances		
– General incentive (23 per cent)		DM23.0 mn
– Equipment incentive (12 per cent)		DM 8.4 mn
– Investment in equipment	DM70.0 mn	
– Less 23 per cent investment	*DM16.1 mn*	
Basis for assessment	*DM53.9 mn*	
Depreciation at 60 per cent rate	DM32.3 mn	
– Tax saving at 50 per cent rate		DM16.1 mn
– Investment in buildings	DM30.0 mn	
– Less 23 per cent investment	*DM 6.9 mn*	
Basis for Assessment	DM23.1 mn	
Depreciation at 54 per cent	DM12.5 mn	
– Tax saving at 50 per cent rate		DM 6.2 mn
– Total Incentives and Tax Savings		DM53.7 mn

Source: Federal Ministry of Economics, 1991b, pp. 27–8

Guarantee banks have been established in the five new *Länder* to assist people without sufficient collateral to start up a business. Members of the liberal professions and small and medium-sized businesses also qualify for these loans. The guarantees cover up to 80 per cent of a loan and the maximum guarantee is DM1 million. The Berlin Bank of Industry and the Federal government also have facilities for supplying guarantees for investment loans.

An assessment of the cumulative benefits of these tax allowances and investment programmes has been devised in the form of two optimal models, one for a small and medium-sized business and the other for a large business. If a large business engaged in an investment project worth DM100 million, it could obtain, in the first year, a total saving of DM53.7 million as a result of investment loans, depreciation allowances and tax relief (see Table 5.1).

The level of state assistance is clearly impressive, but, as yet, the programme lacks a clear, overarching concept and the impact of allowances and incentives is restricted by obstacles such as owner-ship disputes and administrative bottlenecks.

5.2 The Treuhand controversy

The Treuhandanstalt or trusteeship agency (henceforth Treuhand) is at the epicentre of the seismic eruption in the east German economy. Not a formal government agency, it is nevertheless responsible for the controversial implementation of the government's 'miracle cure', that is, the administration of the bitter-sweet medicine of privatization. The controversy is depicted by *The Economist* as follows:

> Investors complain that it [Treuhand] is bureaucratic, economists that it feather-beds firms unfit to survive, trade unions that it is too ready to make quick sales for next to nothing. Tenants and the unemployed call it heartless. All to nods from politicians happy to let the Treuhand take the blame which otherwise would come their way. ['Privatising East Germany', 1991, p. 21]

5.3 The Treuhand under Modrow

The notion of a trusteeship for looking after the 'people's assets' originated with Wolfgang Ullmann of Democracy Now. However, the Treuhand founded by the Modrow government on 1 March 1990 was based on more centralistic notions than had been envisaged by the citizen's movement. According to its statute of 15 March, it was enjoined to administer the corporate assets of the combines, enterprises and institutions in the public interest. It was not, however, designated as the owner of this property and it was subordinated to the government. In keeping with its trusteeship function, the Treuhand was empowered to acquire the shares of the combines, enterprises and institutions after their conversion into limited liability or joint-stock companies. The former were converted from enterprises with more than 2,000 employees and the latter from smaller firms. Nationally-owned companies such as the railways and the post as well as the property of the local and regional authorities could be excluded from this process (Hans Luft, 1991, p. 1271).

Although instrumental in transferring state enterprises into joint-stock companies, the Treuhand was not empowered to intervene in the business operations of the firms under its administration, as had been the practice of the branch ministries in the old command economy. Managers, it was intended, should be largely independent of the higher organs of state and be controlled by their supervisory boards. One important restriction was that nationally owned property could not be purchased by third parties as the necessary legislation was not introduced by the Modrow government. Modrow's own party, the PDS, as well as the SPD and several of the citizens' movements feared that privatization would lead to a sell-off of the GDR and were anxious that the 'people's-own assets' be saved for the people. In keeping with this principle, joint ventures were restricted to East and West German firms. In short, the Treuhand was established by the Modrow government as an agency for the preservation of the GDR's assets, not as an agency for the privatization of the country (Christ and Neubauer, 1991, pp. 116-19; Institut für Angewandte Wirtschafts-forschung, 1991b, p. 12).

Despite these limits on its activities, the Treuhand had much important work to do: for example, aiding firms to evaluate their competitiveness and to clarify their liquidity situation. Recon-struction did not emerge as a major issue during Modrow's pre-miership as the Council of Ministers lacked insight into the real economic condition of the enterprises. The failure to appreciate their desolate state is reflected in the Treuhand statute drawn up by the Council on 15 March which empowered the agency to draw its revenue from the dividends of the companies in its charge. This revenue was intended to prop up the weaker companies (Christ and Neubauer, 1991, pp. 112–13). However, all these plans of the Modrow government were destined for the waste-paper bin, and while Modrow's power crumbled, West German firms such as VW, Daimler Benz and Siemens concluded their own agreements with GDR firms.

5.4 The Treuhand under de Maizière

After the Volkskammer election on 18 March and the subsequent creation of a coalition government under the CDU leader Lothar de Maizière, privatization received the green light. On 17 June 1990, the Volkskammer passed a Treuhand Act, which later was adopted virtually unchanged in the Unification Treaty (see document 4). The Treuhand was authorized to privatize state-owned assets in line with the social-market economy and to promote the restructur-ing of potentially economically viable companies with a view to their privatization (Priewe and Hickel, 1991, p. 165). Privatization enjoyed priority over reconstruction, and the original emphasis was on the private owner to carry out the restructuring of a firm. The crucial paragraph in the Treuhand Act defining the function of the agency, reads:

The Treuhand is an independent government agency established for the privatization and use of state-owned assets based on the principles of the market economy [and] promotes the structural adjustment of the economy to meet market requirements by developing potentially viable firms into competitive enterprises and then transferring them into private ownership. By implementing a program of decentralization and divestment, the Treuhand aims to create competitive corporate structures within an efficient industrial base. [Treuhandanstalt, *Promoting the New Germany*, p. 5]

One alternative to this particular form of privatization, a voucher system, did not receive much consideration as it was felt that it would delay the flow of private capital and the replacement of the old SED cadres by new, more dynamic management teams.

The Treuhand's legal status was defined as that of an independent entity constituted in public law, and since GEMSU it 'reports' to the Federal Finance Ministry. The latter monitors the legal aspects of the Treuhand's activities and, together with the Federal Economics Ministry, is responsible for operational policy. Both ministries are represented on the Treuhand Supervisory Board. This mode of operation has put the Treuhand outside the direct control of parliament, contrary to what Jens Reich of Bündnis 90 had advocated in the Volkskammer debate in April 1990 (Suhr, 1990, p. 66).

The Treuhand Act transferred all state-owned enterprises and property to the Treuhand, in particular the 126 centrally managed and the ninety-five regionally-managed combines, encompassing about 8,000 firms, and 40,000 smaller service outlets such as shops and bars. As a result of the further sub-division of combine enterprises, the number of firms reached 10,344 by the end of June 1991, with the Treuhand being responsible for about 7,200 (Treuhandanstalt, *Informationen*, no. 3–4, July–August 1991, p. 6). In addition, the Treuhand took charge of Schalk-Golodkowski's KoKo, the property of the Stasi and 62,000 square kilometres of real estate amounting to 57 per cent of the surface area of the GDR. It became the employer of about six million people. Charged with disposing of an entire economy, the Treuhand became the world's largest state-holding agency.

The revenue of the Treuhand was expected to come from the proceeds of privatization sales. In October 1990, the then Treuhand President Detlev Rohwedder estimated that the total value of Treuhand firms was DM600 billion (Flug, 1992, p. 32). In anticipation of these proceeds the Treuhand was allowed to draw on DM25 billion credit in 1991 and an anticipated DM32 billion in 1992. The revenue was to be disbursed on the reorganization of the state's assets as well as on the restructuring of the GDR budget. In addition, part of the Treuhand's revenue was designated by the Unification Treaty for the payment of half of the interest on the total GDR state debt until the end of 1993 and from December 1993 a half of the debt servicing on the external liabilities of the former

GDR. In addition, the Treuhand assumed an undefined share of the debt servicing of the Debt Processing Fund and liability for interest payments on the debts inherited by the enterprises until the submission of their opening DM balance sheets. These high expectations were soon to be disappointed: not only were proceeds from privatization far less than had been anticipated, but the whole privatization process proved to be an administrative and political bed of nails.

5.5 Organization of the Treuhand

The Treuhand was at first poorly endowed to cope with its basic tasks: it lacked telephones, fax machines and details about what it owned and it had about 140 officials, most of them East Germans without any experience of a market economy. The Treuhand Act made provision for the establishment of four Treuhand joint-stock companies with responsibility for the heavy-industry, investment goods, consumer goods and service sectors. This plan was soon abandoned by the head of the Hoesch steel group, Detlev Rohwedder, who in August 1990 took over from Rainer Gohlke as President of the Treuhand. After his assassination on 1 April 1991, his work was continued by his deputy and a former Finance Minister of Lower Saxony, Birgit Breuel, whose *modus operandi* soon earned her the label of 'Iron Lady'. Rohwedder, who had also served as a State Secretary in the Federal Economics Ministry, had revamped the entire organizational structure. The Treuhand's staff rapidly increased to over 3,000 highly paid employees, about three-quarters of whom were East Germans (Treuhandanstalt, *Informationen*, no. 5, September 1991, p. 5). The staff were distributed across the eight sections, one each for personnel and finance and six industrial departments. The industrial departments are responsible for several branches: department one, for example, for machine building as well as having overall charge over privatization, while department two deals with precision engineering, vehicle construction and the liquidation of enterprises.

The Treuhand Management Board reports to the Supervisory Board, which is comparable to the board of directors in a joint-stock company. The Supervisory Board, located in the former Luftwaffe headquarters in east Berlin, presides over the industrial departments and must approve major decisions taken by the Management Board. In 1991, the Supervisory Board consisted of twenty-four persons, mainly managers from west Germany, although it did include five east Germans. Other board members included four trade-union, two Federal-government and five

Länder-government representatives (Siebert, 1991, p. 301). The agency was unable to dispense with east German experience and know-how. It recruited ex-SED functionaries such as Dieter Koschella, a former Secretary of State in the Ministry of Light Industry, Erhart Schuler, originally Secretary of State in the Ministry of Machine Tools, and Klaus Klinke and Siegfried Zeisig, both ex-Deputy Finance Ministers (Flug, 1992, p. 18). Twenty-two east Germans occupied a senior position, the leading 'Ossi' being Wolfram Krause, head of the Treuhand finance department, and formerly a deputy chairman of and first SED District Secretary to the State Planning Commission as well as a State Secretary in the Modrow government (Priewe and Hickel, 1991, p. 168; Christ and Neubauer, 1991, p. 127). Krause departed in the summer of 1992 in the wake of controversy surrounding alleged links with the Stasi.

In addition to its east Berlin headquarters, the Treuhand has fifteen regional offices in the main cities of the former GDR. These offices were founded in the spring of 1990 in line with the *Bezirk* structure of the GDR. They were responsible for more than one million workplaces in 6,718 firms as against the two million workplaces in 3,826 firms under the control of the Treuhand headquarters in Berlin (Flug, 1992, p. 97). Experienced west German managers were brought in to direct them, and the offices were given direct responsibility for all the companies in their region employing fewer than 1,500 people, or about two-thirds of the original 8,000. The Liegenschaft, a subsidiary of the Treuhand, assumed responsibility for the sale of real estate.

In the first year of its existence, 120 top west German managers were 'seconded' to the Treuhand. Their salaries were covered by their west German firms for an average of six months. Some of the imported west Germans were plucked from retirement: Werner Lamby, the former chief of the Mischkonzern VIAG, presided over the board of directors of the Stickstoffwerke AG Wittenberg-Piesteritz and Herbert Gienow, ex-chair of the Klockner-Werke, headed the board of directors at the Filmfabrik Wolfen (Holm, 1991, p. 30). Former leading politicians acquired a new lease of life as entrepreneurs in the east, for example, ex-Finance Minister Hans Apel at the Energiewerke Schwarze Pumpe (ibid., p. 31). In order to generate a more entrepreneurial spirit in its enterprises, the Treuhand, between September 1990 and August 1991, introduced about 1,000 west German executives and removed about 1,400 existing managers and members of boards of directors. The head of the Treuhand personnel department, Alexander Koch, estimated that 12,000 east German business leaders out of a total of about 25,000 executives and directors needed to be ousted from the boardrooms of the former people's own enterprises as they were burdened by their political past and lacked professional competence (Suhr, 1991, p. 121; Hans Luft, 1991, p. 1276; Flug, 1992, p. 80). According to Koch's calculations, in July 1991 between 70 per cent and 80 per cent of directors and managers of the Treuhand's firms came from the circle of managers of the former state enterprises (Suhr, 1991, p. 125).

5.6 Privatization or restructuring?

In the October 1990 edition of the Treuhand's glossy *Business Guide* the priority of the Treuhand is specified as the privatization rather than the restructuring of companies or parts of companies – 'in the firm conviction that privatisation is the best way to restructure an enterprise' (Treuhandanstalt, *The Chance of the 90's*, 1991a, p. 10). Sweeping privatization was intended to establish private property as the cornerstone of the new economic order. Treuhand firms with over 500 employees have to establish a supervisory board. These boards are usually dominated numerically by west Germans, whose experience and external links were considered to be crucial in putting firms on a sound commercial basis (Carlin, 1992, p. 340). Companies which had no chance of surviving in a market economy were to be closed down. Initially, little attention was devoted to the full-scale reorganization and retooling of firms in order to make them profitable prior to divestment. It was the new owner who was expected to undertake the necessary restructuring. One member of the Treuhand staff described the atmosphere in the Treuhand as: 'In January 1991 it was almost heretical to speak of restructuring' (Christ and Neubauer, 1991, p. 130). This episode coincided with Bonn's misplaced confidence in the blessings of a market economy and in its inflated expectations of the viability of east German companies. The magnitude of the task is apparent from Hans Luft's estimate that if privatization in east Germany proceeded at the same rate as in Great Britain under the Thatcher administration, it would take about 600 years to complete (Hans Luft, 1991, p. 1270).

A modification of the privatization imperative occurred in the spring of 1991, by which time it had become obvious that the collapse of the east German economy and the mounting social and psychological costs of unemployment could not be solved by a wave of the magic wand of privatization. At Kohl's meeting in March with the leaders of the five new *Länder* and senior Treuhand officials, it was agreed that several billion D-Marks would be released to make viable companies considered to be unready for privatization (Goodhart, 1991c, p. 2). The *Länder* were also given greater leverage over Treuhand decisions in that the newly created Economic Councils in eastern Germany had to be informed of any planned closures (Flockton and Esser, in Smith *et al.*, 1992, p. 290). Neverthless, despite this modification of the Treuhand mode of operation, privatization was still upheld at the meeting as the official aim of the Treuhand, and privatization through divestment has retained its primacy throughout Breuel's stewardship.

The privatization process began hesitantly, partly because of the staff shortages at the Treuhand and partly because of disputes over ownership, the collapse of east German companies in the wake of GEMSU and trading problems within COMECON. In the early chaotic months, the Treuhand was obliged to extend blanket guarantees of short-term liquidity – DM16 billion in July and DM10 billion in August 1990 – simply to keep its hard-pressed companies afloat and to enable them to pay wages (OECD, 1991b, p. 101).

The Treuhand subsequently expanded its management team, removed some of the legal barriers to privatization and developed more sophisticated and more exacting procedures for the implementation of privatization. With regard to legal obstacles, a serious impediment to privatization was the principle enshrined in the Unification Treaty giving restitution of property priority over compensation to former owners. Legislation passed in March 1991 enabled the Treuhand to give priority to investment in that former owners who are unable or unwilling to continue operating a company or unable to submit an investment plan will receive compensation as soon as the new owner undertakes the appropriate investment and secures jobs. Any financial compensation due to former owners is paid from the public purse (Treuhandanstalt, *Promoting the New Germany*, p. 9). Another boost to the pace of privatization was the law enacted in April 1991 allowing the Treuhand to select parts of companies and sell them separately (Goodhart, 1991b, p.25).

In implementing its privatization programme, the Treuhand is willing to consider three types of purchase: the complete firm, individual subsidiaries or plants and parts of the fixed assets and liquid assets. A prospective buyer must submit not only its bidding price but also a concept for the future operation of the firm. The concept should include a business, investment and financial plan, an employment plan and likely transactions with suppliers and customers. In arriving at its decision the Treuhand gives preference to small and medium-sized businesses rather than huge corporations as well as to what it regards as a fair purchasing price. Price, however, is not the only criterion. Of equal importance are investment and job guarantees and the quality of the management team (see Treuhandanstalt, *The Chance of the '90s*, 1991a, pp. 12–14).

Since the advent of GEMSU, the negotiations on a sale are supposed to take into account the DM opening balance of the firms. The GDR firms have been obliged to revalue their assets, debts and their capital resources as of 1 July 1990. This has led to untold difficulties and frequently to long delays in the presentation of balances. Among the main problems have been the lack of knowledge as to whether or not the real estate belonged to an enterprise; the difference between GDR and FRG procedures in assessing the depreciation on machinery and plant; and the devaluation of monetary assets and debts by 2:1 on 1 July 1990 (Flug, 1992, p. 66). Not surprisingly, the original date for the presentation of the D-Mark opening balances had to be extended from 30 October 1990 to 30 June 1991 and for the concerns to 31 January 1992. As late as May 1991, whereas 64 per cent of the firms had presented their balances, only 6 per cent had had them checked by the Treuhand (Sinn and Sinn, 1992, p. 104). The sale of firms was not helped by the sharp increase in wages which meant that the value of a firm to a prospective owner was less than zero. In fact, the liquidation value of a firm – in relation to the value of its real estate – exceeded the value of the firm as a going concern (Carlin, 1992, p. 341).

These factors help to explain why the Treuhand's revenue from sales is often so small, sometimes amounting to only one DM. This kind of transaction tends to occur when a site is heavily polluted or if an enterprise is heavily in debt or if there is no other potential owner willing to undertake the required investment and secure jobs. For example, the West German chemical company BASF paid nothing for a plant at Schwarzheide, near Dresden, in return for a promise to invest at least DM500 million. And although Volkswagen paid only DM150 million for the Sachsenring car firm which used to construct the Trabant, its investment obligation was over DM4 billion (Privatising East Germany', *The Economist*, 14 September 1991, p. 22).

The terms of the sale of the Warnow shipyard illustrates the bait which the Treuhand occasionally feels obliged to dangle in front of potential buyers in order to secure a sale. The purchase of the shipyard in October 1992 cost Kvaerner of Norway little more than a nominal sum of DM1 million plus DM96 million in investments and guarantees for 2,150 jobs. In return, the Treuhand promised to compensate Kvaerner for up to DM500 million in possible losses for a period of four years and to provide DM463 million to modernize the shipyard in addition to the DM73 million commitment by the regional state of Mecklenburg-West Pomerania (Colitt, 1992a, p. X).

In order to promote the flow of investments, the Treuhand is prepared to allow investors to acquire a company without having to purchase the company site. Under certain circumstances, real property can be leased for a limited period with a purchase option. As many east German companies are burdened by inherited debt to the banking system of the former GDR, a remission of the company from existing or inherited debt can be implemented wholly or in part. The Treuhand is prepared to allow outstanding liabilities to remain unsecured for up to six years and to stand surety for outstanding liabilities amounting to DM3 million at commercial banking rates of commission. Potential buyers and owners may also apply for exemption from the terms of the Environmental Act for environmental damage caused before GEMSU. Where an exemption is not granted, the Treuhand is prepared to negotiate a limited liability for the environmental damage in reasonable proportion to the purchase price.

Some idea of the motives for purchasing an east German firm is provided by an inquiry conducted in March 1991 among 174 Treuhand companies of varying size in all five new *Länder*. Most of the purchasers of the firms in the investigation were from west Germany (66.9 per cent). In ranking order the motives included: the development of the east German market; the acquisition of the real estate of east German firms; the exploitation of the East European market; maintaining the purchaser's position in an existing market; expectation of a high profit; the use of the technology and the technical know-how of east German firms; the acquisition of the distribution network of east German firms; and the use of east German firms as suppliers (Institut für Angewandte Wirtschaftsforschung, 1991b, p. 39).

The major obstacles to privatization emerged from the inquiry as: unresolved ownership questions; poor sales prospects; low profitability; debt and environmental liabilities; the cost of reconstruction; valuation problems; workers' qualifications and training; overmanning; wage costs; and inadequate infrastructure. Whereas the problems arising from inherited debt and environmental damage and overstaffing were identified by large firms with over 1,000 employees as the major obstacles to privatization, they were much less significant for small firms with fewer than 100 employees (ibid., p. 40), Looking at the different branches of industry and construction, inherited environmental damage and debt were the primary concerns in the basic materials industry, whereas they were much less pressing in trade and construction. The major obstacle to privatization, according to firms in the investment-goods industry, concerned sale prospects, old debt, environmental damage and surplus labour. Unresolved ownership questions ranked as the most significant obstacle in construction

Table 5.2 Main factors inhibiting investment in east Germany (%)

Economic branch	Legal-uncertainty	Administra-tive short-comings	Infra-structure problems	Ecological liabilities
Industry:	37	25	24	14
Mining	13	0	4	83
Basic materials and producer goods	34	28	17	21
Investment goods	41	24	26	9
Consumer goods	33	28	25	14
Food, beverages, tobacco	42	26	23	9
Construction	42	35	17	6
Trade	42	29	24	5
Services	39	27	26	5
Total	39	27	24	10

Source: Jahresgutachten 1991/92, 1991, p. 76.

(55 per cent) but enjoyed a low rating (10 per cent) in basic materials (ibid., p. 42),

Similar findings were elicited in a survey conducted in the autumn of 1991 by the umbrella organization of the chambers of commerce, the Association of German Chambers of Industry and Trade. The most important factors inhibiting investment in the new Länder were unresolved ownership problems and administrative bottlenecks. Other significant obstacles were infrastructural deficiencies and ecological damage. The significance attached to these factors varied according to economic branch. For example, ecological issues were regarded as one of the four main obstacles by only 10 per cent of all firms in the investigation, whereas 83 per cent of firms in energy placed it among the top four (*Jahresgutachten 1991/92*, 1991, p. 75; and see Table 5.2). The Association was critical of the highly bureaucratic and sluggish manner in which banks have dealt with applications for loans of DM50,000 to DM100,000; a processing period of six months was not regarded as abnormal by the banks. The consequent delay and the banks' conservatism frequently inhibited entrepreneurial activity. Another source of complaint was that the rents for business premises, as demanded by local authorities for instance, were sometimes so high that new businesses were put at risk. The rents were often higher than those charged in compararable west German large cities (*Berliner Zeitung*, 24 July 1992, p.1).

The sheer magnitude of the task of overcomig the obstacles to investment can be illustrated by a detailed examination of owner-ship disputes and the environmental legacy. At the end of December 1992, by which date all restitution and compensation claims had to be made, 1.5 million people had made claims to 2.5 million titles on property. Of that figure, over 119,700 claims for enterprises had been lodged, of which 23.1 per cent had been cleared. Out of the over 2 million claims on houses, only 281,902 had been settled (*Financial Times*, 26 February 1993, p. 2). Clearing this immense backlog will be an extremely time-consuming exer-cise, as can be seen from the experience of the city of Magdeburg. 11,000 restitution claims had been registered there on buildings and real estate by the end of 1991 but virtually none had been settled (Sinn and Sinn, 1992, pp. 86, 94). As has been mentioned earlier, legislation in March 1991 sought to alleviate the situation by modifying the principle of restitution before compensation. Furthermore, in order to speed up an investment while ownership claims are being dealt with, the Law on the Allocation of Formerly State-Owned Real Estate grants the *Länder*, district and municipal authorities the right of disposal of buildings and real estate where those authorities have been entered in the Land Register as being responsible for the property. Although the new legislation has given a much-needed impetus to privatization, many difficulties remain. The former owner still has the right of recourse to the courts, a process which can cause interminable delay. In addition, the offices responsible for the settlement of unresolved property questions frequently lack the necessary information as land regis-ters kept by the GDR were often defective and sometimes non-existent (*Jahresgutachten 1991/92*, 1991, p. 220).

Environmental damage continues to act as a brake on investment despite the new legislation relieving the investor of responsibility for the clean-up and despite reductions in industrial emissions. Most of the improvements have been the result of the closure of some heavily polluting firms in the chemical industry as well as in copper and silver mining. However, the emission density is still many times above that of west Germany. For example, in the Magdeburg district sulphur dioxide emissions exceed 500 t/a and dust 100 t/a per square kilometre. Emissions from motor vehicles and pollution from domestic refuse are fast approaching west German levels. The bill for the clean-up of the former GDR has yet to be paid; one estimate puts it at an alarming DM125 billion (Komar, 1992, pp. 3–4).

Management buy-outs (MBOs) and management buy-ins (MBIs) were at first neglected by the Treuhand but they are now regarded as an important form of privatization for smaller companies. MBOs occur when east German managers take on the task of privatization and MBIs when a west German or a foreign management undertake to make a firm independent. The usual practice in establishing MBOs is for a bank to take an equity stake in the MBO and the managers are given first option on buying out the bank within a few years at an agreed value (Carlin, 1992, p. 344). By the end of June 1992, 1,475 MBOs/MBIs had been registered, of which 138 involved employees' capital shares. Most MBOs/MBIs are located in the service sector, construction and instrument-, machine- and vehicle building. The MBOs/MBIs have produced investment guarantees of over DM1 billion.

While the Treuhand believes that MBOs are particularly suitable for the privatization of those 3,000 or so small firms with less than 250 employees, they do not appear to have fulfilled expectations. Many MBOs were created as an *ad hoc* measure to stave off impending liquidation. From the moment of inception, most MBOs were heavily in debt on account of the owners' lack of capital. New owners frequently inherit the liabilities of the old firm and although the purchasing price is low, investment of up to 95 per cent with outside capital is required, for example, from the ERP credit programme. All this restricts opportunities for financing investments by means of additional outside capital. Furthermore, at the time of privatization, most MBOs had not managed to restructure their product assortment and to find new customers. Numerous MBOs are still bound by contracts with their original parent companies. While this guarantees sales for a limited period of time, unless west German managers are called upon the know-how is usually lacking for the development of new products and finding new customers (DIW and IfW, 1992c, pp. 723–4).

5.7 Evaluation of the Treuhand's work

Obliged to perform a multiplicity of roles, characterized by the *The Economist* as 'a mix of investment banker, buffer between state and business and general economic nanny' ('Reprivatizing East Germany', 1991, p. 24), it is hardly surprising that the Treuhand has attracted fierce criticism from all quarters. Some critics accuse it of dissipating resources on industrial dinosaurs, while others consider that it bears a heavy responsibility for east Germany's de-industrialization and mass unemployment. A standard criticism is that the agency has no clear strategy for the reconstruction of the east German economy beyond that of an overhasty privatization which has accelerated the socio-economic collapse of the new *Länder*. Two *Financial Times* journalists, David Marsh and David Goodhart, sum up well its fundamental problems:

The Treuhand was bound to become the culprit for east Germany's troubled start in the free-market world – partly because it owned a ramshackle empire of state assets built up in 40 years of communism. Overburdened with challenges and short of qualified staff, the Treuhand had to try to privatise as quickly as possible, without selling at knockdown prices. Further, it had to divide up state assets between the different levels of the public sector, distribute liquidity cash, help restructure companies not immediately fit for disbursal, and avoid creating too many pan-German monopolies. [Marsh and Goodhart, 1991, p. 15]

The Treuhand has made determined attempts to present to the outside world a positive picture of its activities, as can be seen from the following extract from one of the agency's information brochures:

In less than two years, the Treuhandanstalt has found new active owners for more than 7,000 businesses or parts of businesses. These new owners have promised 135 billion DM in investments and the maintenance of jobs. As a result, more than 1.1 million jobs have a secure future . . .

In less than 18 months, a permanent dialogue has emerged between the Treuhandanstalt and its businesses. The supervisory boards, the boards of directors and the factory committees are having their voices heard in the privatization process. This was not always so. All parties involved had to get used to a completely altered situation. As a result, some mistakes have also been made. But: We had to learn from our mistakes, and we have done so.

A complete register of all Treuhand companies could not be published until March 1991, 9 months after the beginning of the reconstruction of the economy. At that point, almost 1,000 privatizations had been effected. In the early summer of 1992 more than 7,000 companies were on course for reorganization by new owners. Those businesses under the responsibility of the Treuhandanstalt need a reliable and competent owner. The Treuhand as the owner will actively accompany the modernization of its businesses and with it tender organizational and financial assistance on the basis of viable managerial concepts. This means that active and determined reorganization must be more than mere administration of the businesses . . .

The market and investment orientation transfer of modernization plans can increasingly occur on the basis of audited business concepts and with an ascertained DM opening balance. It must be the decisive criterion for the ability to reorganize and with it for the active support by the Treuhandanstalt owner as to how the business can achieve competitiveness in the foreseeable future, taking account of regional interdependence . . .

The Treuhandanstalt also takes on a responsibility for the national economy. For example, the fact that the means at the disposal of the Treuhand must in the end be provided by the taxpayer ensures reorganization according to high standards. The Treuhand's budget is not unlimited. The expenditure for the reorganization of businesses will, however, rise further in the current year. Cutting unprofitable jobs is one of the most painful but necessary consequences of ensuring the survival of the businesses in the case of reorganization; it is often greater than in the case of privatization.

The fact that the Treuhand now knows its businesses better forces it again and again to let the moment of truth arrive. So far, almost 1,400 companies with about 235,000 employees have been affected by closure. About 63,000 of the jobs concerned can probably be saved by means of relocating business establishments. Whether economically justifiable, we try to maintain an industrial core. This goes for the chemical industry, steel, and for shipbuilding to mention three examples.

At the moment, the Treuhand still has responsibility for about 4,500 businesses. Thousands of small and medium-sized businesses have been created by means of deconcentration of the old combines. Only every other twelfth business has more than 500 employees. As a result, a new managerial middle-class is coming into existence which did not have a chance to develop for forty years. More than 1,200 management buy-outs signal an interest in taking on managerial responsibility.

It is expected that the operative business of the Treuhand will have been concluded at the end of 1993. Right now, the first processes of expansion are starting in Eastern Germany. The seed of a market economy is gradually beginning to grow. The new owners and their highly-motivated and qualified work forces will bring in the harvest. [Treuhandanstalt, *Informationen*, International Edition, July 1992, pp. 3, 5]

The Treuhand, as can be seen from the above document, is not reticent in propagating the statistics of success. It can point to the privatization of the whole retail sector and the divestment of about 4,000 firms within the first eighteen months of its establishment. By early November 1992, 9,500 firms had been privatized, only 3,800 were still on its books and 1,600 had been closed down (Marsh and Colitt, 1992, p. 23). Proceeds from sales had reached DM26.8 billion by the end of March 1992; however, this sum does not include the obligations incurred by the Treuhand, among them contributions toward the clean-up of the environment (Treuhandanstalt, *Informationen*, no. 13, May 1992, p. 4; Siebert, 1992, p. 96).

The Treuhand has enjoyed some success in attracting foreign investors; about every tenth job and every tenth D-Mark invested in the new *Länder* comes from abroad. Among the most spectacular successes have been the sale of the steelworks in Henningsdorf and Brandenburg to the Italian firm Riva and of the Leuna and

Table 5.3 Privatization sales, 1990 – mid-1992

1990	408
1991	
1st qtr	853
2nd qtr	1,322
3rd qtr	1,205
4th qtr	1,422
1992	
1st qtr	1,369
2nd qtr	1,596

Source: Treuhandanstalt, *Informationen*, no. 15, August 1992, p. 1

Zeitz refineries to the French Elf-Aquitaine and Thyssen consortium (Arbeitsgruppe Alternative Wirtschaft, 1992, p. 124). British companies, which by the end of 1991 had acquired only twenty-six Treuhand firms, had increased their purchases to sixty-six three months later. This put them ahead of other foreign buyers in terms of firms purchased but behind their French counterparts according to total investments (DM1.5 billion to DM2.3 billion). British companies offered guarantees for about 14,000 jobs, French companies for over 14,700. The rapid increase in the number of purchases credited to Britain was mainly the result of a change in Treuhand statistics to include partial ownership of firms (Colitt, 1992b, p. 2; Treuhandanstalt, *Informationen*, no. 13, May 1992, p. 3). The number of sales recorded by the Treuhand is by no means negligible, but, as in GDR times, the recitation of statistics should not be allowed to obscure the problems.

The proceeds from sales have been far below the original, admittedly unrealistic target of DM600 billion. For example, by late 1991, when roughly one-third of the privatization process had been completed, the DM15 billion receipts represented a mere 2.5 per cent of what had been anticipated (Sinn, 1992, p. 12). At the present rate of progress, Gerlinde and Hans-Werner Sinn predict that the final total will amount to a mere DM60 billion (Sinn and Sinn, 1992, p. 89). That the Treuhand should have fallen so far short of its target is partly the result of potential buyers being deterred by the desolate state of so much of east Germany's capital stock. The mountain of unresolved ownership claims, high wage increases and the desire of the Treuhand to obtain job and investment guarantees all contribute to pushing down the price of the firms. One further factor indentified by Sinn and Sinn as intrinsic to the unification process itself is the impact of financing unification out of credits. This policy has tended to push up interest rates, thereby not only retarding investment but also reducing the capitalized value of Treuhand assets, Capitalized value is so highly sensitive to changes in interest rates that their increase depresses capitalized value and with it the amount which a potential investor is prepared to expend (ibid., pp. 115, 118). With proceeds so low from privatization sales, one of the main planks of the unification structure has thus been broken.

Employment guarantees given by investors tend to be overoptimistic. For example, while guarantees had been made for 980,000 workplaces by the end of 1991, the real number, in relation to the level of investments, was probably little more than 500,000. This figure is arrived at by dividing the proposed volume of investment of DM84 billion (excluding the DM30 billion in energy) by the required capital outlay per restructured workplace of between DM150,000 and DM200,000. This produces a figure of between 420,000 and 560,000 workplaces (Arbeitsgruppe Alternative Wirtschaftspolitik, 1992, p. 129).

Despite the legal penalties for non-compliance, job guarantees are far from watertight. Investors may seek to reduce their obligations, particulary if they can demonstrate that bankruptcy and the loss of all workplaces would result from Treuhand insistence on the fulfilment of all guarantees. This view is supported by an examination of appeals against dismissal which constitute 75 per cent of all cases brought before the Labour Courts in east Germany as against 40 per cent in west Germany. In the first half of 1992 88,900 new processes were instituted compared to 308,000 cases in 1991. The tendency is increasingly for the new owner rather than the Treuhand to be the subject of complaint. According to a survey by the Institute for Economic Research, Halle, 14 per cent of employees in the first half of 1992 had been dismissed by the new owners. *In toto*, about one-quarter of all workers had not left voluntarily. The Institute concluded that many employment guarantees had not been honoured by the purchaser. The Treuhand disputes this kind of assertion. On the basis of its own investigation into 1,000 privatized firms it expressed satisfaction with the job guarantees, claiming that in 80 per cent of cases they had been overfulfilled and that only 5 per cent of firms were giving cause for concern. However, a Treuhand spokesperson, Franz Wauschkuhn, was obliged to admit that because of the lack of prospective purchasers the Treuhand often had to waive binding job guarantees in order to achieve a sale (Arndt, 1992, p. 4).

The true extent of job losses can be seen from the fate of selected companies. The Iranian government, which bailed out the tyre-maker Pneumant, promised to save 910 out of 1,800 jobs. In 1990, the firm had had 6,000 employees. The Fernsehelektronik works, a manufacturer of television tubes with a labour force of almost

10,000, was purchased by Samsung of Korea. The new owner guaranteed a mere 800 out of the 1,200 jobs remaining in November 1992 (Marsh and Colitt, 1992, p. 23).

As the number of Treuhand enterprises has fallen, so too has their significance for employment. At the beginning of 1991, 2.9 million people had a job in the Treuhand's enterprises; by the spring of 1992, this was down to 1.4 million. The Treuhand expected employment in its enterprises to fall to about 0.8 million by early 1993 ('Die Lage der Weltwirtschaft', 1992, p. 209).

Privatization has progressed unevenly. The sale of real estate in agriculture and forestry has been extremely sluggish, mainly because of the many disputed claims to property. In the first year of the Treuhand's operation, only 3,493 hectares, or 0.3 per cent, of a total of 1.5 million hectares had been sold, for DM199 million (Suhr, 1991, p. 202; Holm, 1991, p. 100). Many newly established units in the trade sector are of the fast-food variety with little beneficial impact on job or wealth creation. Most of the prize assets have been sold off, and it will be difficult to sustain the rapid pace of privatization as the vast majority of the remaining enterprises are burdened by ownership problems. Furthermore, of the Treuhand's most spectacular sales, only one, the sale of the Interhotel chain to the Klingbeil group, was judged to be an unqualified success according to an investigation conducted in the summer of 1992 by the *Manager* magazine. The main reasons cited for this disappointing finding were the breakdown of the markets in the former Soviet Union and Eastern Europe and the escalation of wage costs (*Berliner Zeitung*, 30 July 1992, p. 1). Firms which have been privatized by the Treuhand frequently discover later that they have underestimated the cost and the time required for modernization. In some cases of reprivatization, emotional factors such as the desire to resuscitate a family firm cloud rational decision-making and create financial difficulties (DIW and IfW, 1992b, p. 472).

The Treuhand comes in for severe criticism for its failure to develop a coherent strategy for the active restructuring of its firms, opting either for the liquidation or closure of parts of enterprises or for leaving most of the task of restructuring to the investor after privatization. Even where it retains firms, its critics frequently allege that it adopts too passive a role, simply preserving many of its firms in the hope of an eventual sale. The result is that many firms capable of reconstruction stagnate and have to be closed.

While these criticisms are not without substance, restructuring has been, and remains, a formidable task. Surveys show that hardly any Treuhand firm is competitive owing to overmanning, growing labour costs, obsolescent plant and underinvestment.

One major investigation, conducted by the German Institute for Economic Research in the summer of 1991, depicted a bleak outlook for all those firms in manufacturing industry in the hands of the Treuhand. The survey included 1,488 firms with a total labour force of 850,000. Only 40 per cent had introduced comprehensive rationalization measures, considerably less than was required in the light of the age of the production plant, and many were seriously handicapped by a shortage of investment capital (DIW and IfW, 1991b, pp. 557–9). In general terms, prospects for restructuring and recovery remain extremely unfavourable in chemicals, textiles, and machine building, and the sale of large firms is proving especially difficult among the core parts of the ex-combines in the chemical and investment-goods industries.

The performance indicators of the Treuhand firms make disturbing reading. In 1991, the total losses of the firms were in the region of DM20 billion and about 25 per cent of turnover was swallowed up by labour-force costs (Homann, 1991, p. 1280). Despite the widespread gloom, the Treuhand itself exudes optimism about the proportion of its firms which it believes can be restructured. In 1991, it estimated that 40 per cent could survive with only a little outside help and 30 per cent would require a new partner and new capital. The remaining 30 per cent were deemed incapable of survival, a figure which some experts believe was probably 10 to 20 per cent too high (Siebert, 1992, p. 103; Homann, 1991, p. 1280).

Even in those firms which the Treuhand has identified as suitable for restructuring, progress towards privatization has been sluggish. Although these firms are required, from time to time, to update their restructuring conceptions in order to qualify for credits, some adopt a minimalist approach rather than pursue what would be required under market conditions. For example, many enterprises have released only as many workers as is necessary to prevent wages from running out of control; the application of the market principle would require a ruthless shedding of labour ('Die Lage der Weltwirtschaft', 1992, p. 224).

The relatively low priority assigned by the Treuhand to the direct restructuring of its own firms is apparent from its budgetary expenditure on this item. In 1991, of the DM30 billion in securities for liquidity credits only DM11.5 billion were devoted to restructuring (*Junge Welt*, 16 May 1992, p. 12). Most of the credits which the Treuhand has raised with commercial banks have been allocated to wage payments and have not been linked to binding commitments to the modernization of the production process. One result is underinvestment by the firms. Equipped with liquidity guarantees, firms prefer to adopt a wait-and-see attitude (Flassbeck *et al.*, 1991, p. 576).

Table 5.4 Potential total indebtedness of the Treuhand (DM bln)

Assumption of 'old debt'	80
Annual deficit arising from Treuhand tasks –	
1990	4
1991	20
1992–4, DM30 billion each year, totalling	90
Additional funding requirements (eg liabilities from equalization claims, guarantees and unidentified claims)	26–56
Total	220–250 (by end of 1994)

Source: Marsh and Colitt, 1992, p. 23

Given its multiple obligations and the low level of receipts, it is hardly surprising that the Treuhand's financial condition is so unsound. The Confederation of German Industry's estimate that the Treuhand will have an accumulated deficit of DM250 billion by the time it is due for closure in 1994 was accepted as realistic by the then head of the Treuhand finance department, Wolfram Krause (*Handelsblatt*, 5 February 1992, p. 3). Its credit line for 1991 was DM25 billion and it can draw DM30 billion for each of the next three years. The obligations of the Treuhand are exceptionally onerous, including the interest payments on the inherited debt of its firms, interest payments to the Debt Processing Fund, the costs of liquidation and restructuring and the availment of securities for liquidity credits (see Table 5.4). In 1991, about one-third of its income was absorbed by debt-servicing; this included payments to the Debt Processing Fund (Arbeitsgruppe Alternative Wirtschaft, 1992, p. 128).

Finally, the Treuhand has been bitterly criticized, not without reason, for serious deficiencies in its mode of operation. Its privatization policy is based on the divestment of its firms on an individual basis with a high level of discretion rather than according to a clearly defined sales strategy. Its decisions on the fate of individual firms often seem to outsiders to lack a coherent rationale and transparency, and it has been accused of inadequate consultation with the workforce, of excessive labour shedding and of selling firms at far too low a price. Greater transparency, it has been argued, would have been achieved if a more open bidding process had been implemented through a widespread dissemination of information. As this has been lacking, it is perhaps not surprising that accusations have been made by many east Germans that the Treuhand has deliberately favoured west German industrialists and has depressed privatization receipts far below the fair value of assets (van Brabant, 1992, pp. 230, 234).

Examples of Treuhand neglect abound. One frequent complaint

centres around the delay and confusion in the processing of enquiries. The French mineral oil group Total had to wait for weeks before obtaining an appointment at the Treuhand's Berlin head-quarters (Krumrey, 1992, p. 48). Many cases have occurred where the interests of management consultants used by the Treuhand have overlapped with those of their customers or with firms in the west. For example, on the basis of advice by two experts of the KPMG-Wirtschaftsgesellschaft, one of the Treuhand's most im-portant business consultants, the Treuhand agreed on the sale of a Freiberg paper mill to the Schoeller company in Osnabrück which it was subsequently discovered had been receiving advice from the same two employees. Another example of a possible conflict of interests arises from the position of Jens Odewald, who is head of the large Kaufhof chain of stores as well as a high-ranking Treuhand official (ibid., pp. 50–1). Cases of fraud and embezzle-ment frequently appear in the press. It was reported, for example, that the head of the Treuhand branch in Magdeburg, Andreas Grünebaum, had possibly been responsible for the Treuhand los-ing DM7 million as a result of privatization transactions which favoured a certain Alberto Vulcano (*Berliner Zeitung*, 24 July 1992, p. 21).

5.8 What is to be done?

As the key agent in the transformation process the Treuhand has been embroiled in the passionate debate on the socio-economic modernization of the new *Länder* between the representatives of the structuralist persuasion and the supporters of rapid privatiza-tion (see Section 7.1). A committed adherent of privatization is the Council of Experts, which has advocated that the Treuhand be relieved of its many ancillary functions such as the administration of special funds, the assumption of the debts of the Debt Processing Fund on 1 January 1994, as well as of the tasks which will remain after its privatization brief finishes. One of these tasks is the monitoring of the contracts of those firms which have been completely privatized. The Council has been a particularly fierce critic of those who want the Treuhand or any successor to assume a structure-maintenance role; the danger here is that the Treuhand might be drawn into the administration and the provision of subsi-dies to uncompetitive firms. Its opposition has been based in part on its belief that the Treuhand lacks the resources for such a task but, above all, on its fear that the agency would come under great political pressure to preserve uncompetitive firms and workplaces. Propping up inefficient firms would be a heavy drain on the public purse as well as a drain on the vitality of the national economy. The Council concedes that the Treuhand cannot withdraw entirely from the restructuring of its firms; it has insisted, however, that the financial implications and the duration of its involvement must be clearly defined (*Jahresgutachten, 1991/92*, 1991, pp. 25, 228, 230). Horst Siebert, a member of the Council, and a determined opponent of the provision of subsidies for uncompetitive firms, counters the charge that this kind of policy would lead to a Mezzogiorno scenario by insisting that 'keeping inefficient firms alive implies missing a chance to modernize and actually perpetuates the old structures' (Siebert, 1991, p. 303).

Many proponents of a state-structural policy have urged that the Treuhand become one of the agents of a comprehensive economic reconstruction by the state; others have preferred the withdrawal of ailing firms from the Treuhand portfolio and their transfer to some kind of government holding agency under the control of the Federal government, the *Länder* and other partners. IG Metall, for example, has proposed the establishment of a Treuhand industrial holding which would be orientated towards industrial and regional policy goals during the reconstruction process. All Treuhand firms capable of restructuring in the medium term should be incorporated into the holding. In addition, employees should enjoy equal representation on the Management Board and the trade unions one-third representation on the Treuhand Supervisory Board. In order to ensure a continuous flow of resources into the holding, the union has put forward a variety of suggestions, including the creation of an assets fund: 25 per cent of the shares would be transferred to the industrial holding as would dividend payments and other profits in the later stages of the reconstruction process (Steinkühler, 1991, pp. 10–11).

Among the various objections to the IG-Metall scheme are that potential investors would be deterred by the excessive trade-union influence. Firms in the Treuhand holding would, for example, be less determined than privatized firms in withstanding union pressure for wage increases. In general terms, objections to a special fund are rooted in the fear that it would produce a structural policy geared towards the preservation of old workplaces rather than their restructuring according to market principles (Murmann, 1992, pp. 16–17).

Bündnis 90 and the Greens have advocated the dissolution of the Treuhand and its replacement by *Länder* trustee agencies accountable to the *Länder* parliaments and with a right of say for the district and local authorities. Another participant in the debate, the PDS, has called for the replacement of the central Treuhand in Berlin by regional Treuhand agencies and their incorporation into the decision-making structures of the *Länder* governments and parliaments. Priority, it insists, should be given to restructuring (Flug, 1992, p. 49).

Finally, the German Institute for Economic Research, Berlin, has sought to occupy the middle ground between the privatizers and the structuralists. While recognizing the need to prioritize privatization, it believes that immediate action is essential to help and stimulate the east German economy until long-term policies came to fruition. Among the Institute's proposals are the cancellation of the burden of inherited debt and the transfer from the Treuhand of all those large companies in branches such as steel, chemicals and shipbuilding where closure is politically unacceptable. Such firms ought to be managed as joint-stock companies with the Federal and *Länder* governments as shareholders.

The main thrust of the Institute's scheme was for the workforce of companies undergoing restructuring to receive a wage subsidy equivalent to 50 per cent of the basic wage and declining degressively to nil over a period of between five and ten years. This was to be combined with investment loans and company capitalization up to a fixed limit and linked to the level of non-guaranteed bank loans. Companies would be unable to pursue 'safe' investment programmes and would be required to make a profit by a specified date (Flassbeck *et al.*, 1992, pp. 577–8). The Institute recognized, of course, that wage and investment subsidies lead to labour- and capital-intensive technology but argued that this is unavoidable during the transition from a planned to a market economy. The common objection to wage subsidies, no matter how sophisticated the scheme, is that they undermine the autonomy of the wage negotiators and by cementing supply structures which are not market-orientated impede the necessary structural adjustments (Homann, 1991, p. 1282; *Jahresgutachten 1991/92*, 1991, p. 242; Akerlof *et al.*, 1991, pp. 77–85). However, in the light of the failure of the shock therapy of rapid privatization to revive the former GDR, there seems to be little alternative to the kind of strategy advocated by the Institute, despite the obvious risks inherent in any form of state structural policy, with or without the Treuhand.

6 From Chancellor of unity to Chancellor of debt

6.1 The optimistic scenario

Throughout the spring and summer of 1990, the Federal government and its CDU allies in East Berlin exuded an air of optimism. This mood was embodied in Chancellor Kohl's address to the Bundestag on 21 June 1990 when he reiterated a phrase used earlier by the GDR Minister President, Lothar de Maizière: 'No one will be worse off than before – and for many it will be better', and he predicted that Saxony and the other GDR states would shortly blossom under the beneficent rays of GEMSU (see Presse- und Informationsamt der Bundesregierung, 1991, p. 68). Kohl had expressed a similar sentiment during the Volkskammer election campaign in March 1990 when he had promised that the GDR would become a flourishing region within five years (' "Es gibt keine DDR mehr" ', *Der Spiegel*, 19 March 1990, p. 21). As for West Germans, they were reassured that unification would not entail any sacrifice. Federal Finance Minister Waigel's statement in April 1990 that the reconstruction of the GDR would not require them to pay higher taxes was reinforced a few weeks later by Kohl's denunciation of higher taxes as counterproductive (Christ and Neubauer, 1991, p. 102).

Despite the many warnings issued by the SPD opposition in the Bundestag and the GDR citizens' movements, Bonn continued to take an up-beat approach and government representatives confidently predicted a second economic miracle. Financial arrangements for the transformation of the GDR reflected this optimism. For example, too low a sum was set aside in the German Unity Fund: DM115 billion for 1990–4, including DM35 billion for 1991.

Why did Kohl, Waigel and so many other members of Bonn's political elite fail to address the problems of unification before the spring of 1991? Party-political considerations undoubtedly played an important role: with unification impending and the Bundestag election towards the end of 1990, it behoved Kohl and his col-

leagues to continue what had already proven a remarkably successful political and electoral course since early 1990, even though
this involved underplaying the unification burden. This neglect
was subsequently subjected to fierce criticism, with the President
of the Republic, Richard von Weizsäcker, to the fore. He attacked
the narrow vision of the political parties and politicians and their
hunger for power, which, in von Weizsäcker's opinion, had stifled
the necessary debate on the costs and the sharing of the financial
burden of unification ('Die verfeindeten Nachbarn', 1992, pp. 18,
21). A public debate at a time when popular opinion was receptive
and a candid admission that the financial cost of unification could
not simply be achieved out of extra economic growth or a higher
public-sector deficit might, in Weizsäcker's view, have mobilized
broad support for sacrifices among the West German population
(*Richard von Weizsäcker*, 1992, pp. 35–42). Here was Kohl's second
window of opportunity; but, unlike in his foreign policy, he neglected to take advantage of the relatively favourable circumstances
for an East–West German solidarity pact.

The President of the Treuhand, Birgit Breuel, added her voice to
the swelling chorus of criticism:

Many citizens of the old Federal Republic had assumed that a triumphal
march of the market economy would sweep away the evil empire of the
planned economy and that would be it . . . Thoughtful people were
quickly silenced in 1990. Nobody wished to sin against the great work of
unity. Problems were suppressed rather than analyzed soberly.

Because everything went and had to go at such a frantic speed, much
remained unsaid, in the hope that it would not have to be said. It
remained unsaid that the rebuilding of a country's entire economy would
take not months and years but decades . . . And above all, it remained
unsaid that the basic experience of all those concerned was virtually nil.
Nobody knew for sure how things might go. [Breuel, 1992, p. 30]

Throughout 1990, Bonn overestimated both the recovery powers
of the East German economy and the efficacy of market instruments to transform the socialist system. At the same time, it also
overestimated the willingness and capacity of private investors to
stimulate recovery. In his governmental statement to the
Bundestag on 4 October 1990, Kohl had anticipated that a short-
lived economic downturn would be followed by vigorous economic growth driven by heavy West German private investment
and substantial public infrastructure investment (Presse- und
Informationsamt, 1991, p. 271). The extra demands on the Federal
budget would, it was hoped, be largely covered by the elimination
of costs related to ending the division of Germany and by addi-

tional tax revenues generated by higher incomes and business profits (ibid., pp. 275–6). In short, the government's inflated expectations of private investment flows and the regenerative power of the market mechanism produced a flawed and inadequate strategy for the transformation of the GDR economy. As a result another problem soon arose: the high level of transfers required to subsidize social consumption. In 1991, a provisional calculation by the Federal Statistical Office estimated that the production of goods and services in east Germany was DM193 billion (adjusted for prices) but that demand was DM361 billion. The gap in production had to be covered by west Germany, thus underlining the heavy dependence of the new *Länder* on their western counterparts.

The defects in Bonn's strategy can be seen in the overloading of the Treuhand and the underfunding of the German Unity Fund. The State Treaty, the Treuhand Law and the Unification Treaty all envisaged that the Treuhand would obtain sufficient funds from privatization sales to enable it to fulfil a series of formidable tasks (see chapter 5). The German Unity Fund, created by the State Treaty, was intended to support the unfunded deficit of the east German public authorities. This provided for DM115 billion between 1990 and 1994, rising from DM22 billion in 1990 to a peak of DM35 billion in 1991 and then falling rapidly to DM10 billion in 1994. Of this sum, DM95 billion would come from credits raised on the capital markets, and the central government would contribute the remaining DM20 billion out of budgetary cuts and from savings made from the financial burden of the division of Germany (Priewe and Hickel, 1991, pp. 136–7). This relatively low level of provision was based on the expectation that an increase in tax yields in the east German *Länder*, as a spin-off from economic growth, would synchronize with a fall in transfer payments from the Fund. The Federal government and the *Länder* governments were each to bear a half of the debt servicing (Arbeitsgruppe Alternative Wirtschaftspolitik, 1992, p. 161).

The Unity Fund was intended as a provisional measure until the west German system of financial horizontal equalization between the *Länder* and vertical financial equalization between the Federation and *Länder* came into operation in the former GDR in 1995. Nevertheless, its design imposed too high a burden on the Federal budget: the west German *Länder* share in the Fund was fixed at DM47.4 billion, an arrangement that should have been finalized only if the exact costs of unification had been predictable. As this was palpably not so, the agreement with the *Länder* on the sharing of the financial burden should have left open the question of the vertical distribution of turnover tax, thereby enabling the Federal government to renegotiate the distribution of the tax once the DM115 billion ceiling was exceeded (see *Jahresgutachten 1991/92*, 1991, p. 186).

6.2 Erosion of the policy of unification on the cheap

As the costs of the transformation from the administrative-command system ballooned, it soon became apparent that unification was not to be had on the cheap and that a course correction was imperative. The rapid collapse of east German production, escalating unemployment, rising wages and the adoption of the west German social-security system were reflected in a dramatic increase in transfers from west to east and put Bonn under greater pressure to revise its policy. Whereas the total transfers to the east in 1991 amounted to DM170 billion gross from all sources, the provision of only DM35 billion was envisaged from the German Unity Fund (Priewe and Hickel, 1991, p. 133).

Previous critics of the government now regarded themselves as vindicated. The Council of Economic Experts, which in 1990 had advised the Chancellor against an overhasty monetary union, poured scorn on those who had believed that GEMSU and the infusion of start-up finance would transform the GDR into a flourishing social-market economy. It reproached those who had invested their hopes in economic growth generating sufficiently high tax yields to obviate the need for an increase in the rate of taxation. And it was particularly critical of the policymakers' failure to revise policy once it had become apparent that an alternative financial strategy was essential. Had the nettle been grasped earlier, a crisis of confidence might have been avoided (*Jahresgutachten 1991/92*, 1991, pp. 14, 130).

The widespread criticism of Bonn's lack of candour about the drawbacks of economic and monetary union and its reluctance to implement course correctives was well articulated by the SPD Finance Minister of the *Land* Brandenburg, Klaus-Dieter Kuehbacher, an 'import' from west Germany:

. . . risks [of economic unification] were identifiable in qualitative terms. Their possible dimensions were frankly and rationally quantified, especially among scientists. If the relevant politicians had admitted this to the people in both western and eastern Germany and pointed out the tremendous economic and sociopolitical pressure to adjust associated with economic unification, especially with rapid monetary union, the corresponding effective countermeasures could have [been] taken much earlier.

To preclude misunderstanding, I do not wish to stand up as a critic of unity. There were, as we know, a number of overriding political aspects which demanded German unification at a fast pace. However, I have always advocated honesty in politics, and it would have been honest to inform the people as comprehensively as possible about what they could expect and about what was already foreseeable at that time. [Kuehbacher, 1992, p. 135]

Bonn did not remain completely inactive: its initial response to the escalation of the costs of unification was to introduce three supplementary budgets of DM3.9 billion, DM13 billion and about DM15 billion in the summer and autumn of 1990; however, it made no attempt to reassess its general policy, preferring piecemeal adjustments and putting its faith in the market and the Treuhand. In the first supplementary budget, pensions and unemployment insurance were barely considered, but in the second budget assistance was increased by DM11.5 billion. It was not until the third budget that DM4 billion was released for health insurance (Priewe and Hickel, 1991, p. 138), another sign of Bonn's lack of an overall strategy.

By the beginning of 1991, the financial position of the east German regional and local authorities was so precarious that they were barely able to support even the most urgent tasks. Their predicament is illustrated by a comparison of revenue from taxation in 1991: per head of population the east German *Länder* tax revenue was only 34.8 per cent of west Germany's and that of the local authorities a mere 11.5 per cent. The situation was exacerbated by the fact that a fixed proportion of community taxes had to be paid to the Federal exchequer, for example, 42.5 per cent of income tax and 65 per cent of turnover tax. This was tantamount to forcing the new *Länder* into penury and indebtedness (ibid., pp. 142–3). In the spring of 1991, problems continued to multiply: unemployment soared, the industrial and agricultural structures were disintegrating and the popular mood was becoming ever more depressed. In March, Leipzig and other east German cities echoed once more to popular protests, this time against the arbitrariness of the Treuhand, the closure of kindergartens, the colonization tactics of west German firms and West German arrogance (Pollack, 1992a, p. 54).

Although the Federal government was not prompted into a major rethink, it did at least introduce three policy innovations: the Upswing East programme, legislation to speed up the resolution of property disputes and a greater emphasis by the Treuhand on regional and social issues in the restructuring of its companies.

In order to provide some relief for the hard-pressed east German authorities, it was announced at the Minister Presidents' conference with Chancellor Kohl in February 1991 that the new *Länder* would receive the 15 per cent share of the German Unity Fund (DM5.25 billion) originally allocated to the Federal government to meet public requirements at public level (OECD, 1991b, p. 67; Priewe and Hickel, 1991, p. 146). In addition, the new *Länder* were allowed a full participation in the *Länder* share of the turnover tax yields, rather than the gradual increase envisaged in the Unification Treaty from 55 per cent in 1991 to 100 per cent in 1994. The new arrangement represented a DM10 billion gain for the new *Länder* in 1991 and more than DM30 billion until 1994 (Pilz and Ortwein, 1992, p. 198).

At the end of February, Bonn's announcement of a tax package heralded its retreat from the policy of no tax increases. The most important measures were a 7.5 per cent solidarity surcharge on income tax and corporation tax liabilities from 1 July 1991 to 30 June 1992, a 25 per cent increase in the tax on tobacco from 1 January 1992, an increase by 1.5 per cent net of contributions to social-insurance funds, and a 35 per cent average increase in various fuel and energy taxes from 1 July 1991 (Priewe and Hickel, 1991, p. 154). The taxes enabled the government to limit recourse to the capital market, but they were still no substitute for a structured transformation policy. One year later, in February 1992, the rate of turnover tax was raised from 14 per cent to 15 per cent for 1993 in order to cover the need for extra resources with the termination of the solidarity charge (Arbeitsgruppe Alternative Wirtschafts-politik, 1992, p. 164). However, the lower rate of turnover tax on clothes remained unchanged. Revenue from the solidarity charge amounted to about DM22 billion in 1991 and 1992. If other sources of revenue from the tax increases are included, the additional receipts were expected to reach DM40.35 billion in 1992, still a long way from the predicted total transfers of over DM200 billion (Sakowsky, 1992, p. 1263).

Although the government had bowed to the inevitable, it sought to keep the overall tax load and the duration of the tax increases within clearly prescribed limits as it feared that higher income, wealth and other direct taxes dampened work performance and investment. One alternative which commands much support is for greater weight to be placed on indirect taxes, for example turnover tax and the tax on fuel (Siebert, 1992, pp. 159–60). Unfortunately, this solution has its drawbacks, too: raising turnover tax and other taxes on articles of consumption hits lower-income households disproportionately hard as consumption represents a high pro-portion of the household budget and, second, it diminishes pur-chasing power and demand (Pilz and Ortwein, 1992, pp. 224–5).

Finally, in March 1991, the Upswing East package was announced. This authorized DM24 billion support in 1991 and 1992 for stimulating infrastructure investment at regional and municipal level. DM5.5 billion were to be invested in job creation schemes, DM6.3 billion in roads and railways and DM2.2 billion in housing and urban development. Other areas included in the programme were the local-authority investment programme, private investment, the environment and higher education (Bundesminister der Finanzen, 1991, p. 31). Despite the considerable financial flows involved in this and other programmes, the outlays fell well short of the requirements for the social and economic reconstruction. Developments in the labour market illustrate this: by the beginning of September 1991, the outlays on job-creation schemes planned for the whole of 1991 had already been distributed, including the DM2.5 billion from the Upswing East programme (Priewe and Hickel, 1991, p. 153).

6.3 Total west German transfers to the new *Länder*

Although calculations on the magnitude of the financial transfers from west to east Germany vary slightly from one statistical body to another, it is clear that they have escalated far beyond Bonn's least sanguine prediction. Second, relative to the *Länder* share a disproportionate financial burden is borne by the Federal government and private investment flows have been far less than anticipated. And third, while social transfers have helped to maintain social and political stability, their high level constitutes lost potential for urgently needed investment.

Since GEMSU, the Federal government, with some assistance from the west German *Länder* governments and local authorities, has been responsible for a wide range of support schemes: the expansion of the east German public administration, the improvement of the infrastructure, the bailing out of firms threatened by collapse, the securing of exports, the provision of investment assistance, payments for job-creation measures and the financing of social transfers. Because a considerable proportion of the transfers – such as unemployment benefit and pensions – is linked to wage level developments in east Germany, the pronounced increase in wages has meant that the transfer payments have an inbuilt tendency to rise ('Die Lage der Weltwirtschaft', 1992, p. 211).

The financial transfers from West German public budgets to East Germany in 1990 amounted to DM45 billion. This figure included DM22 billion from the German Unity Fund, a DM10 billion grant to the GDR state budget and DM3.1 billion, DM2.9 billion and DM2.0 billion for covering the deficit on pensions, health and unemployment insurance respectively ('Die Lage der Weltwirtschaft', 1991a, p. 244; Boss, 1990, p. 58).

Transfers rocketed in 1991 to DM170 billion gross. As the east German *Länder* paid DM30 billion in taxes the net shift was DM140 billion. Predictions for 1992 were about DM218 billion gross and DM180 billion net. Some idea of the magnitude of this assistance can be gauged by the fact that whereas Marshall Aid after the establishment of the FRG accounted for less than 2 per cent of national product, west German public-sector transfers represent about 80 per cent of east German GDP (Siebert, 1992, p. 142). The Bundesbank's detailed breakdown of financial flows appears in Table 6.1 from which it can be seen that in comparison to the Federal government the west German *Länder* governments and local authorities contributed relatively little to the flow. Their DM8 billion contributions in 1991 represented only 2 per cent of their combined budget volume, whereas about 20 per cent of Federal expenditure was destined for the new *Länder* (*Monthly Report of the Deutsche Bundesbank*, vol. 44, no. 3, 1992, pp. 17, 19; *Jahresgutachten 1991/92*, 1991, p. 132).

The east German *Länder* are clearly heavily dependent on their rich western siblings. The tax receipts of the east German public authorities have been very modest: the per capita yields from income tax and corporation tax comprised only 12 per cent of the west German level. This difference was the result not only of the economic depression in the east but also of the fact that income tax yields were lower as gross wages and salaries lagged such a long way behind those in west Germany. An additional factor was the inefficiency of the embryonic east German financial administration (*Jahresgutachten 1991/92*, 1991, p. 138). The new regional and local authorities were expected to be able to meet only 30 per cent of requirements from their own revenues in 1992; the remaining 70 per cent would have to come from transfers from the west (Sakowsky, 1991, p. 1261).

Economists and government representatives frequently lament that far too high a proportion of the financial transfers is devoted to social consumption to the detriment of the modernization of the east German capital stock. And as the transfers are to a great extent based on credits, rising public-sector deficits and debt servicing restrict the room for manoeuvre in fiscal policy and impose a heavy burden on future generations (Siebert, 1992, pp. 145–6). The Bundesbank, a persistent critic of government policy, has calculated that about DM60 billion were transferred to support private consumption alone in the new *Länder* in 1991. To this sum should be added the Federal government's administrative spending on the new *Länder* and interest spending and current transfers to

Table 6.1 West German public-sector payments to eastern Germany in 1991 and 1992 (in DM bln)

Payments	1991	1992
Gross payments by the Federal government*	81	109
Payments by the West German *Länder* governments and local authorities	8	12
Expenditure on the German Unity Fund financed on credit	31	24
Loans of the ERP Special Fund and specialized banks (interest-subsidized by means of public funds)	21	25
Gross payments from the EC budget	4	4
Deficit of the Federal Labour Office in East Germany	25	30
Deficit of the statutory pension insurance funds in East Germany	–	14
Gross payments, total	170	218
of which:		
Expenditure	(164)	(210)
Shortfalls in tax revenue in West Germany	(2)	(4)
Waiver of share in turnover tax	(4)	(42)
less:		
Tax revenue of the Federal government in East Germany	-28	-35
Tax revenue of the EC in East Germany	-3	-3
Net payments, total	139	180
of which:		
Federal government	53	74
West German *Länder* governments and local authorities	8	12
German Unity Fund	31	24
ERP Special Fund, specialized banks	21	25
EC	1	1
Federal Labour Office	25	30
Pension insurance funds	–	14

Source: *Monthly Report of the Deutsche Bundesbank*, vol. 44, No. 3, 1992, p. 16. (all figures are part estimates)

* Expenditure due to unification (1992 target), excluding expenditure on the CIS, and after deduction of the *Länder* governments' refunds to the German Unity Fund in respect of debt service payments and of payments from the EC budget, plus shortfalls in tax revenues owing to tax concessions. In 1992 including the transfer to finance the 1992 deficit of the Federal Labour Office, which was included in the 1991 budget.

Table 6.2 Gross payments primarily for social security purposes by the Federal government to eastern Germany envisaged in the budget (DM bln)

Purpose	1991	1992
General subsidies to the social-security funds	9.8	14.9*
Child benefits	6.0	6.0
Child-rearing benefits	0.6	0.8
Housing assistance	0.3	1.4
Training promotion	0.8	0.8
Unemployment assistance	0.7	1.5
War victims' welfare	0.6	2.2
Early retirement pension	4.4	4.8
Social bonus	0.8	0.3
Supplementary retirement pension	0.7	1.6

Source: Monthly Report of the Deutsche Bundesbank, vol. 44, no. 3, 1992, p. 17

* = Including transfers of DM4.9 billion to the Federal Labour Office to finance spending in 1992, which were included in the 1991 supplementary budget.

enterprises of about DM25 billion. Finally, the transfers serving the general financing of the east German public sector, mainly from the German Unity Fund and from the waiving of turnover tax by the west German *Länder* can also be defined as consumption. The overall share of gross transfers represented by these three categories was in the region of two-thirds, leaving the remaining quarter – or about DM45 billion – for investment purposes. A similar ratio was expected in 1992 (*Monthly Report of the Deutsche Bundesbank*, vol. 44, no. 3, 1992, pp. 20–1). One cautionary note: this sum is necessarily an approximate guide, as some transfers overlap the border between the investment and social categories.

Government spending on what may be defined as 'social purposes' (see Table 6.2) includes – in addition to traditional cash benefits, among them child benefit and housing assistance and transfers to the social security funds – special payments like retirement and unemployment benefits, all of which cushion the integration process. Furthermore, the Federal government is temporarily responsible for the obligations inherited from the GDR system relating to maternity benefits, supplementary old-age benefits and care of sick children. In 1991, the Bundesbank estimated that social expenditures were about DM30 billion and anticipated a rise to DM40 billion in 1992 (*Monthly Report of the Deutsche Bundesbank*, vol. 44, no. 3, 1992, p. 17).

In addition to the public-sector authorities, the social funds make heavy contributions to the new *Länder*. The Federal Labour Agency provides funds for unemployment and short-time work benefits, as well as for retraining and job-creation measures. In 1991, the expenditure of the Agency amounted to DM30 billion, only DM4.5 billion of which was financed from contributions paid in the new *Länder*. This meant transfers from the west to the east of about DM25 billion. With no improvement in sight, the Federal Labour Agency's commitments were likely to increase to DM45 billion in 1992. As the contributions from the new *Länder* were expected to be DM10 billion and DM5 billion respectively, the transfer payments were expected to increase to about DM30 billion (ibid., p. 20). Finally, there will be a need for transfers to the statutory pension-insurance funds of about DM15 billion in 1992. In 1991, pension payments, which in principle were still based on GDR law, were made from contribution revenue accruing in the new *Länder* and from regular Federal government payments. Heavy additional demands were anticipated in 1992 owing to the introduction of west German pension law. Financial requirements will have to be met out of current revenue in the old *Länder* and the fluctuation reserves which the pension funds have built up in the west.

Although not inconsiderable, capital investment has fallen far short of the level required for an appreciable narrowing of the gap in economic performance and living conditions with west Germany. The IMF has estimated that an annual DM120 billion of private capital will be needed to close this gap ('Scheinblüte', 1992, p. 100 and Section 7.1). In 1991, total private and public investment in the new *Länder* was about DM82 billion (Kühn, 1993, p. 3) and was expected to increase to between DM87 billion and DM90 billion in 1992. The state's share has been considerably higher than that of private investors, a trend that would continue into 1992, when, according to the Institute for Economic Research (Ifo) in Munich, the state sector would be responsible for DM54.5 billion and west German firms for DM32.5 billion. Public investment would be concentrated in the railways (DM10 billion), post (DM10 billion), housing construction (DM5.0 billion), gas supply (DM2.0 billion), electricity supply (DM3.5 billion) and infrastructure (DM24 billion). Private investment would flow into manufacturing industry (DM18 billion), housing construction (DM5.0 billion), banks and insurance (DM1.8 billion) and construction (DM1.5 billion) (ibid., p. 100). The flow of investment by west German firms to east Germany has been attacked as far too low by the deputy-chair of the Federation of German Trade Unions (DGB), Ulf Fink. According to the Ifo, west German firms invested DM8 billion in the manufacturing sector of the new *Länder* in 1991 and

DM16.5 billion in 1992; a modest increase to DM17.5 billion is projected for 1993 (*Handelsblatt*, 20 January 1993, p. 5). In per capita terms investment by west German firms in the new *Länder* was one-third less than in the old *Länder*. One remedy, according to Fink, is to force each west German firm to contribute 5 per cent of net profit or invest twice that sum in east Germany (ibid., p. 101).

In 1991, the investment ratio in east Germany – that is, fixed investment in relation to GNP – was about 40 per cent, or twice the west German ratio. However, this indicator distorts the relative level of investment; more pertinent was the prediction for 1992: investment per gainfully employed person and per inhabitant in east Germany was not expected to exceed the west German levels by two-thirds and one-half respectively (DIW and IfW, 1992a, p. 132). This low ratio partly explains why an economic upswing has not occurred in the former GDR (Kühn, 1993, p. 3).

6.4 The rising tide of public debt

With public-sector net transfers of about DM140 billion in 1991, the costs of unification have imposed considerable strain on the public-sector budgets. The Finance Ministry anticipated that unification-related outlays in 1992 would account for one in every four D-Marks on the expenditure side of the Federal budget (Bundesministerium der Finanzen, 1991, pp. 11–12). In 1991, the deficit of the central, regional and local authorities in the financial balance was DM120 billion (see Table 6.3), an increase of DM15 billion on the previous year. The main share of the newly incurred debt was borne by the Federal government. Its deficit rose by DM52 billion as against the DM16 billion of the *Länder* governments and the DM6 billion of the local authorities in west Germany. In east Germany the deficit of the *Länder* was about DM9 billion while that of the local authorities was relatively small. The German Unity Fund must be added to this total: loans amounting to DM31 billion were raised in 1991 compared to DM20 billion in 1990 (*Report of the Deutsche Bundesbank for the Year 1991*, pp. 27–8).

The official financial balance represents only a part of a complex overall picture as it is also necessary to take into account the requirements of the Treuhand and those institutions which are regarded as Federal enterprises – the German Federal Post Office, the German Federal Railway and the German National Railway. The impact of their inclusion in the net borrowing of the central, regional and local authorities in 1991 is to push the requirement up from DM102 billion to DM141 billion (ibid., p. 30).

Although the public-sector debt is resourced by domestic rather

Table 6.3 Public sector finance, 1991 (DM bln, partly estimated)

Central, regional and local authorities:	
Expenditure:	
Personnel expenditure	288.5
Other operating expenses	141.5
Transfers*	293.5
Interest	76.5
Fixed capital expenditure	86.5
Financial aid	
Total expenditure	957
of which:	
Federal government	405.5
West German *Länder* governments	322.5
East German *Länder* governments	75.5
West German local authorities	227.5
East German local authorities	46
EC**	33
Receipts:	
Tax revenue	661.5
Other receipts	182.5
Total receipts	837
of which:	
Federal government***	353.5
West German *Länder* governments	306.5
East German *Länder* governments	66.5
West German local authorities	221.5
East German local authorities	45
EC	33
Surplus (+) or deficit (-)	−120
of which:	
Federal government***	−52
West German *Länder* governments	−16
East German *Länder* governments	−9
West German local authorities	−6
East German local authorities	−1
German Unity Fund	−30.5
Debt Processing Fund	+0.5
ERP Special Fund	−6.5
Social security funds	
Expenditure	544
Receipts	557
Surplus (+) or deficit (-)	+13
Public sector, total	
Expenditure	1,431
Receipts	1,323
Deficit (−)	−108

Source: Report of the Deutsche Bundesbank for the Year 1991, 1992, p. 29
* mainly social expenditures and current grants to the enterprise sector
** EC expenditure financed out of EC revenue in Germany
*** The Bundesbank profit transfer is included in the figure as government revenue

than foreign creditors, overall prospects for public finance in the short to medium term are a matter of widespread concern, even alarm. The Council of Economic Experts predicted that in 1992 the public-sector deficit would rise to DM131 billion, and the state's recourse to the capital markets would be in the region of DM200 billion (*Jahresgutachten 1991/92* 1991, p. 13. This estimate includes the railway, post and Treuhand). Additional burdens arising in 1992 include the social costs arising from the merger of the east and west German insurance systems, higher payments to the EC, aid to the CIS and East European states, export credit guarantees, the environmental clean-up and restitution payments (*Report of the Deutsche Bundesbank for the Year 1991*, 1992, p. 32; 'Die Lage der Weltwirtschaft', 1992, pp. 222–3).

With the deficit continuing to rise in 1992 – possibly to DM200 billion – it was estimated that by the end of the year the country's total public debt stock, including the Treuhand, the German Unity Fund and the ERP Special Fund would be around DM1.39 trillion or 45.4 per cent of GNP ('West-Ost Transfers', 1991, p. 5). This is a higher proportion than that of Great Britain (38 per cent), although lower that of the United States (59 per cent), Japan (61 per cent) and Italy (106 per cent) ('Der Staat und seine Verschuldung', 1992, p. 8). The magnitude of the net debt in 1991 pushed up the interest-payment requirement by an additional DM10 billion. The interest load quota – interest in relation to expenditure – was 8 per cent and is predicted to increase to 12.5 per cent in 1996 (Arbeitsgruppe Alternative Wirtschaft, 1992, p. 165).

The costs of unification will undoubtedly continue to soar: the Federal government will have to assume most of the debts and the servicing of the debt when the Debt Processing Fund is due to be dissolved at the end of 1993 and the Treuhand closes its doors one year later. The deficit of the latter may reach DM250 billion in 1994 and that of the Debt Processing Fund DM100 billion in 1993. Yet another burden will be the DM51..5 billion liabilities from the GDR housing sector (Donhöff *et al.*, 1992, p. 38). The stock of public debt will climb to around DM1.9 trillion in 1995, and the interest payment on the debt will absorb 25 per cent of all tax receipts (' "Eine grausame Dynamik" ', 1992, pp. 110–11). This will impose severe restraints on the government's ability to carry out its fiscal and political goals. It is hardly surprising that Kohl was dubbed 'Chancellor of debt' by the weekly magazine *Der Spiegel* (ibid., p. 110).

The Bundesbank regards a public-sector deficit and a debt stock of this magnitude as unsustainable over a prolonged period and argues that monetary policy would be overtaxed if it were expected, single-handed, to perform the task of durably containing the present relatively strong price upsurge. It has also been alarmed by wage increases outstripping productivity gains and it is ever fearful of an excessive growth of the money supply. It has therefore sought to combat inflationary risks by using the instrument of higher interest rates (Donhöff *et al.*, 1992, p. 41) while urging a moderate wage policy and budgetary consolidation (*Report of the Deutsche Bundesbank for the Year 1991*, 1992, p. 30 and see documents 10 and 13).

Budgetary consolidation must include not only the public-sector budgets but also the deficits of the Treuhand, the Debt Processing Fund, the German Unity Fund and the liabilities of the former GDR housing sector. The West German *Länder* and local authorities should not be excluded from the exercise, and determined efforts must be made to reduce subsidies and to shift the emphasis in transfers from consumption to investment. Under great pressure, the Finance Ministry launched a budgetary consolidation exercise in 1992. The Ministry set as its goal a reduction of the budget deficit of the central, regional and local authorities to 2.5 per cent of GNP by 1995. Theo Waigel regarded the target as realistic and, given a cut in subsidies, would enable the Federal government to finance 80 per cent of the unification-related deficit by 1995. The success of the whole exercise depended on the achievement of an average economic growth of 2.5 to 3 per cent (' "Es besteht kein Anlaß zum Ächzen" ', 1992, p. 3). The Ministry's goals appeared to be unrealistic, particularly as the Federal outlays on the Treuhand and the Debt Processing Fund were incorporated into the 2.5 per cent target. Manfred Kolbe, a CDU Bundestag deputy from Saxony, believed that the omission of these crucial funds threatened to dynamite Waigel's plan. And the Federal government's hope for a significant contribution by the new *Länder* to the servicing of the debt was wishful thinking (Kolbe, 1992, p. 30).

The Federal government has not enjoyed much success in persuading the *Länder* governments to shoulder a greater share of the burden. The West German regional and local authorities have made only a modest contribution to the financing of German unification: in 1991, they were responsible for DM8 billion transfers and an additional DM1 billion for administrative assistance. This was extremely low in view of the fact that their tax revenue of about DM312 in 1991 was almost as much as that of the Federal government (Gurtz, 1992, p. 15). The latter's plan to shift one-half of the Treuhand and the Debt Processing Fund liabilities on to all the *Länder* and the entire debt of the GDR housing sector on to the new *Länder* alone was rejected by the *Länder* Finance Ministers at their annual meeting on 3 July 1992 on the grounds that the inherited liabilities of the former GDR were the responsibility of the Federal government (*Junge Welt*, 4 July 1992, p. 2).

Central to Waigel's consolidation strategy and the Federal government's economic reconstruction programme in east Germany is the continuation of economic growth in the old *Länder*. At the time of the dismantling of the Berlin Wall, the Federal Republic was still experiencing the economic boom which had commenced in 1982. Since about mid-1987, economic growth had been more vigorous than at any time since the upswing began. Growth was particularly buoyant in 1989 when total exports rose by 10.4 per cent and the unemployment rate of 5.6 per cent was about 0.5 per cent lower than in 1987 and 1988. The Federal budget deficit was reduced to DM20 billion or less than 1 per cent of GNP (OECD, 1990, pp. 13, 19, 39). The absorption of the GDR gave a further boost to the west German economy. A simulation study by the German Institute for Economic Research has estimated that unification boosted real economic growth by 2.3 per cent in the twelve months after GEMSU despite higher interest rates and a temporary increase in the value of the D-Mark. Without this bonus, economic growth would have been about 2 per cent rather than the 4 per cent actually achieved (Horn and Zwiener, 1991, pp. 451–2). This was a fortunate coincidence for west German business as the west German economic boom had been showing clear signs of faltering: in 1990, the demand from abroad for tradeable goods had begun to slacken. Foreign demand had been the main pillar of the economic expansion of the 1980s (Priewe and Hickel, 1991, p. 234).

The German Institute of Economic Research has traced the end of the economic boom to the summer of 1991 (Arbeitskreis Konjunktur im DIW, 1992, p. 7). The prospects for growth, according to the Bundesbank, depended partly on a cyclical revival in major partner countries such as the United States and the United Kingdom and partly upon domestic factors such as the acceleration of economic development in east Germany. The Institute warned, however, of the implications for the east German economy if a clash between labour and capital hit labour productivity and west German exports. Heavily dependent on west Germany for private and public investment, a slackening or decline of economic growth in the old *Länder* would endanger the convergence in living conditions and impose an even greater burden on public-sector finance in the form of social transfers (ibid., pp. 7–8 and section 7.1).

By the autumn of 1992, the Chancellor was indeed reaping 'reunion's bitter harvest' (headline in *The Guardian*, 11 September 1992, p. 19). By late 1992, in the west public-sector debts were accumulating, interest payments on the debt servicing were spiralling, the clouds of economic recession were gathering; in the new *Länder* de-industrialization showed little sign of slackening, prospects for an upsurge in output were remote, large-scale unemployment had become a structural phenomenon and east German towns such as Rostock and Eisenhüttenstadt had experienced the scourge of racist violence. According to an Allensbach opinion poll published in September 1992, 70 per cent of west and 75 per cent of east Germans were alarmed by the threat of economic recession or collapse. The political forces of the extreme right continued to make inroads into the electorate while the Federal government, torn by policy disagreements between coalition members, seemed to have lost its sense of direction. A traditional policy glue, European integration, was also losing much of its adhesive properties for the Chancellor. European integration was being called into question in the wake of the turmoil on the currency markets and growing reservations both within and outside Germany about the Maastricht treaty. The D-Mark's replacement by a single European currency was running into widespread opposition. In one opinion poll in autumn 1992, 68 per cent in west and 75 per cent in east Germany were opposed to the demise of the D-Mark (Peel, 1992b, p. 2). Seeking a way out of this impasse, the Chancellor at last, in September 1992, floated the idea of a solidarity pact between unions, employers, local and regional governments, the coalition in Bonn and the opposition. All were called to make sacrifices in the general interest. It remains to be seen whether or not this is two years too late (see Section 7.2).

7 Germany divided

7.1 Modernization thwarted?

Two years after German unification it is painfully obvious that the former GDR will not become a flourishing part of the new Germany within the immediate future. The most highly optimistic reading of the economic tea leaves suggests that living conditions and economic performance will not approach those of west Germany until about the year 2010 at the earliest. And even then, an appreciable gap, it is predicted, will exist between the individual east German *Länder*, with Saxony and Mecklenburg-West Pomerania at the two extremes. While a more realistic scenario is that an appreciable degree of convergence will require at least three decades, even this may err on the side of optimism. In the present climate of post-unification blues, some commentators predict that, except for pockets of prosperity in Leipzig, Berlin and Dresden, the former GDR might become Germany's Mezzogiorno, thereby confirming the warning of the PDS leader, Gregor Gysi, at the SED–PDS Extraordinary Congress in December 1989, that unification would reduce the GDR to an underdeveloped *Land*, the poorhouse of the FRG (*Außerordentlicher Parteitag der SED/PDS*, 1990, p. 76).

The elusiveness of economic recovery can, as has been discussed earlier, be attributed to a combination of factors. The original conception of monetary and economic union was badly flawed, to a great extent 'a victim of its own optimism' (Wehner, 1991, p. 115), of a belief that the economic boom in west Germany was normal and that western firms would be eager to invest in the new Eldorado. As a result, the sheer complexity of transplanting the social market economy into the ailing body of the planned economy was seriously underestimated by many politicians. Furthermore, with wage costs accelerating, west German firms became increasingly disinclined to undertake the risk of investing in a region beset with a myriad of problems, some of them inherited from the old system such as an obsolescent capital stock, a delapidated infrastructure and widespread environmental degradation and others, like the immediate collapse in demand for east German products and disputes over ownership, the result of

GEMSU's shock therapy. With production declining at home and the traditional COMECON markets disintegrating at the same time as wages were rising, Bonn countenanced vast public-sector financial transfers as a social cushion but to the detriment of capital investment and public-sector finance.

Ingenious efforts have been made to determine the period of time required for convergence on the basis of key criteria like labour productivity and the level of capital investment. For example, the Institute for Economic Research, Halle, has calculated that fixed-assets investment of DM1.2 trillion would spur GNP and productivity to an average annual growth rate of 9.5 per cent and 8 per cent respectively. As a result, the level of productivity would be within 20 per cent of West Germany's by the year 2000 (Institut für Angewandte Wirtschaftsforschung, 1991a, p. 10). This may be regarded as the most optimistic scenario. Another sanguine interpretation has also been sketched by Meinhard Miegel of the Institute for Economics and Society in Bonn. Given transfers from west to east Germany of DM1.2 trillion throughout the 1990s – that is, about 5 per cent of GNP during this period – he considers it feasible for per capita GNP and the employment rate in the new *Länder* to attain two-thirds and three-quarters of the respective west German levels by the end of the century. In his view, this would represent a considerable achievement and produce the kind of regional economic gap which has been by no means unusual in German history. In the case of Saxony and Bavaria, it would reverse their respective positions in 1900 (Miegel, 1992, pp. 89, 91).

A more realistic and sober assessment comes from two Munich-based economists, Gerlinde and Hans-Werner Sinn. They have attempted to calculate the total investment required for the new *Länder* to attain west Germany's 1989 level of capital endowment per workplace. Should west German capital endowment stagnate, then DM50 billion per annum would be needed over a period of twenty years – or DM100 billion for ten years – to enable east Germany to catch up with the west. However, as west German capital stock increased by DM200 billion per annum in the period before unification, they reckon with a continuation of growth in the old *Länder*. Thus for east Germany simply to keep pace with this growth rate in relation to the size of population, an additional annual investment of DM50 billion would probably be necessary. In short, at 1989 prices, the total investment needed for the convergence of east Germany's economic potential with that of the west within ten to twenty years would be between DM100 billion and DM150 billion per annum, a sum which they regarded as far too great to be raised in so short a time span (Sinn and Sinn, 1992, pp. 150–1). Similar scepticism characterized the assessment by Priewe and Hickel of the Alternative Economic Policy Working Group. Shortly after GEMSU, they calculated that about DM2 trillion would be required to raise east German living standards to west German levels, to modernize and create new workplaces and to tackle the environmental, housing and telecommunications problems. Given a growth in west German GNP of about 2.5 per cent during the 1990s, they concluded that the average annual growth of GNP in the new *Länder* would have to reach 15.8 per cent if the former GDR were to catch up with the west by the year 2000 (Priewe and Hickel, 1991, pp. 123–4).

Such calculations are clearly mechanistic and, given the unpredictability of economic developments, it is impossible to predict with confidence the likely level of investment flows and the rates of growth of GNP and labour productivity. Perhaps, as Edmund Fawcett has argued in *The Economist*, it is time to redefine what counts as success in integrating the two economies (Fawcett, 1992, p. 13). It is becoming increasingly unrealistic to treat success as bringing the average east German living standards up to west German levels within the next ten or even twenty years. Bonn should make it clear once and for all that even if this was once a policy goal, then it must be revised, even dispelled.

Whatever the exact length of time required to transform the former GDR economy, the outcome of the process will depend on several key preconditions: first and foremost, the modernization of the capital stock through the infusion of massive public and private investment; an improvement in marketing skills and the establishment of a network of small and medium-sized firms which can respond quickly and flexibly to market trends and customer requirements; a high level of demand at home and abroad for east German products; the emergence of a suitably qualified and highly motivated management and labour force; the development of a strong R & D base; the clean-up of the environment; the creation of an efficient and responsive regional and local administration; the removal of infrastructure obstacles to growth, especially in communications; a more rapid processing of property claims; the creation of an attractive living environment by means of urban renewal and housing reconstruction; and the moderation of wage demands (see Priewe and Hickel, 1991, pp. 206–10; Becker, 1992, p. 470).

Although these factors should operate across each of the five new *Länder*, the rate of recovery will undoubtedly differ according to factors such as location and the existing level of economic development. Some areas, for example Berlin and parts of Saxony, can be expected to benefit from their central location whereas those situated on the Czech and Polish borders will be relatively disadvantaged. Old industrial centres face formidable adjustment problems, especially those trapped in the mono-structural legacy of the GDR. In these regions the hitherto dominant industry cannot expect to survive, as is likely to be the case in the shipyards on the Baltic, the Saxon textile industry and the steel industry around Eisenhüttenstadt.

Until such time as the new *Länder* achieve self-sustaining economic growth, they will be heavily dependent on west German assistance and thus on the health of the west German economy. At the time of German unification, the vigour of the FRG's economic performance was one of Chancellor Kohl's trump cards. Two years later, economic gloom had descended on the old *Länder*. The growth of GNP, which dropped to 0.8 per cent in 1992, was expected to fall to around zero or even lower in 1993. Prices were rising by 3.7 per cent and were expected to climb to over 4 per cent in 1993, about two points higher than desired by the Bundesbank. The money supply was expanding by 10.4 per cent, almost twice as high as its target, wages were rising to 5.5 per cent above the 1991 level and unemployment in 1993 was forecast to increase by between 150,000 and 300,000 (Parkes, 1993, p. 2; Hanke, 1993, p. 17). Orders in manufacturing industry, which had been falling since early 1992, showed no sign of improving, and equipment investments at the end of the third quarter of 1992 were about 5 per cent lower than in the corresponding period in 1991 (Müller-Krumholz, 1992b, p. 625). With even such giants as Daimler Benz and Volkswagen experiencing collapsing profits, capital investment in the recovery of east Germany was likely to be reduced. Hopes for recovery were pinned on a general recovery of world trade led by the United States and on an easing of monetary policy by the Bundesbank. However, the central bank was reluctant to commit itself to appreciable cuts in interest rates until it saw evidence of wage moderation and fiscal consolidation (Walter, 1993, p. 26). This in turn depended very much on the establishment of a broad consensus by the Federal government, the *Länder* governments, unions and the opposition on a solidarity pact for financing unification.

While there is widespread agreement on which factors are crucial to the reconstruction of the east German economy, opinion diverges sharply on what kind of overall economic strategy should be pursued. As outlined in the chapter on the Treuhand, structuralists call for a more vigorous role by the state and privatizers for restructuring and recovery principally through the operation of market forces. The differences between the two camps sparked off a lively discussion in the pages of *Der Spiegel* (' "Die Industrie muß ran" ', 1992) between Professor Rudolf Hickel of the University of Bremen and Hans Karl Schneider, formerly president of the Rhine-

Westphalian Institute for Economic Research and between 1985 and February 1992 the director of the Council of Experts. Hickel is one of the co-authors of the annual memoranda of the Alternative Economic Policy Working Group, a regular critic of the Council's policy recommendations. Hickel, while recognizing that the state could not strip management of the responsibility for business decisions, argued strongly against abandoning restructuring to the markets. Recovery, he insisted, could not be achieved simply by the application of traditional west German steering instruments. The consequences of such a policy would be the destruction of the east German economy rather than a Schumpeterian process of creative destruction. He called upon the government to devise a five-year medium-term financial programme, which would give east German firms a much needed breathing space. As west German investors had shown relatively little interest in the economic restructuring of the new *Länder* (he reckoned that DM25 billion had been invested in east Germany in 1991 compared to about DM100 billion outside Germany), he proposed that the Federal government impose a levy on those west German firms which had eschewed investment in the new *Länder* and that the yield from this levy be used for the creation of new workplaces. Anticipating that about DM150 billion per annum would be needed over the next ten years for social and economic reconstruction, he looked to the west German public-sector budgets to bear a high proportion of the burden. Finally, he recommended the conversion of the Treuhand into an industrial holding for a specific period of time and with the power to decide on which firms should be restructured.

Schneider took issue with most of Hickel's ideas. Although critical of government inaction in the early stages of economic and monetary union, he rejected direct steering by the state. In his view, the state's task is to provide the framework and the essential preconditions for recovery by removing bottlenecks and legal con-traints and by improving infrastructure and administration. Investments would then start to flow. State intervention of the kind envisaged by Hickel, for example an increase in Hermes credits to stabilize trade with the former COMECON countries, was no guarantee of success. East German firms needed to adjust to the demands of international markets rather than rely on subsi-dies and the old structures. Schneider argued that where the public authorities are needed to prevent the sudden collapse of entire branches of east German industry, the main responsibility should rest with the *Länder* governments. He did not indicate, however, how bodies so strapped for cash could undertake this task. One of Schneider's main fears, which he saw in Hickel's proposal for a

Treuhand industrial holding, was that resources would be dissipated on subsidies to unprofitable firms. Finally, he warned that unless the west German authorities reduced the present level of transfers 'the rich West would very soon no longer be rich' (ibid., p. 155). If, however, priorities were set correctly, then ruin need not occur. Priorities in financial policy should encompass a radical cut in existing public subsidies, no increases in taxation rates and a reduction in the public deficit.

This allergy to state intervention is a thread which runs through the writings of Horst Siebert, the President of the Kiel Institute for World Economics and a member of the Council of Economic Experts:

If political demands are allowed to influence the course of events and to dominate the markets, old inefficiencies will continue to prevail. As before, firms will face soft budget constraints and the necessary adjustment will not come about. The government will take over the role of evaluating the potential development of sectors and firms, which it clearly cannot do. Structural change in the ex-GDR will take place along lines similar to West Germany's experience with sectoral policy for ailing industries. Financial resources will be wasted, the tax burden will rise and the supply-side effect will be severely inhibited. [Siebert, 1991, p. 316]

Another participant in the debate is Harry Maier, a former leading GDR political economist who moved to the west before the Wende. The Council of Experts, he believes, has drawn too sharp a line between privatization and a state structural policy. Maier advocates restructuring on the basis of private, state and mixed ownership forms, with the privatization of 80 per cent of east Germany's firms as the ultimate target, a figure which corresponds to the international norm. Total privatization he ruled out as an illusion: it would divert such a large flow of investments as to reduce united Germany into a second-class economic power. He warned, too, against the excessive financial burden of dismantling workplaces regarded as uneconomic according to strict business criteria. Estimating in mid-1991 that 2.5 million workplaces were at risk at a probable cost to the tax payer of about DM500 billion, he argued that it was preferable to redirect resources towards the modernization of existing workplaces and the production structure (Maier, 1991, pp. 6–8).

In a joint paper, the influential German Institute for Economic Research, Berlin, and the Kiel Institute of World Economics sought the *via media* in policy. They accepted that firms must be closed down where restructuring was impossible but, as a matter of the utmost urgency, called for a halt to the de-industrialization of the new *Länder*. Pleading for a combination of policy measures, the two institutes proposed the expansion of existing investment grants and a more active intervention by the state. The latter should formulate a restructuring policy for industry by branch and region specifying which projects should be the beneficiaries of investments. In order to underpin recovery, they recommended a reduction in the sale price of firms, the granting of subsidies for a clearly defined period of time, degressively graduated wage subsidies and the removal by the state of infrastructure bottlenecks (DIW and IfW, 1992b, pp. 490–2).

7.2 In search of solidarity

Much of the wide-ranging debate on the reconstruction of the east German economy has undoubtedly been shaped by earlier West German discussions on the role of the state in economic policy-making as well as by traditional notions of financial rectitude, discipline and consolidation. With regard to the latter, the Bundesbank's efforts to impose financial discipline in monetary and economic policy are rooted in the trauma of the Weimar Republic. It is not surprising, therefore, that the strength of the D-Mark is regarded – to quote Josef Joffe – as 'almost a Calvinist sense of redemption at the end of the century which, until 1945, was but an endless chain of national disaster' (Joffe, 1992, p. 9).

In the 1980s, an animated debate took place on 'Location Germany' prompted by fears that Germany was losing its competitive edge. The Federal government came under heavy fire for its unwillingness to challenge vested interests and for a lack of bold leadership in economic policy. Critics were disappointed with the failure of the Kohl government to achieve a substantial scaling down of the role of the state in the economy. Heavy public subsidies in coal, shipbuilding, air and space, steel and agriculture were regarded not only as a burden on the public budgets but also as a damper on entrepreneurial spirit. The subsidies increased by about 50 per cent between 1980 and 1989. Other matters which gave cause for concern were high labour costs, competition from Japan, sluggish investment, relatively heavy insurance, social-security and transport costs and a shortfall in R & D (for details, see Smyser, 1992, pp. 108, 110; Dyson, in Smith *et al.*, 1989, pp. 150, 153).

German unification has sharpened this earlier debate on structural policy as the government is no longer in a position to continue all the old subsidies and meet its many new commitments. In principle, Bonn favours financial discipline, the application of the instruments of the market and a reduction in subsidies; in practice, it has found itself boxed into a corner as it needs to pump vast sums into the new *Länder* not only to help reconstruct the economy but also to maintain social and political peace. Attempts to reduce subsidies, particularly in early 1991 by the then Economics Minister Möllemann, were frustrated by entrenched opposition from the industrial, agricultural and defence lobbies (Smyser, 1992, pp. 121–2). The problem is partly of the government's own making for after his bold strike for German unity in 1990, Kohl reverted to type, seeking consensus, anxious not to disturb the political and economic instititions which had served the old FRG so well.

But with unification stalling so badly, Kohl was obliged to change tack. In order to mobilize wider support and additional resources for the reconstruction and modernization of the new *Länder*, he proposed, in September 1992, a solidarity pact among unions, employers, local and regional governments, the Federal government and the opposition. The pact, as put together in March 1993, was designed as the main instrument for overcoming the unification crisis until the next Bundestag election in 1994. As originally conceived, the main elements of the pact were to include wage restraint in east and west, a revision of the system of revenue sharing between the Federal government and the sixteen *Länder* and a curtailment of the public deficits. In the negotiations leading up to the pact, it was described by *The Economist* as 'neither the Gordian egg nor the knot of Columbus' ('German's knot of Columbus', 1993, p. 41).

When, in January 1993, the coalition government in Bonn made its first significant move to construct the pact, its proposals were greeted with much dismay. With the government's net-borrowing requirement expected to rise to DM53 billion in 1993 – or about DM18 billion more than predicted – Bonn sought to make cuts in social payments such as children's allowance and unemployment benefit. The package also included a road and petrol tax increase from 1994, a reduction in subsidies and the introduction of an income and corporation tax supplement from 1995. The popular reaction to the package was summed up in the headline 'Alle sauer' (*Bild*, 21 January 1993, p. 1). Some pulled a longer face than others. The CDU Minister President of Saxony-Anhalt, Werner Münch, feared that the package was yet one more page in the chapter of deteriorating relations between the new and old *Länder* over the reallocation of shrinking resources (*Neue Zeit*, 23 January 1993, p. 1).

To the surprise of most observers, the politicians managed to cut the Gordian knot. An agreement concluded in March between the coalition government, the SPD and the *Länder* was based on a compromise between the various interested parties and signified the ability – and need – of the leaders of the political parties to strike a deal. The government, under pressure from the SPD, abandoned its aspirations to make deep cuts in social security and agreed to give the *Länder* about DM20 billion in extra tax revenues to enable them to pay transfers to the east. This was to be done by raising the *Länder* share of VAT receipts from 37 to 44 per cent. The new arrangements for financial equalization, to come into effect from 1995, incorporated the new *Länder* into the system and, by putting their finances on a sounder footing, it was hoped to relieve them of the embarassment of continually approaching Bonn as supplicants. Taxpayers were asked to dig deeper into their pockets. From January 1995, taxes would be raised by a massive 7.5 per cent charge on income tax and an increase in the wealth tax. These increases were twice as high as the Finance Ministry thought desirable. The Treuhand's borrowing limit was to be increased significantly within an agreed limit of DM8 billion per annum for 1993 and 1994 in addition to its current annual credit line of DM30 billion. It was intended that this extra financial provision would enable it to help clean up the ecological damage and to pursue a more active restructuring of the 'core industries' which it was unable to sell off. The Bank for Reconstruction was empowered to raise its borrowing limit from DM30 billion to DM60 billion to finance housing modernization in eastern Germany. An extra DM2 billion would be released for job-creation measures (see Peel, 1993c, p. 13 and *Frankfurter Allgemeine Zeitung*, 18 March 1993, p. 13).

The overall impact of the package entailed an increase in the 1993 borrowing requirement of the Federal government from DM51 billion to DM53 billion. Business leaders, notably Tyll Necker, the chairman of the Federation of Industry, regretted the pact's failure to make greater cuts in state spending and predicted that the DM2 billion increase towards job-creation schemes would discourage investment. Perhaps the most serious drawbacks are that the financing of the pact will essentially be through new credits and that a disproportionate share will be borne by central government. The Federal budget deficit is expected to climb to a record DM65 billion in 1995 and whereas in 1995 the old *Länder* governments are expected to be contributing only DM4.9 billion towards the net transfers to the east, Bonn will be responsible for DM51 billion (*Frankfurter Allgemeine Zeitung*, 18 March 1993, p. 13; *The European*, 18–21 March 1993, p. 2).

Entailing sacrifices by all, it remains questionable, however, whether the constellation of interests makes the pact a viable long-term proposition. One serious fault line is between capital and labour. While the Chancellor and employers are eager for severe wage restraint in both east and west Germany, the unions are still committed to parity and insist on a substantial increase in the contributions of industry and the better-off to investment in the new *Länder*. Even the individual negotiating parties are internally divided: the Federation of German Trade Unions (DGB) struggles to strike a balance between the interests of the employed and those out of work. It also has to calm the fears of west German trade unionists that cheap workplaces in the new *Länder* might endanger jobs in the west (Mehr, 1993, p. 2). It also remains to be seen in the present period of recession how willingly the 'Wessis' will continue to bear the brunt of the financial burden.

As part of the bait to attract support for his solidarity pact, Chancellor Kohl intimated that the 'industrial cores' of east Germany would not be allowed to disappear, a belated recognition that reconstruction could not continue to proceed through rapid privatization by the Treuhand (Arbeitskreis Konjunktur im DIW, 1993, p. 13). He did not, however, make clear what he had in mind by 'industrial cores'. One interpretation was that it was tantamount to a blank cheque for all those industries which were considered vital for the economy of the individual *Länder*. It certainly aroused expectations among east German CDU Bundestag representatives that permanent subsidies would be available for virtually all firms not reprivatized but regarded as capable of restructuring. And it encouraged the eastern *Länder* to initiate discussions with the trade unions on which firms might constitute the industrial core. Saxony-Anhalt, for example, issued an extensive list which included every firm with more than 250 employees. The Atlas project in the *Land* Saxony, though less comprehensive, was used by the regional government as a lever to persuade the Treuhand to release more resources for firms which the agency has deemed to be incapable of restructuring but which are designated by the *Land* as crucial to the region (Weidenfeld and Kessler, 1993, pp. 12, 16).

Treuhand scepticism about the economic value of such subsidies is shared by the four main employers' bodies. As part of the negotiations for the solidarity pact, they insisted that subsidies be of limited duration, degressive and linked to firms' competitiveness and market performance. They also pressed for greater pay restraint in east and west Germany. In return, they offered to encourage western firms to purchase more goods from the new *Länder* as well as to raise private investment from DM110 billion in 1992 to DM130 billion in 1993 (Gow, 1993, p. 9).

Another indicator of what Bonn might be envisaging as part of its retreat from its trust in the regenerative powers of the market is the establishment of limited partnerships (*Kommanditgesellschaften*, KGs). In order to halt de-industrialization, Bonn is considering active state involvement in the restructuring of the 70 per cent of the remaining Treuhand firms which are regarded as capable of resurrection. Responsibility for their administration is to be withdrawn from the Treuhand; in the case of medium-sized firms, they will be organized into groups of ten and placed in the control of a KG. The KG-firms, it is hoped, will soon be transformed into viable units. Trade union co-determination rights are largely absent in this kind of legal entity. As for the larger concerns, Bonn desires to keep the state shareholding to below 50 per cent and to encourage a fusion between east and west German firms. Western managers will undertake the restructuring and the taxpayer will cover a high proportion of the costs. In addition, western firms must purchase a specific percentage of their goods – perhaps 20 per cent – from east German firms (*Der Spiegel*, 14 December 1992, pp. 19–20). If these ideas are developed further, they will constitute a shift, however modest, towards neo-Keynesianism and perhaps sustain the solidarity pact. On the other hand, the Treuhand, which has set up six management KGs – two were actually functioning by the start of 1993 – remains cool towards the incorporation of the KGs into any general restructuring package. The agency still prefers to seek individual solutions and to encourage firms to develop their own business and restructuring plans (see the interview with Breuel in *Wirtschaftswoche*, vol. 47, no. 3, 1993, pp. 16–17).

7.3 Germany divided

The euphoria which swept through the GDR after the crumbling of the Wall has been superseded by deep-seated and well-founded anxieties over the general economic situation, jobs, political extremism and individual well-being. Public opinion surveys conducted in the GDR between February and October 1990 captured the initial optimism: between 62 per cent and 72 per cent responded that they were 'optimistic' or 'optimistic rather than pessimistic' about their personal future. Belief in an economic miracle in East Germany was widespread: 13 per cent confidently expected one and 51 per cent believed it probable' (see 'Das Profil der Deutschen, Was sie vereint' 1991, p. 80). Asked their opinion on the situation in September, 23 per cent discerned more advantages than disadvantages; 21 per cent held the opposite view. The percentages were markedly different when the interviewees were asked to predict the situation two years later: the pluses were expected to outweigh the minuses by 51 per cent to 8 per cent.

Table 7.1 Indicators of alienation in east and west Germany, 1990 (%)

	Social Isolation (i)		Meaningless (ii)		Work-alienation (iii)		Indigence (iv)	
	++	–	++	–	++	–	++	–
West	6	54	3	61	4	56	-(v)	-
East	10	54	12	25	8	53	34	6

++ = 'completely true; – = 'completely untrue'
(i) 'I often feel lonely.'
(ii) 'Things have become so complicated today that I don't understand just what's going on.'
(iii) 'I don't really enjoy most of the work I do.'
(iv) 'I am not able to solve our present problems.'
(v) Not defined.

Source: Landua, in Ghassy and Schäfer, 1993, p. 102.

Among the anticipated drawbacks were a rise in crime, unemployment, drug abuse, violence, and AIDS (ibid.).

Although unification began to lose some of its glitter during 1991, public opinion surveys continued to register a high level of expectation (about half of east Germans interviewed) of an improvement in the economic situation in the near future (see, for example, the results of the Mannheim Research Group in Jung and Roth, 1992, p. 6). This was testimony to the continuing strength of the commitment to German unity. However, an investigation conducted in June 1991 among 4,200 east Germans by the Socio-Economic Panel of the German Institute for Economic Research traced a growing disenchantment: within twelve months the proportion of those expressing confidence in the future had fallen by 10 per cent; the fall was much more pronounced among the unemployed and short-time workers (Arbeitsgruppe Sozialberichterstattung, 1992, p. 71).

A Social Welfare Survey carried out in the new *Länder* in the second half of 1990 on the pattern of those conducted for many years in the old FRG gives an insight into the worries of east Germans and reveals a sharp difference between the two parts of Germany as regards emotional well-being. Whereas about one-sixth of people polled in eastern Germany stated that they were 'very or fairly unhappy', only one in twenty westerners did so (Landua, in Ghassy and Schäfer, 1993, p. 101). In east Germany, feelings of disorientation, loneliness, anxiety and a lack of purpose were more widespread than in the west (see Table 7.1)

Given the traumatic impact of the transformation process, it is hardly surprising that nostalgia for GDR times has been picked up in a number of investigations (see Merkl, in Smith *et al.*, 1992, p. 347). For example, in a survey conducted for *Der Spiegel* in November–December 1992 among 2,000 western and 1,000 eastern Germans the Emnid Institute registered that 13 per cent of the Ossis 'mourn' for the passing of the GDR. Although the over-whelming majority of the easterners rejected Honecker's GDR and its associations with the Stasi and oppression, 49 per cent wished that a democratic GDR had managed to survive for an undefined period after October 1990. Most of them admitted, however, that they were not of this opinion at the time. The kind of system which they favoured in late 1992 was much influenced by the authoritar-ian paternalism of the old GDR which in the light of their experi-ences in real existing capitalism now seemed to have certain social and economic benefits. The eastern German respondents tended to prefer a system without extremes of wealth and one which pro-vided a secure and orderly existence. Seventy-nine per cent, as opposed to 56 per cent of the west Germans, wanted the state to play an active role in economic affairs ('Erst vereint, nun entzweit' 1993, pp. 56, 59, 62).

Central to east German apprehension has been the loss of job security and the implications for their standard of living. Throughout 1991, unemployment was regarded as the most im-portant problem by more than 60 per cent of the east German population; well over half thought that their job was in jeopardy. With unemployment on the increase and production collapsing, it is not surprising that the economic climate was judged to be 'bad' by between 60 and 80 per cent of the respondents in the Mannheim surveys. In sharp contrast, 90 per cent of the west Germans regarded their jobs as safe (Jung and Roth, 1992, p. 5). Age influ-ences perceptions, too. In the Socio-Economic Panel survey in June 1990, 8 per cent of the under-30s as opposed to 30 per cent of those aged forty-five to sixty-four held out little hope of finding a com-parable job if they were made redundant (Christian Holst, 1991, p. 35).

Expectations of convergence between east and west German living standards have become more sober. In September 1990, whereas 21 per cent of west Germans in a *Spiegel* survey believed that convergence would take at least eleven years, only 2 per cent of the east Germans expected such a lengthy process (ibid., p. 29). In surveys conducted by Infratest, three-quarters of east Germans in February–March 1990 were of the opinion that the west German standard of living would be attained 'certainly' or 'perhaps' within one to two years. By July–August, the proportion had fallen to 63 per cent. Other investigations indicate that expectations of the average length of time required was tending to increase: 7.3 years

Table 7.2 Ossis and Wessis divided, 1992 (%)

Statement	In agreement	
	east Germans	west Germans
Do the billions transferred to east Germany endanger west German prosperity?	21	54
Despite their prosperity, Germans in the west have not learned how to share	68	43
How great a burden on west German citizens is the cost of reunification?		
– low	33	2
– average	49	35
– high	16	62
How many west Germans would have preferred reunification not to have taken place?		
– a majority	39	28
– about a half	40	38
– a minority	20	34

Source: 'Erst vereint, nun entzweit', 1993, p. 58.

in October–November 1990 and eight years in June–July 1991 (ibid., p. 30).

Another cause for concern has been the emergence of a clear east–west divide. Between 75 and 80 per cent of east Germans have been disappointed with the Federal government's efforts at equalizing living conditions. This kind of attitude is regarded as unwarranted by about two-thirds of west Germans; in fact, 15 per cent maintained that Bonn had already done too much (Jung and Roth, 1992, p. 5). Western resentment against vast financial transfers to the east has been quickened by the slackening of growth and an increase in job losses in the old *Länder*. The Emnid survey in November–December 1992 revealed east and west Germans far apart on many issues (see Table 7.2).

One British journalist found the mood in the Ruhr confirmed this sharp east–west German divide: 'Local people are enraged at having to dip constantly into their pockets to finance unification when their own jobs are at stake and rents are soaring. The generosity released by unification applies to Bosnians and Somalis now, not Ossis' (Gow, 1992b, p. 25).

The inferiority complex harboured by so many east Germans before the *Wende* has been reinforced by their personal experiences in the new Germany as well as, in some cases, by feelings of guilt by association with the GDR. About 75 per cent of Ossis in October 1990 and 91 per cent in March 1991 regarded themselves as second-class

citizens (Christian Holst, 1991, p. 41). This attitude is rooted not only in
the palpable disparity in living standards and Ossi perception of being
colonized by west Germans but also in east German sensitivity to
accusations of collusion and double-think under the SED regime.

The socio-economic and psychological wall which still divides
the new and old *Länder* is vividly illustrated by the Emnid survey
referred to earlier. Sixty-four per cent of the Wessis and 74 per cent
of the Ossis agreed with the statement that 'The Wall has gone but
the wall in people's heads grows' ('Erst vereint, nun entzweit',
1993, p. 52). A survey conducted in Berlin by the public-opinion
research institute FORSA gives added weight to the notion of an
east–west gulf. Of the 618 west Berliners and 385 east Berliners
who were asked in July 1992 to comment on the political and
economic situation, 67 per cent of the former and 62 per cent of the
latter thought that east and west Berlin had not yet grown
together. Only 8 per cent were sufficiently optimistic to anticipate
the emergence of a truly united Berlin within three years; about
one-third expected it to take longer than nine years. 71 per cent of
west Berliners and 69 per cent of east Berliners believed that
political unity was barely discernible. 87 per cent of all those
questioned saw little or no sign of a true economic unification.
Finally, the vast majority (85 per cent) perceived little or no indi-
cation of any common feelings and thought between the inhabitants in both parts of the city (Bauschke, 1992, p. 5).

7.4 Xenophobia and the crisis of the party system

Despite the east–west divide and the gathering gloom in the new
Länder, no broad movement of well-organized social and political
protest has yet emerged. This is in part the result of what von
Beyme has called the weak east German resistance to 'cultural
imperialism' rooted in the fact the the FRG had served as a reference culture for four decades (von Beyme, 1992, p. 175). In addition, the heavy financial transfers have helped to maintain
stability.

But how long can social and political stability be maintained if
recovery in east Germany continues to be so elusive and if west
Germans prove reluctant to shoulder an even heavier burden in
the rebuilding of the new *Länder*? The wave of strikes among west
German public-service workers in May 1992 was an early signal of
the potential for conflict inherent within a redistribution of resources between east and west. Another early sign of the crack in
consensus politics was the advance of the Republican Party in the
first all-Berlin borough elections since 1946 – it obtained 8.3 per

cent of the vote – and the creditable performance of the PDS in east Berlin. As in the west German *Länder* elections in Baden-Würtemberg and Schleswig-Holstein in April 1992, these results underlined a growing disenchantment with the governing parties and the SPD. Although the commitment to the principles of democracy are widespread, an ALLBUS (Allgemeine Bevölkerung-sumfrage der Sozialwissenschaften) survey in spring 1992 found that satisfaction with the operation of the democratic system was 20 per cent lower in the new than in the old *Länder*, by 62 per cent to 80 per cent (Statistisches Bundesamt, 1992, p. 645).

In the east, parties of the radical and extreme right such as the Republicans and the DVU and cadre groups like the banned Nationalist Front and German Alternative have sought to establish a viable organizational network and expand their membership. The influx of foreign workers into Germany has provided them with an effective lever for mobilizing disenchanted and vulnerable east Germans. Foreign workers, never fully integrated into GDR society as a group, now find themselves in an increasingly margi-nalized position and, along with the flood of *émigrés* and asylum-seekers into Germany, the target of racial abuse and violence.

Before 1989, anti-Semitic outbursts and attacks on foreigners were infrequent and quickly suppressed by the GDR security forces. However, sociological data published since the *Wende* re-veal a growing support among young people for radical and ex-treme right-wing views and activities as well as a greater willingness to resort to violence. It is estimated that between 15 per cent and 20 per cent of east German pupils, apprentices and young workers have an authoritarian, nationalistic and xenophobic orien-tation (Schubarth, in Heinemann and Schubarth, 1992, p. 87). According to a sociological investigation conducted in Saxony and Saxony-Anhalt in March–April 1992 among 4,300 young people aged fourteen to twenty-five, 54 per cent of the young Saxons were negatively disposed towards foreigners. This represented an in-crease of between 5 and 8 per cent since a comparable study in December 1990.

Hostility towards foreigners is rooted in the belief that not only do they exacerbate the housing shortage (74 per cent) and wish to live well at Germany's expense (58 per cent), but that they also deprive German workers of jobs (55 per cent) and are predisposed to criminality (38 per cent) (Hennicke, 1992, p. 2). Turks, Poles, Roma and Sinti arouse the greatest antipathy (Müller and Schubarth, 1992, p. 18). Among other disturbing findings are the by no means inconsiderable level of support for the reincorpo-ration of the 'Eastern territories' into Germany (35 per cent of all the young people and 43 per cent of the apprentices) and for the statement that 'Fascism had its good side' (25 per cent of the pupils and 40 per cent of the apprentices). Six per cent of the pupils and 11 per cent of the apprentices favoured a seizure of power by a new National Socialist party and 11 per cent of the pupils and 29 per cent of the apprentices considered the Jews to be Germany's 'misfortune' (Hennicke, 1992, p. 3). Overt anti-Semitism has been spreading: since 1990 the percentage of apprentices supporting the latter statement rose by 10 per cent (Müller and Schubarth, 1992, p. 22). Social-Darwinist tendencies are also apparent in the 24 per cent who believed that, as in nature, the stronger emerge victorious (Förster and Friedrich, 1992, p. 7). In addition to exhibiting such a high propensity for radical and extreme-right positions, 11 per cent of the group (27 per cent of the male apprentices) expressed sympathy for the Republicans. Skinheads, hooligans and Fascists (*Faschos*) attracted sympathy ratings of 5 per cent each. About 3 per cent of the young people, including 5 per cent of the males, admitted to being members of at least one of these groupings (Müller and Schubarth, 1992, p. 22).

The sympathizers with radical and extreme-right attitudes constitute a small to medium-sized pool of potential support for organized groups such as the Republicans, the DVU and the NPD or the militant cadre groups like the Nationalist Front. The influence of these groups and parties must not be exaggerated, however. According to official figures, the supporters of these groups numbered, at the start of 1991, 30,000 in the old *Länder* and 15,000 in the new *Länder* (Leenen, 1992, p. 1043). And it is estimated that in 1991 the number of those disposed to resort to violence, such as the loosely organized right-wing skinheads, was about 3,000 in the east and 1,200 in the west. In 1992, these numbers may have risen to 3,800 and 2,600 respectively (Klinger, 1993, p. 156). What is more worrying at the moment is the radicalization and growing militancy of broad sections of east German youth culture outside the direct influence of the organized far-right groups.

Why have extreme right-wing attitudes, beliefs and groups gained a foothold in the new *Länder*? As a preliminary observation, it should be stressed that such ideas have engendered a similar degree of sympathy not only in the old *Länder* but also throughout Western Europe, a manifestation of what Scheuch once called the 'normal pathology of liberal industrial societies' (quoted by Leenen, 1992, p. 1041). Well before the collapse of communism, the new right in West Germany was seeking to reconstitute cultural and national identity against what was perceived to be the disruptive and threatening tendencies of universalism and the cultural deficits of modern industrial societies. In order to preserve Germany's cultural heritage, the new right called for an end to the influx of foreigners into the FRG, to the 'foreignization' of language and culture and to the division and occupation of Germany. The right-wing critique of modernity was frequently associated with a vitriolic attack on the United States, which was seen as the source of the modern values infecting German culture. The accelerated modernization of West Germany in the 1980s produced a number of serious problems such as structural unemployment, social fragmentation and marginalization. The inability of the established parties to mollify the anxieties of the electorate was partly responsible for the growing dissatisfaction with politicians and their parties and the rise in the number of floating voters during the 1980s. Among the political forces of the radical and extreme right, it was the radical populist Republicans, founded at the end of 1983, who enjoyed most success in exploiting the mixture of fear and resentment. They sought to mobilize support through appeals to the conservative values of law and order and through warnings of the threat to prosperity posed by the growing influx of foreigners. And they sought to restore German self-confidence by, for example, calling for an end to the stigmatization of German history.

At first glance, it came as a surprise to discover that many young east Germans, the children of a self-proclaimed anti-Fascist state, should show a proclivity to extreme right-wing ideas and groups. There is no satisfactory body of theory which satisfactorily accounts for the development of this complex phenomenon. Instead, there are a series of partial explanations, some of which carry a high level of conviction but which do not represent an integrated theory, and much research remains to be done to reconcile seemingly incompatible data within a comprehensive theoretical framework.

One popular explanation for the emergence of the right-wing extremism in east Germany is that it is the result of the inadequacy of political education and political socialization in the GDR. Having been raised in an authoritarian system, which suppressed open political debate and frequently imposed restrictions on direct contacts with people from other countries, young east Germans, so this argument runs, were ill-prepared for the psychological and cultural shock of the sudden opening to the outside world (see Gow, 1992c, p. 15). However, the political-culture argument can only be a partial explanation as the sociological research conducted by the Leipzig youth researchers shows that a clear majority of the young Saxons reject racism and xenophobia. The complexity of the whole issue is shown by some of the results emerging from a representative study by the Institute for Empirical Psychology: while 62 per cent of young east Germans believed that no more foreigners should be allowed into Germany, 70 per cent regarded hostility to foreigners as an aggravating problem (Klinger, 1993, p. 157). And it needs to be stressed that the civic culture of Western democracies has not proved to be an adequate antidote to intolerance in its various guises.

The current wave of violence and the attraction of radical and extreme right-wing views is partly accounted for by the disenchantment with the existing political system: only 39 per cent of the young Saxons in the survey discussed above (Förster and Friedrich, 1992, p. 12) expressed satisfaction with it. The overthrow of the old SED state has not been followed by a thorough democratization of the citizens of the former GDR. It is, of course, far too early in the unification process to expect Germans in the former GDR fully to absorb the political values and norms which their western counterparts have internalized in the course of four decades. At best, one can only speak of a partial emancipation of the political subject (see Schubarth, in Heinemann and Schubarth, 1992, pp. 94–7).

A standard explanation for the emergence and spread of extreme-right views in the new *Länder* is that it represents the classic reaction of vulnerable social strata to abrupt economic and social dislocation as their society undergoes the painful process of modernization. If one recalls the experiences of young east Germans since 1988, they have experienced not only the frustration of the SED's intransigence over reform but also the euphoria of their own peaceful toppling of the *ancien régime* and then the ambivalence of the new order. The new, united Germany may well have brought many benefits – freedom of travel, a wider range of consumer goods and political openness – but it has also produced spiralling unemployment, a rising crime rate, an increase in the cost of living and a reinforcement of feelings of inferiority towards Wessis. The old SED system was a form of authoritarian paternalism in which many basic necessities were taken care of and, though the individual might resent their tutelage, life seemed to follow a predetermined path from school to retirement. Since 1990 most of the collective props of the old system have disappeared or are fast disappearing. These include the extensive network of youth clubs, sports clubs and many leisure and sports activities once run by the enterprises and the mass organizations like the FDGB and the German Gymnastics and Sports Association but which the new local authorities can no longer sustain. Despite greater opportunities for self-determination, the individual east German now faces far greater existential uncertainties and the threat or the reality of serious status deprivation. In the case of the former GDR frustrated modernity has exacerbated the difficulties of the transformation into the 'modern', the modern in this case being the economic, political and social welfare system of the FRG. Some of the 'losers' in the modernization process, either real or perceived, find in the parties of the radical and extreme right a vehicle for expressing their protest against the existing political and economic order as represented by the mainstream parties. Others express their alienation in what is often a vicious and brutal manifestation of a youth revolt.

Finally, another contributory factor to the growth of xenophobia may lie in the search by young east Germans for a clear national identity hitherto denied to them by the ambiguities of SED policy on the national question. The slogan 'Germany for the Germans' received 40 per cent of support from the young Saxons in 1992, while 34 per cent agreed with the statement 'The Germans have always been the greatest in history' (Förster and Friedrich, 1992, p. 6). The former slogan received the approbation of over 90 per cent of members and sympathizers of the Republicans, skinheads, hooligans and fascists (Müller and Schubarth, 1992, p. 23).

Hostility to foreigners has become the central issue around which the the radical and extreme right-wing groups and parties like the DVU and the Republicans have sought to exploit the politically disaffected and the socially vulnerable, although the degree of control exercised by these organizations over what has been equated with the broader manifestation of youth revolt should not be overestimated. The record influx of foreign asylum-seekers and refugees into Germany since the end of the cold war has inflamed the issue and provided the extreme right with an exposed target. By the end of October 1992, 370,000 foreigners had sought political asylum in the country, an increase of 81 per cent over the corresponding period in the previous year (Tomforde, 1992, p. 9). As we have seen above, certain groups of foreigners are perceived as denying east Germans housing as well as jobs. They have thus become the targets of what Leenen has called a 'prosperity-chauvinism' motivated by envy and fear (Leenen, 1992, p. 1043). People adversely affected by material and ideological change and by the disintegration of traditional values and social ties are particularly susceptible to simplistic solutions and the designation of 'outsiders' as scapegoats.

The first of the disturbing explosions of open xenophobia and racial violence in the former GDR was the week-long siege by extreme right-wing groups to an apartment block for asylum-seekers in September 1991 in the town of Hoyerswerda. Even more disturbing was the 'orgy of terrorism and intimidation' (Sherwell, 1992, p. 15) by local right-wing youths and western neo-Nazis which broke out eleven months later against more than 200

Romanian gypsy asylum-seekers and about 150 Vietnamese workers and their children in a hostel in the Lichtenberg district in Rostock. The terrorizing of the asylum-seekers and the foreign workers was reported to have been supported by 'thousands of cheering, chanting, beer-swilling onlookers' (ibid.). Soon afterwards racial violence flared up in east German towns such as Eisenhüttenstadt, Cottbus and Leipzig. It is estimated that over 800 people had been seriously injured and 17 killed in both parts of Germany during the first eleven months of 1992 (Juhnke, 1992, p. 12). And according to official statistics, by early December 1992, about 2,000 acts of violence had been committed by right-wing extremists. Around 70 per cent of those apprehended were aged sixteen to twenty-one. Only a small minority of the attacks – up to 10 per cent – had been committed by organized right-wing extremists (' "Bestie aus deutschem Blut" ', 1992, p. 23).

7.5 No need to fear the Germans?

Reactions in the West to German unification were characterized by a mixture of delight, unease and even fear: delight at the crumbling of the Berlin Wall and the collapse of the SED autocracy as a confirmation of the superiority of the market and liberal democracy over 'real socialism'; unease among many Europeans and Americans about the possibility of German economic hegemony with the accession of the Soviet bloc's leading economic power and its 16.4 million inhabitants, many of them highly skilled; and fears that Germany, psychologically unprepared for her new role as a European economic and political superpower and perhaps no longer so tightly bound by the institutional straps of NATO and the EC, might become less predictable, less stable. Some envisaged the revival of chauvinism and the darker forces of German nationalism (see Glaeßner, 1992, pp. 17–26 and Wolffsohn, in Grosser, 1992, pp. 159–76). The Italian Foreign Minister Giulio Andreotti spoke for many Western politicians when in the mid-1980s he remarked that 'Pangermanism must be laid to rest. There are two German states and there should remain two German states' (quoted in Glaeßner, 1992, p. 18). Fear of the future was very much determined by memories of the Third Reich, the Irish writer and politician Conor Cruise O'Brien envisaging 'a statue of Hitler in every town' in Germany (O'Brien, in James and Stone, 1992, p. 223) and the Israeli Prime Minister Shamir raising, in November 1989, the spectre of a united Germany once again trying to murder millions of Jews (Wolffsohn, in Grosser, 1992, p. 172).

British attitudes to German unification have been distinguished by a combination of *Angst*, resentment, and admiration. In the euphoria after the disintegration of SED rule, popular reaction to the fall of the Berlin Wall was initially positive, although not without some reservations. Headlines such as 'Passport to freedom' (*Sunday Times*, 17 September 1989, p. B1) and 'The best Germany we've got' – the title of Tim Garton Ash's article in *The Spectator*, 21 July 1989, p. 14 – encapsulated popular perception of the start of the East German transition from a totalitarian dictatorship into a liberal democracy. In an opinion poll conducted by *The Economist* and *The Los Angeles Times*, 45 per cent of a British sample welcomed unification, 30 per cent opposed it. Poles, by comparison, harboured more doubts: 44 per cent were opposed and 41 per cent were in favour ('United Germany', 1990, p. 49).

The reaction of the political elite in Britain was hesitant and confused (see Rae, 1991, pp. 28–33). The then Prime Minister, Margaret Thatcher, while welcoming the breaching of the Wall as 'a great day for freedom, a great day for democracy' (quoted in Glaeßner, 1991, p. 180), sought on sober reflection, once unification rather than democratic reform in the GDR appeared to be the likely outcome, to slow down the pace of unification; she urged restraint in the interest of economic and political stability and until a new security system had been designed. Much to the annoyance of the West German government (see Teltschik, 1991, pp. 115–16), she preferred unification to be located at the end of the process of economic and democratic reform in Eastern Europe (Padgett, 1990, p. 29).

The British Prime Minister's coolness revealed just how difficult it was for her, as for many other West European political leaders, to cast off the psychological fetters of the cold war. Relationships both within and between the two major alliance systems had achieved a comfortable predictability and sustained the British illusion of being a medium-sized power with an appreciable influence on global events. Moreover, the old system had the added bonus of keeping Germany on a rein within NATO and the EC, even if the leash was becoming ever looser. Untie Germany and Britain would not only have to come to terms with the demise of the so-called German political dwarf and a demographically and economically enlarged Germany but also with the further erosion of her special relationship with the USA. Furthermore, Britain would be called upon to review with even greater urgency its role within the European Community, whatever that body's eventual organizational complexion, for it seemed likely that a united Germany could be expected to push harder for the closer degree of European integration favoured by Chancellor Kohl in contrast to the British government's preference for a looser confederation and for greater national control over economic policy. In short, the British government felt that too rapid a change, including the rush for German unity, might so destabilize the existing political order that new and unforeseen dangers could emerge. Germany might even be tempted into neutrality and become a 'loose canon' (*The Economist*, quoted in Glaeßner, 1992, p. 190), thereby undermining NATO, the cornerstone of Western security.

Another factor which inclined Thatcher to a slower rate of change in Eastern Europe and the Soviet Union was her belief that too hasty a retreat from empire might jeopardize the position of Gorbachev in his struggle with his opponents in the Soviet military and political elite. Would it not, asked Mrs Thatcher, be better if German unification could be delayed for ten to fifteen years? (' "Mrs Thatchers tadelnder Ton" ', 1990, p. 160). This cautious policy simply could not be sustained, however, once the GDR entered into its terminal crisis. In the early spring of 1990, the British government was obliged to adjust its policy to the reality of German unity; it continued, none the less, to harbour many doubts and fears as to its consequences.

After her forced retreat from high office, Mrs Thatcher, still not reassured by developments, became a rallying point for disaffected Conservatives who feared a deepening of European integration in the wake of German unity. She stated her views on Germany and European integration with great force in an address delivered at The Hague in May 1992:

Germany's new pre-eminence is a fact . . . and its power is a problem – as much for the Germans as for the rest of Europe. Germany is too large just to be another player in the European game, but not large enough to establish unquestioned supremacy over its neighbours . . .

Germany's preponderance in the [European] Community is such that no major decision can really be taken against German wishes. In these circumstances, the Community augments German power rather than containing it. [extract from speech in *The Daily Telegraph*, 16 May 1992, p. 9]

Perceptions of Germany among some members of the British political elite have been determined not simply by this kind of *Realpolitik* but also by a crude stereotyping. The classic case of 'Kraut-bashing' occurred in the rambling interview given by the then Secretary of State for Trade and Industry, Nicholas Ridley. Worried about the 'German menace', he warned against an economically dominant Germany and against the proposed European Monetary Union as: '. . . a German racket designed to take over the whole of Europe. It has to be thwarted. This rushed take-over by the Germans on the worst possible basis, with the French behaving like poodles to the Germans, is absolutely intolerable' ('Saying the unsayable . . .', 1990, p. 8). And he added for good measure that if sovereignty were to be surrendered to the European Commission, 'you might just as well give it to Adolf Hitler, frankly' (ibid.). Although Ridley was forced to resign after the international furore caused by his remarks, Mrs Thatcher was most probably sympathetic to the sentiments if not the tone (Reynolds, 1991, pp. 286–7).

The allegedly negative side to the 'Germany character' was subjected to scrutiny at a meeting held in March 1990 between Mrs Thatcher and six historians, including two Americans and Lord Dacre. One sentence in the published memorandum was particularly provocative: 'Some even less flattering attributes were also mentioned [at the meeting] as an abiding part of the German character: in alphabetical order, angst, aggressiveness, assertiveness, bullying, egotism, inferiority complex, sentimentality' [sic] (quoted by Ash, 1990a, p. 65).

Although one of the participants in the meeting, Tim Garton Ash, has protested that this did not reflect the tone of the discusion, with the positive features far outweighing the negative ones, there was an undeniable congruence between the negative aspects and the stereotypical characterization of Germans often found in sections of Britain's popular press. Moreover, the historians expressed great concern over a German tendency 'to over-estimate their own strength and capabilities' and over 'a capacity for success, to kick over the traces' (' "Wer sind die Deutschen?" ', 1990, p. 110). Together, the Chequers episode and the Ridley interview uncovered what one observer has called 'a Fawlty Towers tendency within the Cabinet' (Sassoon, in James and Stone, 1992, p. 240).

Popular concern in Britain was pinpointed in *The Economist/Los Angeles Times* opinion poll, in which 50 per cent of the British respondents expressed their anxiety over Germany becoming once more the dominant power in Europe. Their main worries included 'Return of fascism' (53 per cent), 'Might try to expand territory' (28 per cent) and 'Economy too strong' (41 per cent) ('United Germany', 1990, p. 49). At the start of 1990, a leader article in *The Economist* summed up this *Angst* over the re-emergence of a 'bigger, mightier' Germany: '[the] . . . most challenging element of policy on Germany is to ensure that its power stays channelled into benign use such as supporting economic growth in Western Europe, and putting Eastern Europe back on its feet, and does not turn malign' ('Germany benign', 1990, p. 15).

A negative attitude to Germany and German unification is, of course, by no means universal. Sir Edward Heath's retort to Mrs

Thatcher's Hague speech can be quoted as evidence of a warm appreciation of German political culture. He distanced himself consciously from bouts of xenophobia and complimented the Federal government on its policy: 'They have taken complete responsibility for the people in the former East Germany. They are now rebuilding that part of the country, have given it democracy and taken it into their system. What more could one ask of them to do?' (see *Daily Telegraph*, 22 May 1992, p. 12).

Sir Edward Heath's warmth notwithstanding, British popular attitudes to Germany are often characterized by the features which the Chequers memorandum alleges are typical of Germans. An inferiority complex and *Angst* towards Germany's economic performance intermingles with an admiration for German efficiency and the virtues symbolized by the D-Mark. Respect for German efficiency was expressed in the confident predictions in many sections of the British press of a second economic miracle, this time in east Germany after the infusion of D-Marks and west German know-how and technology. On the other hand, displays of German economic prowess often encounter antipathy. Thus when one of Britain's leading travel firms, Thomas Cook, was taken over by German owners, *The Sun* reported a travel staff man lamenting that not only do 'the Germans already get the best deckchairs by the swimming pool' but also that 'now British holidaymakers will have to pay them to get to the hotel in the first place' ('Taken over by Germans', *The Sun*, 5 June 1992, p. 12).

However, as 'Wunderkohl' turned into 'Blunderkohl' (*The Economist*, 6 April 1991, p. 45), many commentators were not too disturbed too see 'the new Sigfried humbled' ('Chancellor of Angst', 1991, p. 11). A certain *Schadenfreude* was apparent in the reactions to the spread of the so-called British disease when public-sector strikes affected major German cities in the spring of 1992. A correspondent of the daily newspaper *Today* wrote of the shock of widespread strike chaos which 'has deeply truamatised a nation used to having its economic successes trumpeted like an oompah band'. Stereotypical notions of German adherence to order were explicit in the reference to 'the explosion of pent-up aggression when a nation used to getting to work with slavish punctuality is plunged into travel misery' (Yarranton, 1992, p. 4). A JAK cartoon (*The Express and Star*, 29 April 1992, p. 9) depicted jack-booted strikers in serried ranks marching down east Berlin's Unter den Linden, yet another potent reminder that the British image of Germany is still deeply impregnated by memories of the Third Reich and the Second World War (see Kettenacker, in Trautmann, 1991, p. 202).

Symptomatic of Britain's difficulties in coming to terms both with the new united Germany and the momentous changes in the broader economic and political landscape of Europe has been the question of Britain's position within the European Monetary System and the impact of high German interest rates on Britain's economic prospects. These are highly sensitive economic antennae to the state of Anglo–German relations. The Conservative government under John Major was at first determined to combat inflation and to attain financial stability by linking the pound to the D-Mark at an original, and what was subsequently recognized as too high, entry rate of DM2.95 in the Exchange Rate Mechanism (ERM). Britain joined the ERM in October 1990. Keeping within the ERM bands was seen as the discipline required to attain Major's target of zero inflation. In accordance with the new political virility, devaluation was ruled out as a soft option, 'a betrayal of our future', according to the Prime Minister in an address to the Scottish CBI on 10 September 1992 (quoted by Keegan, 1992, p. 20). By making the defence of sterling's ERM parity the main plank of economic policy and by linking the pound to what appeared as an almost inflation-proof D-mark would, it was hoped, create a stronger, more stable British economy. By ruling out devaluation and more flexible exchange rates, British policy was linked even more closely to the key currency in the ERM and to developments in German fiscal and economic policy. But what Major and his Chancellor of the Exchequer, Norman Lamont, had not anticipated was that German unification would prove to be such a stormy process. Thus when the Bundesbank pursued a tighter monetary policy and pegged interest rates at a high level in order to maintain financial stability in a sea of rising public-sector deficits and inflation as well as demonstrating in public its own independence, Britain was unable to escape from its straitjacket. The damaging impact of German unification was analysed in a *Financial Times* leader:

The challenges for all ERM members have risen greatly because of the Bonn government's policy errors over German unification. Large German deficits have given an inflationary boost to German growth. This has forced the Bundesbank to raise interest rates far higher than foreseen two years ago. Countries – within and outside the ERM – which had hoped to hitch a ride to price stability on the Bundesbank's coat tails have suffered a bumpier journey than they imagined. [*Financial Times*, 17 September 1992, p. 24]

The fixation in Whitehall and the City of London on Germany and the monetary policy of the Bundesbank is testimony to German hegemony in the European financial order. Britain, therefore, could not avoid being drawn into the orbit of what *The*

Guardian called 'Germany's digestion problems with the east' (17 July 1992, p. 20). At the same time, the paper fulminated against the Bundesbank as 'the last outpost of monetarism which Britain had tried and discarded in the 1980s' and pleaded for Germany to devalue against everyone else, thereby applying deflationary pressure to Germany and offering interest rate cuts all round (*The Guardian*, leader, 17 July 1992, p. 20). However, with the Federal government failing to control public borrowing and the Bundesbank unable to bring money supply down from its 9 per cent growth of M3 to within the Bank's target range of 3.5 to 5.5 per cent, the prospects in the summer of 1992 for a significant fall in German interest rates were gloomy – and guaranteed further British agonizing. The apparent refusal of Germany at a meeting of the EC finance ministers in Bath at the beginning of September to countenance interest-rate reductions at a time of turbulence on the exchange markets in the run-up to the French referendum on the Maastricht treaty only deepened British worries and was greeted on the front page of the 6 September issue of *The Sunday Telegraph* with the headline of 'Germans say all Europe must suffer'.

The ignominious retreat of the Major government from keeping Britain within the ERM and its U-turn on a realignment of sterling, both precipitated by the unprecedented financial turmoil on 16 September 1992, unleashed an open bout of Germanophobia in government circles as it sought scapegoats for its policy reversal and for spending billions of pounds defending an unsustainable exchange rate. The crash of confidence in the pound was attributed by the Chancellor of the Exchequer, Norman Lamont, with the backing of the premier, in no small measure, to Germany's commitment to high interest rates and to the widely reported remark by Helmut Schlesinger, the Bundesbank President, in an interview on 15 September with *Handelsblatt* and *The Wall Street Journal* that a comprehensive realignment of currencies would have been preferable to the recent lowering of German interest rates by 0.25 per cent in return for a devaluation of the Italian lira as a means of reducing pressure on the market. This remark, which first appeared in an advance story and without the final authorization of the Bank and though it did not specifically refer to sterling, was listed by Downing Street as one of five instances since late August of Bundesbank members or senior officials briefing sterling into a crisis. The Deputy Chairman of the Conservative party, Gerry Malone, blamed 'the clear briefing that came from the Bundesbank, one way or another, and got into the financial markets that they were seeking a devaluation of the pound' (Wintour, 1992, p. 5). When the Bundesbank shortly afterwards defended the French franc when it too came under pressure, the *Sunday Times* reported 'renewed fury with the Bundesbank in government circles' and with 'senior sources' complaining that this confirmed the British government's view that the Bundesbank had engaged in a deliberate campaign to undermine sterling (Hughes and Grice, 1992, p. 1).

Major's predecessor could not restrain herself from intervening. In an address to the World Economic Development Congress in Washington, she welcomed the suspension of Britain's membership of ERM and the breaking free of 'largely self-imposed constraints' and advised a complete reversal of policy on Maastricht (Grice, 1992, p. 3). And in an interview in *Le Figaro* shortly before the French referendum on Maastricht, she once again warned of the twin dangers of a federal Europe and of an overmighty Germany while conveniently overlooking Britain's responsibility for its own chronic economic condition:

They claim that the federalism of Maastricht will contain German power which is already dominant. It has been us, rather than the taxpayers of Germany, who have had to bear the costs of reunification. We were not consulted when their interest rates were set, we have suffered from inflation and our interest rates have been raised, with the consequences of unemployment and recession! But if you look at the balance of power within a future federal structure, Maastricht would not be able to counter-balance the growth of German power. People are aware of that. In the early days of the European Community, Germany was not dominant. Now, if we accept federalism, the balance will be distorted by German domination. [quoted in *The Guardian*, 19 September 1992, p. 25]

Former members of Thatcher's cabinet such as Kenneth Baker and Lord Tebbit banged the national drum. Rejecting Maastricht and the pooling of sovereignty, Baker launched an attack against the inflationary effect of Kohl's decision on the one-to-one conversion of GDR Marks into D-Marks and on paying for unification by borrowing. The consequence, higher German interest rates just when Europe wanted lower ones, 'meant that the people of Europe, rather than the German taxpayer, were paying for German reunification. Herr Kohl consulted no one outside Germany on these matters but these decisions had a profound effect upon jobs in Yorkshire, London and Surrey' (Baker, 1992, p. 18).

The furore was subjected to analysis in a *Financial Times* article headed 'British guns target Germany':

. . . just two years ago, comments by Mr Nicholas (now Lord) Ridley, a cabinet minister, that Germany was 'already running most of the

Community' were deemed too intemperate to allow him to stay in the government.

Today, however, beleagured Britain appears to have lost its inhibitions and declared an open season of vituperation on the awesome might of the Teuton power – mainly on that of the boys from the Bundesbank.

. . . there is no doubt that several senior British government officials, ministers, and MPs would have little argument with the headline in one mid-market tabloid newspaper yesterday morning: 'Sabotage by the Germans'.

The view, as one Tory MP put it, that 'we are paying for East German reconstruction and the expansion of Germany into Eastern Europe' also has widespread resonance nightly in public houses across Britain. [Dawney, 1992, p. 2]

The stereotypical view of Germany was vividly illustrated in Sir Peter Tapsell's comments in the House of Commons during the ERM debacle:

Germany will not change its personality. It has two great characteristics which have been clear throughout its history. First the Germans have an instinctive urge to dominate Europe; and second – they set about that by appointing groups of élites which were not answerable to anybody. Between 1860 and 1945, that élite was the German general staff. Since 1950 the élite that has replaced the German general staff has been the Bundesbank. [quoted in Burns, 1993, p. 28]

British criticism of the Bundesbank is one of several instances of the British being beastly to the Germans. The German government was castigated for its overbearing behaviour in pushing its reluctant EC partners into recognizing Croatia and Slovenia and for its lack of full solidarity during the Gulf War (Horsley, 1992, pp. 225–41). And relations were soured by controversy over the erection of the Bomber Harris statue in The Strand and over the throwing of eggs at the Queen on the occasion of her visit to Dresden in October 1992. One tabloid praised the Queen's courage in confronting the neo-Nazis of Dresden:

It took a special kind of bravery to face the wave of hatred the Queen ran into in Germany yesterday. But then she has always been a brave lady.

As the mob of baying neo-Nazis in Dresden threw eggs, yelled *Sieg Heil* and gave her Hitler salutes, she hit back at them with the one weapon that has laid waste so many.

Unshakeable dignity. [Arnold, 1992, p. 6]

These and other events have helped to raise 'the art of Kraut-bashing to new heights' (Hume, 1992, p. 4). British *Angst* has been quickened by the upsurge of right-wing extremism against asylum-seekers and foreign workers in Rostock, Cottbus and many other German towns and by the gains of the far-right in *Länder* elections in the west. In its leader of 26 August 1992, *The Independent* warned of 'Echoes from a dark past' and that the violence in Rostock was 'a warning of what could happen if the stresses of the past few years are allowed to increase'. The article continued:

Racial hatred is far from unique to Germany, but its manifestations under the Nazis were so appalling that any re-emergence is bound to carry echoes of the past. It helps to remember that until reunification Rostock had not known democracy for 60 years. Its inhabitants have no tolerance and little understanding of constitutional means of redressing grievances. The collapse of Communism has left them disorientated, humiliated and in large measure unemployed. Studies have also shown that the young have little trust in the older generation, whom they regard as responsible for Communism. They resent the money and attention devoted to refugees. Probably they would like to seek asylum from their own lives.

Behind these feelings flicker an older xenophobia. Historically the Germans have defined themselves by reference to the tribe, not to the state, because they lived for so long amid fragmented power. Their nation state, which never encompassed all Germans, lasted only from 1871 to 1945 and was a disaster. Where identity is bound up with ethnicity, outsiders pose a special threat. [*The Independent*, 26 August 1992, p. 28]

A *Sunday Times* leader, though readily conceding that Britain is in no position to preach to Germany about civil disorder, also pursued the theme of a resurrection of Fascism in that 'Rostock's rioting has reminded the world of nightmares it thought were behind it (*The Sunday Times*, 30 August 1992, p. 3, Section 2). While the newspaper hoped that the new Germany, once east Germany was completely absorbed by the west, would become a massive force for good, it saw this hope being negated by the racial violence in Rostock as well as by 'the nationalist policies being pursued by the Bundesbank to Europe's detriment and Germany's own peril' (ibid.). Warming to the theme of an overmighty Germany and the dual threat of German nationalism as exemplified by racial intolerance and the mighty D-Mark, it argued that Germany should lower interest rates to everyone's advantage. The Bundesbank, it argued, was pursuing an anti-inflationary policy as revenge against Kohl for overruling its warnings against the real cost of unification:

Mr Kohl sold Germany a pup which has become a rottweiler. The mechanics of taming it may be difficult, but it must be done before it devours us all. The Bank must be persuaded of its duties to a wider world as well as Germany's narrow self-interest. That would be in Germany's interests as well as everyone else's. Helmut Schlesinger, the bank president . . . would warm all our hearts if he persuaded his board to cut interest rates forthwith and put a less rigid timeframe on their aim to cut inflation below 2% . . .

We all live in an extended democracy these days. The D-Mark would not escape the convulsions caused by the collapse of Europe's monetary system. Germany's central bankers should use their power to prevent it. So should the German government to prevent more Rostocks. Neo-Nazi street fighters and an overmighty D-Mark bode ill for the new Germany. There are other ways. [ibid.]

Ian Buruma reflected on this amalgam of the past and present in the columns of *The Spectator*:

Every newspaper photograph of a screaming German thug can, if one wishes, serve as a cosy reminder that Germans will be Germans, and we Brits, or Dutch or even French are still on the side of the angels, or at least of the Spitfires. It is presumably why wartime metaphors come to the fore as soon as there are problems with Germany over finance, security or trade. [Buruma, 1992, p. 10]

The gains of Schönhuber's Republicans in the local elections in the federal state of Hesse in March 1993, they obtained just over 8 per cent of the vote, set the alarm bells ringing once more. The *Daily Mail* warned of the danger to Germany's democratic system arising from the 'Advance of the ex-nazi with no regrets' (Pukas, 1993, p. 10). Emphasizing popular antipathy in west Germany to Maastricht and to being the milk cow of Europe and to the burdens of unification, one correspondent feared that if the Republicans were the only party effectively 'to articulate the weariness of the West German taxpayer with the costs of German and European unification . . . Germany's neighbours will shrink further and further back from closer ties and Chancellor Kohl's dream will lie shattered by the ugly shadows of the swastika and the jackboot' (Almond, 1993, p. 6).

From the preceding discussion of British reactions to German unification, it can be seen that attitudes and policies are partly determined by an allergy, based on historical memory, against extreme nationalism in Germany. However, a good deal of domestic political manoeuvring is involved: whereas some Eurosceptics warn against the dangers of German nationalism as a reason against too close an association with the EC in which Germany is the major player, others favour closer European cooperation as a means of controlling Germany.

Many British anxieties are by no means unjustified. The sluggish nature of economic growth in east Germany and the manifest structural problems of the west German economy ensure that the unification bill will be a continuing and perhaps unacceptable burden for many well into the 1990s (Gow, 1992a, p. 13), and possibly delaying Europe's hopes for greater monetary stability. Although many reactions to German unification are impregnated with stereotypical images of German nationalism and militarism, concern about the stirrings of the far right in Germany and the stability of the post-war German political system are entirely legitimate. However, in this difficult situation, greater understanding needs to be shown for Germany's predicament as it seeks not only to modernize the east German economy but also to absorb the torrent of refugees and asylum-seekers attracted by Germany's material prosperity and liberal democratic culture. In this transitional stage for the west as well as the east German system, a spirit of tolerance and solidarity is required not only within Germany but also between Germany and her neighbours; otherwise, as Martin Kettle has argued, both Germany and the European project might wreck themselves upon the same xenophobic rock (Kettle, 1993, p. 18).

Bibliography

'3154 DM Einnahmen im Monat' 1992. *Zahlen – Fakten – Trends. Monatlicher Pressedienst des Statistischen Bundesamtes*, July, pp. 2–4.

Adler, Frank 1991. 'Das "Bermüda-Dreieck" des Realsozialismus: Machtmonopolisierung – Entsubjektivierung – Nivellierung', *BISS public*, No. 2, pp. 5–46.

Aganbegyan, Abel and Timofeyev, Timor 1988. *The New Stages of Perestroika*, New York, Institute for East–West Security Studies.

Agrarbericht 1992. Agrar- und ernährungspolitischer Bericht der Bundesregierung 1992, Bonn, Verlag Dr. Heger.

Akerlof, George A., Rose, Andrew, Vellen, Janet, L. and Hessenius, Helga 1991. 'East Germany in from the Cold: The Economic Aftermath of Currency Union', *Brookings Papers on Economic Activity*, no. 1, pp. 1–105.

Almond, Mark 1993. 'Maastricht and the rise of an ex-SS officer', *Daily Mail*, 9 March, p. 6.

Arbeitsgruppe Alternative Wirtschaftspolitik (ed.) 1992. *Memorandum '92 gegen den ökonomischen Niedergang – Industriepolitik in Ostdeutschland*, Cologne, PapyRossa.

Arbeitsgruppe Sozialberichterstattung 1992. 'Stimmungseinbruch in Ostdeutschland', *WZB Mitteilungen*, no. 56, pp. 69–71.

Arbeitsgruppe Wirtschaftsreform beim Ministerrat der DDR (ed.) 1990. *Regierungskonzept zur Wirtschaftsreform in der DDR*, Berlin, no publisher.

Arbeitskreis Konjunktur im DIW, 1992. 'Grundlinien der Wirtschaftsentwicklung 1992', *DIW Wochenbericht*, vol. 59, no. 1–2, pp. 1–19.

Arbeitskreis Konjunktur im DIW 1993. 'Bundesrepublik Deutschland: Rezession in Westdeutschland und anhaltende Krise in Ostdeutschland', *DIW Wochenbericht*, vol. 60, no. 1–2, pp. 8–23.

Arndt, Heinz-Peter 1992. 'Arbeitsgerichte überlastet', *Berliner Zeitung*, 8–9 August, p. 4.

Arnold, Harry 1992. 'Happy and glorious', *Daily Mirror*, 23 October, p. 6.

Ash, Timothy Garton 1990a. 'The Chequers Affair', *New York Review of Books*, vol. XXXVII, no. 14, p. 65.

Ash, Timothy Garton 1990b. 'Germany Unbound', *New York Review of Books*, vol. XXXVII, no. 18, pp. 11–15.

Assmann, Georg, Backhaus, Klaus and Hilker, Jörg (eds) 1991. *Deutschdeutsche Unternehmen. Ein unternehmenskulturelles Anpassungsproblem*, Stuttgart, C.E. Poeschel Verlag.

Außerordentlicher Parteitag der SED/PDS. Partei des Demokratischen

Sozialismus 8./9. und 16./17. Dezember 1989 1990. Berlin, Dietz Verlag.

Baker, Kenneth 1992. 'Europe at the right price', *The Daily Telegraph*, 22 September, p. 18.

Balkhausen, Dieter 1992. *Gutes Geld und schlechte Politik. Der Report über die Bundesbank*, Düsseldorf, Vienna, New York and Munich, ECON Verlag.

Bark, Dennis L. and Gress, David R. 1993. *A History of West Germany. Volume 2: Democracy and its Discontents 1963–1991*, 2nd edn, Oxford and Cambridge, Massachusetts, Blackwell.

Batt, Judy 1991. *East Central Europe from Reform to Transformation*, London, The Royal Institute of International Affairs and Pinter.

Baumann, Claus 1992. 'Verkauf von Leuna und Minol ist jetzt perfekt', *Berliner Morgenpost*, 24 July, p. 23.

Bauschke, Christian 1992. 'Einig in der Beurteilung der Uneinigkeit', *Berliner Zeitung*, 27 July, p. 5.

Becker, Harald 1992. 'Wirtschaft in den neuen Bundesländern. Strukturwandel und Neuaufbau', *Deutschland Archiv*, vol. 25, no. 5, pp. 461–75.

'Bei den Lebensmitteln läuft der Aufschwung Ost' 1992. *Berliner Zeitung*, 6 August, p. 30.

Bentley, Raymond 1992. *Research and Technology in the Former German Democratic Republic*, Boulder, San Francisco and Oxford, Westview Press.

Berger, Horst and Hinrichs, Wilhelm 1992. 'Erwerbs- und Wohnverhältnisse im Wandel', *BISS public*, no. 7, pp. 61–8.

' "Bestie aus deutschem Blut" ', *Der Spiegel*, 7 December 1992, pp. 22–32.

Beyme, Kurt von 1992. 'The Effects of Reunification on German Democracy: A Preliminary Evaluation', *Government and Opposition*, vol. 27, no. 2, pp. 158–76.

Biedenkopf, Kurt H. 1990. *Offene Grenze, offener Markt: Voraussetzung für die Erneuerung der DDR-Wirtschaft*, Wiesbaden, Gabler.

Biedenkopf, Kurt H. 1992. 'Die geeinte Nation im Stimmungstief', *Die Zeit*, 2 October, pp. 3–4.

Blaschke, Dieter, Buttler, Friedrich, Karr, Werner, Klauder, Wolfgang and Leikeb, Hanspeter 1992. 'Der Arbeitsmarkt in den neuen Bundesländern – Zwischenbilanz und Herausforderungen', *Mitteilungen aus der Arbeitsmarkt- und Berufsforschung*, vol. 25, no. 2, pp. 119–35.

Boden, Steffen and Zimmermann, Henry 1992. 'Weitere Stellenabbau bis Ende 1993 erwartet', *Berliner Zeitung*, 5 August, p. 30.

Boss, Alfred 1990. 'Budgetdefizite und Finanzpolitik in der Bundesrepublik Deutschland', *Die Weltwirtschaft*, no. 2, pp. 58–70.

Braun, Albert and Obenau, Hans 1992. *Landesreport Mecklenburg-Vorpommern*, Berlin and Munich, Die Wirtschaft.

Brabant, Jozef van 1992. *Privatizing Eastern Europe. The Role of Markets and Ownership in the Transition*, Dordrecht, Boston and London, Kluwer.

Breuel, Birgit 1992. 'Grenzenlos überfordert', *Die Zeit*, 13 November, p. 30.

'Brief des Sachverständigenrates zur Begutachtung der gesamtwirtschaftlichen Entwicklung' 1990. *Deutscher Bundestag 11. Wahlperiode. Bundesdruksache 1/8472*, Bonn, Verlag Dr. Hans Heger.

Brocke, Rudolf Horst 1990. 'Thesen zur Situation von FuE in den neuen Bundesländern – FuT-Herausforderungen im Vereinigungsprozeß', *IGW-report über Wissenschaft und Technologie in Ostdeutschland*, vol. 4, no. 4, pp. 41–9.

Brown, J.F. 1991. *Surge to Freedom. The End of Communist Rule in Eastern Europe*, Twickenham, Adamantine Press.

Bryson, Phillip 1992. 'The Economics of German Reunification: A Review of the Literature', *Journal of Comparative Economics*, vol. 16, no. 1, pp. 118–49.

Bryson, Phillip and Melzer, Manfred 1990. *The End of the East German Economy. From Honecker to Reunification*, Basingstoke and London, Macmillan.

Brzezenski, Zbigniew 1989. *The Grand Failure. The Birth and Death of Communism in the Twentieth Century*, New York, Charles Scribner's Sons.

Buechtemann, Christoph F. and Schupp, Jürgen 1992. 'Repercussions of reunification: patterns and trends in the socio-economic transformation of East Germany', *Industrial Relations*, vol. 23, no. 2, pp. 90–106.

Bundesminister der Finanzen (ed.) 1991. *Finanzbericht 1992*, Bonn, Bonner Universitäts-Buchdruckerei.

Bundesministerium für innerdeutsche Beziehungen (ed.) 1987. *Materialien zum Bericht zur Lage der Nation im geteilten Deutschland 1987*, Bonn, Verlag Dr. Hans Heger.

Bundesministerium für Wirtschaft 1992. 'Wages and the Labour Market in the New Länder', *Supplement to Monthly Review 2 '92*, pp. 1–41.

Burda, Michael 1990. 'The Consequences of German Economic and Monetary Union', *Centre for Economic Policy Research*, Discussion Paper No. 449, London, Centre for Economic Policy Research.

Burns, Bob 1993. 'Stereotype unfounded', *The Times Higher Education Supplement*, 26 February, p. 28.

Buruma, Ian 1992. 'Germany's deep well of hate', *The Spectator*, 5 December, pp. 9–11.

Carlin, Wendy 1992. 'Privatization in East Germany, 1990–92', *German History*, vol. 10, no. 3, pp. 335–51.

'Chancellor of Angst' 1991. *The Economist*, 6 April, pp. 10–11.

Chodak, Szymon 1973. *Societal Development*, New York, Oxford University Press.

Christ, Peter and Neubauer, Ralf 1991. *Kolonie im eigenen Land. Die Treuhand und die Wirtschaftskatastrophe der fünf neuen Länder*, Berlin, Rowohlt.

Clasen, Lothar 1992. 'Tarifverträge 1991. Schrittweise Angleichung', *Bundesarbeitsblatt*, no. 4, pp. 5–11.

Colitt, Lesley 1992a. 'Optimists repeatedly disappointed', *Financial Times, Survey: Germany*, 27 October, Section 3, p. X.

Colitt, Lesley 1992b. 'UK interest rises in East German companies', *Financial Times*, 1 May, p. 2.

Cornelsen, Doris 1985. 'Bilanz des Fünfjahrplans', *FS-Analysen*, vol. 12, no. 4, pp. 39–69.

Cornelsen, Doris 1987. 'The GDR Economy in the Eighties: Economic

Strategy and Structural Adjustments', *Studies in Comparative Communism*, vol. XX, no. 1, pp. 39–53.

Cornelsen, Doris 1990. 'Die Wirtschaft der DDR in der Honecker-Ära', *Vierteljahreshefte für Wirtschaftsforschung*, vol. 59, no. 1, pp. 70–9.

Cornelsen, Doris, Melzer, Manfred and Scherzinger, Angela 1984. 'DDR-Wirtschaftssystem: Reform in kleinen Schritten', *Deutsches Institut für Wirtschaftsforschung Vierteljahrsheft*, no. 2, pp. 200–23.

'Das Profil der Deutschen. Was sie vereint, was sie trennt' 1991. *Der Spiegel-Spezial*, no. 1, Hamburg, SPIEGEL-Verlag Rudolf Augstein.

' "Das reale Bild war eben katastrophal!" Gespräch mit Gerhard Schürer' 1992. *Deutschland Archiv*, vol. 25, no. 10, pp. 1031–9.

Dawney, Iwo 1992. 'British guns target Germans', *Financial Times*, 17 September, p. 2.

'DDR schon 1989 "von kapitalistischen Kreditgebern abhängig" ' 1990. *die tageszeitung*, 19 March, p. 4.

Dennis, Mike 1984–5. 'The Red Robots Are Here!' *GDR Monitor*, no. 12, pp. 1–17.

Dennis, Mike 1987–8. 'Economic and Social Challenges of the 1990s', *East Central Europe*, vols. 14–15, pp. 49–80.

Dennis, Mike 1988. *German Democratic Republic. Politics. Economics and Society*, London and New York, Pinter.

'Der Arbeitsmarkt in Ostdeutschland' 1992. *Deutschland Archiv*, vol. 25, no. 3, pp. 231–2.

Der Fischer Weltalmanach. Sonderband DDR 1990. Frankfurt on Main, Fischer Taschenbuch Verlag.

'Der Staat und seine Verschuldung' 1992. *Das Parlament*, no. 5, 21 February, p. 8.

Derix, Hans-Heribert 1990. 'A Bureaucratically Regulated Market Economy between Inertia and Liquidation', *Aussenpolitik*, vol. 41, no. 4, pp. 351–65.

Deutsches Institut für Wirtschaftsforschung (ed.) 1984. *Handbuch DDR-Wirtschaft*, 4th edn, Reinbek bei Hamburg, Rowohlt Taschenbuch Verlag.

Deutsches Institut für Wirtschaftsforschung, Berlin, and Institut für Weltwirtschaft an der Universität Kiel 1991a. 'Gesamtwirtschaftliche und unternehmerische Anpassungsprozesse in Ostdeutschland', *DIW Wochenbericht*, vol. 58, no. 24, pp. 323–46.

Deutsches Institut für Wirtschaftsforschung, Berlin, and Institut für Weltwirtschaft an der Universität Kiel 1991b. 'Gesamtwirtschaftliche und unternehmerische Anpassungsprozesse in Ostdeutschland', *DIW Wochenbericht*, vol. 58, no. 39–40, pp. 553–74

Deutsches Institut für Wirtschaftsforschung, Berlin, and Institut für Weltwirtschaft an der Universität Kiel 1992a. 'Gesamtwirtschaftliche und unternehmerische Anpassungsprozesse in Ostdeutschland', *DIW Wochenbericht*, vol. 59, no. 12–13, pp. 131–62.

Deutsches Institut für Wirtschaftsforschung, Berlin, and Institut für Weltwirtschaft an der Universität Kiel 1992b. 'Gesamtwirtschaftliche und unternehmerische Anpassungsprozesse in Ostdeutschland', *DIW Wochenbericht*, vol. 59, no. 39, pp. 467–92.

Deutsches Institut für Wirtschaftsforschung, Berlin, and Institut für Weltwirtschaft an der Universität Kiel 1992c. 'Gesamtwirtschaftliche und unternehmerische Anpassungsprozesse in Ostdeutschland', *DIW Wochenbericht*, vol. 59, no. 52, pp. 709–38.

'"Die Industrie muß ran"' 1992. *Der Spiegel*, 4 May, pp. 146–7, 149, 152–3, 155–6.

'Die Lage der Weltwirtschaft und der deutschen Wirtschaft im Herbst 1990' 1990. *DIW Wochenbericht*, vol. 57, no. 43–44, pp. 605–35.

'Die Lage der Weltwirtschaft und der deutschen Wirtschaft im Frühjahr 1991' 1991a. *DIW Wochenbericht*, vol. 58, no. 18–19, pp. 227–58

'Die Lage der Weltwirtschaft und der deutschen Wirtschaft im Herbst 1991' 1991b. *DIW Wochenbericht*, vol. 58, no. 42–43, pp. 587–622

'Die Lage der Weltwirtschaft und der deutschen Wirtschaft im Frühjahr 1992' 1992. *DIW Wochenbericht*, vol. 59, no. 16–17, pp. 199–233.

'Die verfeindeten Nachbarn' 1992. *Der Spiegel*, 22 June, pp. 18–19, 21, 23–6.

'Die wirtschaftliche Entwicklung im Deutschland im ersten Quartal 1992. Erste Ergebnisse der volkswirtschaftlichen Gesamtrechnung' 1992. *DIW Wochenbericht*, vol. 59, no. 20–21, pp. 263–72.

Dohnanyi, Klaus von 1990. *Das deutsche Wagnis*, Munich, Droemer Knaur.

'Dokumentation. Erich Honecker vor den 1. SED-Kreissekretären' 1987. *Deutschland Archiv*, vol. 20, no. 4, pp. 436–44.

Dölling, Irene 1991. 'Between Hope and Helplessness: Woman in the GDR after the "Turning Point" ', *Feminist Review*, no. 39, pp. 3–15.

Donhöff, Marion *et al.* 1992. *Ein Manifest. Weil das Land ändern muß*, Reinbek bei Hamburg, Rowohlt Verlag.

Donovan, Barbara 1990. 'The East German Election Results', *Radio Free Europe. Report on Eastern Europe*, vol. 1, no. 12, pp. 15–17.

'"Eine grausame Dynamik"' 1992. *Der Spiegel*, 24 February, pp. 110–13.

'Einkommen Ost. Produktivität hinkt nach' 1991. *iwd. Informationsdienst des Instituts der deutschen Wirtschaft*, vol. 17, no. 37, p. 6.

Ellman, Michael 1989. *Socialist planning*, Cambridge, Cambridge University Press.

Ellmann, Michael and Kantorovitch, Vladimir (eds) 1992. *The disintegration of the Soviet economic system*, Routledge, London and New York.

Elsner, Eva-Maria and Elsner, Lothar 1992. *Ausländer und Ausländerpolitik in der DDR*. Forscher- und Diskussionskreis DDR-Geschichte: hefte zur ddr-geschichte, Abhandlungen, 2, Berlin, Gesellschaftswissenschaftliches Forum.

Erich Honecker zu dramatischen Ereignissen 1992. Hamburg, W. Runge.

'ERP-Kredite 1993' 1992. *Die Wirtschaft*, vol. 41, no. 31, p. 2.

'Erst vereint, nun entzweit' 1993. *Der Spiegel*, 18 January, pp. 52–3, 56, 58–9, 62.

' "Es besteht kein Anlaß zum Ächzen" ' 1992. *Die Zeit*, 8 May, pp. 3–4.

' "Es gibt keine DDR mehr" ' 1990. *Der Spiegel*, 19 March, pp. 20–33.

' "Es reißt mir das Herz kaputt" ' 1991. *Der Spiegel*, 9 September, pp. 88, 92–3, 96, 99, 101, 104.

Fach, Wolfgang and Ringwald, Annette 1991–2. 'Curing Germany, Saving Europe', *Telos*, no. 90, pp. 89–100.

Faulner, Harald 1992. 'Die Lausitzer Textil-Industrie liegt im Sterben', *Berliner Morgenpost*, 26 July, p. 8.

Fawcett, Edmund 1992. 'A Survey of Germany. Not as Grimm as it looks', *The Economist*, 23 May, pp. 1–28.

Federal Institute for Soviet and International Studies (ed.) 1990. *The Soviet Union 1988–1989, Perestroika in Crisis?*, Boulder, Westview.

Federal Ministry of Economics 1991a. *Economic Assistance in the new German Länder*, Bonn, Federal Ministry of Economics.

Federal Ministry of Economics 1991b. *Investing in the Future. Germany's New Federal States*, Bonn, Federal Ministry of Economics.

'Ferngespräch mit Gerhard Schürer' 1992. *Deutschland Archiv*, vol. 25, no. 2, pp. 143–5.

Fink, Hans-Jürgen 1990a. 'Bündnis '90. Die Revolutionäre der ersten Stunde verloren die Wahl', *Deutschland Archiv*, vol. 23, no. 4, pp. 515–17.

Fink, Hans-Jürgen 1990b. 'Die SPD in der DDR', *Deutschland Archiv*, vol. 23, no. 2, pp. 180–5.

Flassbeck, Heiner, Horn, Gustav, Scheremet, Wolfgang and Zwiener, Rudolf 1991. 'Subventionierung und Privatisierung durch die Treuhandanstalt: Kurswechsel erforderlich', *DIW Wochenbericht*, vol. 58, no. 41, pp. 575–9.

Fleissner, Peter, and Ludwig, Udo 1992. *Ostdeutsche Wirtschaft im Umbruch. Computersimulation mit einem systematischen Modell*, Brunswick and Wiesbaden, Vieweg.

Flug, Martin 1992. *Treuhand-Poker. Die Mechanismen des Ausverkaufs*, Berlin, Ch. Links.

Forschungsstelle für gesamtdeutsche wirtschaftliche und soziale Fragen (ed.) 1989. *Glasnost und Perestroika auch in der DDR?*, Berlin, Berlin Verlag.

Förster, Peter and Friedrich, Walter 1992. 'Politische Einstellungen und Grundpositionen Jugendlicher in Ostdeutschland', *Aus Politik und Zeitgeschichte*, no. 38, pp. 3–15.

Förster, Peter and Roski, Günter 1990. *DDR zwischen Wende und Wahl. Meinungsforscher analysieren den Umbruch*, Berlin, LinksDruck Verlag.

Förtsch, Eckhard 1990. 'Auf dem Weg zur Wirtschaftsunion', *Deutschland Archiv*, vol. 23, no. 11, pp. 1198–1200.

Freeman, Christopher 1982. *The Economics of Industrial Innovation*, 2nd edn, London, Frances Pinter.

Garland, John 1987. 'The GDR's Strategy for "Intensification" ', *Studies in Comparative Communism*, vol. XX, no. 1, pp. 3–7.

Gati, Charles (ed.) 1974. *The Politics of Modernization in Eastern Europe. Testing the Soviet Model*, New York, Washington and London, Praeger.

Geißler, Rainer 1991. 'Transformationsprozesse in der Sozialstruktur der neuen Bundesländer', *BISS public*, no. 2, pp. 47–78.

Geißler, Rainer 1992. *Die Sozialstruktur Deutschlands. Ein Studienbuch zur Entwicklung im geteilten und vereinten Deutschland*, Opladen, Westdeutscher Verlag.

Gerber, Margy (ed.) 1989. *Studies in GDR Culture and Society 9*, Lanham and London, University Press of America.

Gerber, Margy (ed.) 1991. *Studies in GDR Culture and Society 10*, Lanham and London, University Press of America.

'Germany benign?' 1990. *The Economist*, 27 January, pp. 15–16.

'Germany's knot of Columbus' 1993. *The Economist*, 6 March, pp. 41–2.

Ghaussy, Ghanie A. and Schäfer, Wolf (eds) 1993. *The Economics of German Unification*, London and New York, Routledge.

Gibowski, Wolfgang 1990. 'Demokratischer (Neu-)Beginn in der DDR. Dokumentation und Analyse der Wahl von 18. März 1990', *Zeitschrift für Parlamentsfragen*, vol. 21, no. 1, pp. 5–22.

Giesen, Bernd and Leggewie, Claus (eds) 1991. *Experiment Vereinigung. Ein sozialer Großversuch*, Berlin, Rotbuch Verlag.

Glaeßner, Gert-Joachim 1991. *Der schwierige Weg zur Demokratie. Vom Ende der DDR zur deutschen Einheit*, Opladen, Westdeutscher Verlag.

Glaeßner, Gert-Joachim 1992. *The Unification Process in Germany. From Dictatorship to Democracy*, London, Pinter.

Glaeßner Gert-Joachim and Wallace, Ian (eds) 1992. *The German Revolution of 1989. Causes and Consequences*, Oxford and Providence, Berg.

Goldman, Marshall I. 1992. *What Went Wrong with Perestroika?*, New York and London, W.W. Norton.

Goodhart, David 1991a. 'Germany's public sector debt will top DM 200bn', *Financial Times*, 2 August, p. 20.

Goodhart, David 1991b. 'So much to do, so little time', *Financial Times*, 9 April, p. 25.

Goodhart, David 1991c. 'Treuhand about-turn on plant closures likely to cost billions', *Financial Times*, 16–17 March, p. 2.

Gornig, Martin 1992. 'Perspektive Ostdeutschland: Zweites Wirtschaftswunder oder industrieller Niedergangsprozeß', *Konjunkturpolitik*, vol. 38, no. 1, pp. 1–14.

Görzig, Bernd and Gornig, Martin 1991. *Produktivität und Wettbewerbsfähigkeit der Wirtschaft der DDR. Deutsches Institut für Wirtschaftsforschung. Beiträge zur Strukturforschung*, Berlin, Duncker and Humblot.

Götz-Coenenberg, Roland 1990. 'Währungsintegration in Deutschland: Alternativen und Konsequenzen', *Berichte des Bundesinstituts für ostwissenschaftliche und internationale Studien*, Cologne, Bundesinstitut für ostwissenschaftliche und internationale Studien.

Gow, David 1992a. 'Europe may have to foot the bill of unforeseen costs of unification', *The Guardian*, 22 July, p. 13.

Gow, David 1992b. 'Kohl's glow in the West', *The Guardian*, 4 September, p. 25.

Gow, David 1992c. 'Why racism ran riot in Rostock', *The Guardian*, 25 August, p. 15.

Gow, David 1993. 'Bonn recovery pact in danger', *The Guardian*, 26 January, p. 9.

Gräf, Gerd 1993. 'Nie wieder wettbewerbsfähig', *Neue Landwirtschaft*, no. 1, pp. 10–12.

Grass, Günter 1991. 'What Am I Talking For?' *new german critique*, no. 52, pp. 66–72.

Greulich, Matthias 1992. 'Außenhandel 1991', *Wirtschaft und Statistik*, no. 2, pp. 96–107.

Grice, Andrew 1992. 'Thatcher warning for Major as she rounds on Maastricht', *The Sunday Times*, 20 September, p. 3.

Gröbner, Gerhard 1992. 'Arbeitsmarktpolitik Ost. Hilfen für den Umbruch', *Bundesarbeitsblatt*, no. 1, pp. 5–6.

Groß, Heinz 1985. 'Die innerdeutschen Wirtschaftsbeziehungen', *FS-Analysen*, vol. 12, no. 5. pp. 27–48.

Grosser, Dieter (ed.) 1992. *German Unification. The Unexpected Challenge*, Oxford and Providence, Berg.

Grundman, Siegfried, Müller-Hartmann, Irene and Schmidt, Ines 1991. 'Ausländer in Deutschland', *BISS public*, no. 3, pp. 5–75.

Gurtz, Johannes 1992. 'In den alten Ländern boomten die Budgets', *Die Wirtschaft*, vol. 41, no. 32, p. 15.

Haase, Herwing H. 1990. 'Finanzpolitik vor der Öffnung', *FS-Analysen*, vol. 17, no. 2, part 1, pp. 25–37.

Habermas, Jürgen 1991. 'Yet Again: German Identity – A Unified Nation of Angry DM-Burghers', *new german critique*, no. 52, pp. 84–101.

Hanke, Thomas 1993. 'Auf rascher Talfahrt', *Die Zeit*, 1 January, p. 17.

Häder, Michael (ed.) 1991. *Denken und Handeln in der Krise. Die DDR nach der 'Wende': Ergebnisse einer empirisch-soziologischen Studie*, Berlin, Akademie Verlag.

Härtel, Hans-Hagen and Krüger, Reinald 1991. 'Aktuelle Entwicklungen von Marktstrukturen in den neuen Bundesländern', *Aus Politik und Zeitgeschichte*, no. 29, pp. 13–25.

Haendke-Hoppe, Maria 1990. 'Außenhandel. Umbewertung der Außenhandelsstatistik', *Deutschland Archiv*, vol. 23, no. 9, pp. 651–2.

Hasse, Rolf 1992. 'German Unification and European Upheavals', *Aussenpolitik*, vol. 43, no. 2, pp. 122–33.

Haupt, Christine, Haupt, Hans-Georg and Hövelmans, Kurt 1988. 'Einige Aspekte der gegenwärtigen Entwicklung des sozialistischen Weltsystems', *Deutsche Zeitschrift für Philosophie*, vol. 36, no. 7, pp. 588–98.

Haupt, Hans-Georg and Hövelmans, Kurt 1988. 'Zu ausgewählten Entwicklungsproblemen des sozialistischen Weltsystems', *Wirtschaftswissenschaft*, vol. 36, no. 7, pp. 961–77.

Heimpold, Gerhard, 1991. 'Wirtschaftsförderung in den neuen Bundesländern', *IAW-Kurzinformationen*, no. 9, pp. 3–4.

Heinemann, Karl-Heinz and Schubarth, Wilfried (eds) 1992. *Der antifaschistische Staat entläßt seine Kinder: Jugend und Rechtsextremismus in Ostdeutschland*, Cologne, PapyRossa.

Heisenberg, Wolfgang (ed.) 1991. *German Unification in European Perspective*, London, Washington and New York, Brassey's.

Helwig, Gisela 1992a. 'Soziale Sicherheit', *Deutschland Archiv*, vol. 25, no. 3, pp. 228–30.

Helwig, Gisela 1992b. 'Dramatische Lage am Wohnungsmarkt', *Deutschland Archiv*, vol. 25, no. 8, pp. 788–90.

Hennicke, Petra 1992. 'Tendenz steigend: Flucht in Rechts-/Links-Extreme', *Junge Welt*, 23 June pp. 2–3.

Herles, Helmut and Rose, Ewald (eds) 1990. *Parlaments-Szenen einer deutschen Revolution. Bundestag und Volkskammer im November 1989*, Bonn, Bouvier Verlag.

Herr, Hansjörg 1992. 'The new Federal states after the shock of unifica-
tion', *Employment Observatory East Germany*, no. 1, pp. 3–4.
Hertle, Hans-Hermann 1992a. 'Der Weg in den Bankrott der DDR-
Wirtschaft. Das Scheitern der "Einheit von Wirtschafts- und
Sozialpolitik" am Beispiel der Schürer/Mittag Kontroverse im Politbüro
1988', *Deutschland Archiv*, vol. 25, no. 2, pp. 127–31.
Hertle, Hans-Hermann 1992b. 'Staatsbankrott. Der ökonomische Untergang
des SED-Staates', *Deutschland Archiv*, vol. 25, no. 10, pp. 1019–30.
Hesse, Jörg 1990. 'Die Allianz für Deutschland', *Deutschland Archiv*, vol.
23, no. 4, pp. 502–6.
Heym, Stefan 1991. 'Ash Wednesday in the GDR', *new german critique*, no.
52, pp. 31–5.
Hilmer, Richard and Köhler, Anne 1989. 'Die DDR läuft die Zukunft
davon. Die Übersiedler-/Flüchtlingswelle im Sommer 1989', *Deutschland
Archiv*, vol, 22, no. 12, pp. 1383–93.
Hirzowicz, Maria 1981. *Industrial Society. An Introduction*, Oxford,
Blackwell.
Holm, Knut 1991. *Treuhand oder Ramschhand? Zitate-Fakten-Gedanken*,
Berlin, SPOTLESS-Verlag.
Holst, Christian 1991. *Ein Jahr Umfragen in den Neuen Bundesländern –
Themen und Tendenzen*, AG Sozialberichterstattung, Wissenschafts-
zentrum Berlin für Sozialforschung (WZB), P91–102.
Holst, Elke 1991. 'Frauenpolitische Aspekte der Arbeitsmarktentwicklung
in Ost- und Westdeutschland', *DIW Wochenbericht*, vol. 58, no. 30, pp.
421–6.
Holst, Elke and Schupp, Jürgen 1992. 'Umbruch am ostdeutschen
Arbeitsmarkt benachteiligt auch die weiterhin erwerbstätigen Frauen –
dennoch anhalted hohe Berufsorientierung', *DIW Wochenbericht*, vol.
59, no. 18, pp. 235–41.
Homann, Fritz 1991. 'Treuhandanstalt: Zwischenbilanz, Perspektiven',
Deutschland Archiv, vol. 24, no. 12, pp. 1277–87.
Horn, Gustav and Zwiener, Rudolf 1991. 'Vereinigung wirkt positiv auf
Weltwirtschaft. Ergebnisse einer ökonometrischen Simulationsstudie',
DIW Wochenbericht, vol. 58, no. 32, pp. 447–56.
Horsley, William 1992. 'United Germany's Seven Cardinal Sins',
Millenium: Journal of International Affairs, vol. 21, no. 2, pp. 225–41.
Hughes, David and Grice, Andrew 1992. 'Interest rate action on the way',
The Sunday Times, 20 September, pp. 1–2.
Hume, Mick 1992. 'Kraut-bashing: the British disease', *Living Marxism*, no.
49, November, pp. 4–5.
' "Ich sterbe in diesem Kasten" ' 1992. *Der Spiegel*, 31 August, pp. 38–53.
'Im blauen Dunst' 1992. *Der Spiegel*, 27 April, pp. 76, 78.
Institut für Angewandte Wirtschaftsforschung (ed.) 1991a. *Ostdeutschland:
Der mühsame Aufstieg. Gutachten zur Lage und zu Aussichten der Wirtschaft
in den neuen Bundesländern*, Berlin, Institut für Angewandte
Wirtschaftsforschung.
Institut für Angewandte Wirtschaftsforschung (ed.) 1991b. *Strategie und
Verlauf der Privatisierung in den neuen Bundesländern*, Berlin, Institut für
Angewandte Wirtschaftsforschung.

Institut für Angewandte Wirtschaftsforschung (ed.) 1992. *Landesreport Brandenburg*, Berlin and Munich, Die Wirtschaft.

Institut für Umweltschutz (ed.) 1990. *Umweltschutzbericht der DDR. Informationen zur Analyse der Umweltbedingungen in der DDR und zu weiteren Maßnahmen*, Berlin, Verlag 'visuell'.

'IWH-Gutachten vom Dezember 1992. "Ostdeutschland 1992 und 1993. Zwischen Skepsis und Hoffnung" – Eine Kurzfassung' 1993. *IWH-Kurzinformation*, no. 11, 19 January, pp. 1–8.

Jahresgutachten 1990/91 des Sachverständigenrates zur Begutachtung der gesamtwirtschaftlichen Entwicklung 1990. Bundestagsdrucksache 12/1618, Bonn, Verlag Dr. Hans Heger.

Jahresgutachten 1991/92 des Sachverständigenrates zur Begutachtung der gesamtwirtschaftlichen Entwicklung 1991. Bundestagsdrucksache 11/8472, Bonn, Verlag Dr. Hans Heger.

James, Harold and Stone, Marla 1992. *When the wall came down: reactions to German unification*, London, Routledge.

Janson, Carl-Heinz 1991. *Totengräber der DDR: Wie Günter Mittag den SED-Staat ruinierte*, Düsseldorf, Vienna and New York, ECON Verlag.

Jeffries, Ian 1990. *A Guide to the Socialist Economies*, New York and London, Routledge.

Jesse, Eckhard and Mitter, Armin (eds) 1992. *Die Gestaltung der deutschen Einheit. Geschichte – Politik – Gesellschaft*, Bonn, Bundesanstalt für politische Bildung.

Joffe, Josef 1992. 'Getting that sinking feeling', *The European*, 18–21 June, p. 9.

Johnson, Chalmers (ed.) 1970. *Change in Communist Systems*, Stanford, Stanford University Press.

Juhnke, Andreas 1992. 'The hydra-headed monster of Germany', *New Statesman and Society*, 4 December, pp. 12–13.

Jung, Matthias and Roth, Dieter 1992. 'Politische Einstellungen in Ost-und Westdeutschland seit der Bundestagswahl', *Aus Politik und Zeitgeschichte*, no. 19, pp. 3–16.

Kaiser, Jens 1991. 'Zwischen angestrebter Eigenständigkeit und traditioneller Unterordnung. Zur Ambivalenz des Verhältnisses von sowjetischer und DDR-Außenpolitik in den achtziger Jahren', *Deutschland Archiv*, vol. 24, no. 5, pp. 478–95.

Kalmbach, Peter 1991. 'Die Produktivität ist kein geeigneter Maßstab für die Lohnentwicklung', *Zeitschrift für Wirtschaftspolitik*, vol. 71, no. 1, pp. 11–14.

Kasek, Leonhard 1990. 'Die Entwicklung arbeitsbezogener Werte zwischen 1986 und 1990 auf dem Gebiet der ehemaligen DDR', *Informationen zur soziologischen Forschung*, vol. 26, no. 6, pp. 50–9.

Keegan, William 1992. 'Get our economy moving', *The Observer*, 20 September, p. 20.

Keren, Michael 1973. 'The New Economic System in the GDR: an Obituary', *Soviet Studies*, vol. XXIV, no. 4, pp. 554–87.

Kettle, Martin 1993. 'Refuge from the asylum-seekers', *The Guardian*, 9 March, p. 18.

Bibliography 199

Kieselbach, Thomas and Voigt, Peter (eds) 1992. *Systemumbruch, Arbeitslosigkeit und individuelle Bewältigung in der ex-DDR*, Weinheim, Deutscher Studien Verlag.

Klinger, Fred 1987. 'Die Krise des Fortschritts in der DDR: Innovationsprobleme und Mikroelektronik', *Aus Politik und Zeitgeschichte*, no. 3, pp. 3–19.

Klinger, Fred 1990. 'Subventionen und Leistungsprinzip – Anmerkungen zur aktuellen Reformdiskussion in der DDR', *FS-Analysen*, vol. 17, no. 3, pp. 51–62.

Klinger, Fred 1993. 'Soziale Konflikte und offene Gewalt. Die Herausforderungen des Transformationsprozesses in den neuen Bundesländern', *Deutschland Archiv*, vol. 26, no. 2, pp. 147–61.

Knabe, Hubertus (ed.) 1989. *Aufbruch in eine andere DDR*, Reinbek bei Hamburg, Rowohlt Taschenbuch Verlag.

Knop, Hans 1990. 'Staatliche Hilfen und Kapitalimporte im Angleichungsprozeß der DDR', *Zeitschrift für Wirtschaftspolitik*, vol. 39, no. 3, pp. 339–48.

Kolbe, Manfred 1992. 'Konzept mit Schieflage', *Die Zeit*, 15 May, p. 30.

Komar, Walter 1992. 'Umweltprobleme schrittweise lösbar', *IWH-Informationen*, no. 0, pp. 3–4.

Krakat, Klaus 1986. 'Elektronisierungs- und Automatisierungsplanungen der DDR', *FS-Analysen*, vol. 13, no. 2, pp. 39–54.

Krakat, Klaus 1990a. 'Mikroelektronik in der DDR unter Wirtschaftlichkeitsaspekten', *FS-Analysen*, vol. 17, no. 2, pp. 51–93.

Krakat, Klaus 1990b. 'Schlußbilanz der elektronischen Datenverarbeitung in der früheren DDR', *FS-Analysen*, vol. 17, no. 5, pp. 1–59.

Krambach, Kurt 1991. 'Genossenschaftsbauern im Umbruch', *Utopie kreativ*, no. 5, pp. 5–34.

Kretzschmar, Albrecht 1985. 'Sozialistische Persönlichkeit und intensiv erweiterte Reproduktion', *Deutsche Zeitschrift für Philosophie*, vol. 33, no. 1, pp. 21–30.

Kretzschmar, Albrecht 1991a. 'Zur sozialen Lage der DDR-Bevölkerung (Teil I)', *BISS public*, no. 4, pp. 38–97.

Kretzschmar, Albrecht 1991b. 'Zur sozialen Lage der DDR-Bevölkerung (Teil II)', *BISS public*, no. 5, pp. 77–106.

Kretzschmar, Albrecht 1992. 'Massenarbeitslosigkeit – gewichtiger Posten in der Zwischenbilanz sozialen Wandels', *BISS public*, no. 7, pp. 5–12.

Krüger, Peter Thomas 1990. 'Programmatik der stärksten Bürgerbewegung. Demokratie braucht Initiative und Phantasie. An der Wiege der Wende stand das Neue Forum', *Das Parlament*, no. 8, 16 February, p. 8.

Krumrey, Henning 1992. *Aufschwung Ost. Märchen oder Modell*, Frankfurt on Main, Fischer Taschenbuch Verlag.

Küchenmeister, Daniel 1993. 'Wann begann das Zerwürfnis zwischen Honecker und Gorbatschow?' *Deutschland Archiv*, vol. 26, no. 1, pp. 30–40.

Kuehbacher, Klaus 1992. 'German Unification: A Long-Term Task', *Aussenpolitik*, vol. 43, no. 2, pp. 134–43.

Kühn, Wolfgang 1993. 'Investitionen machen es nicht allein', *Die Wirtschaft*, vol. 42, no. 3, p. 3.

Kurjo, Andreas 1992. 'Der ostdeutsche Weg der Landwirtschaft – Herausforderung und Chance für die europäische Agrarpolitik', *FS-Analysen*, vol. 19, no. 1, part 1, pp. 57–67.

Kusch, Günter, Montag, Rolf, Specht, Günter and Wetzker, Konrad 1991. *Schlußbilanz-DDR. Fazit einer verfehlten Wirtschafts- und Sozialpolitik*, Berlin, Duncker and Humblot.

Lambrecht, Horst 1990. 'DDR-Landwirtschaft vor erneutem Umstrukturierungsprozess', *DIW Wochenbericht*, vol. 57, no. 33, pp. 468–72.

Lapp, Peter Joachim 1990. 'Ehemalige DDR-Blockparteien auf der Suche nach Profil und Glaubwürdigkeit', *Deutschland Archiv*, vol. 23, no. 1, pp. 62–8.

Lapp, Peter Joachim 1992. 'Die neuen Bundesländer. IV. Sachsen', *Deutschland Archiv*, vol. 25, no. 3, pp. 242–7.

Leenen, Wolf Rainer 1992. 'Ausländerfeindlichkeit in Deutschland. Politischer Rechtsruck oder Politikversagen?', *Deutschland Archiv*, vol. 25, no. 10, pp. 1039–54.

Leptin, Gert 1980. *Deutsche Wirtschaft. Ein Ost-West-Vergleich*, Opladen, Leske and Budrich.

Leptin, Gert and Melzer, Manfred 1978. *Economic Reform in East German Industry*, tr. Roger A. Clarke, Oxford, Oxford University Press.

Lipschitz, Leslie and McDonald, Donogh (eds) 1990. *German Unification: Economic Issues*, Washington, International Monetary Fund.

Livingston, Robert Gerald 1992. 'United Germany: Bigger and Better', *Foreign Policy*, no. 87, pp. 157–74.

Loke, Matthias 1992. 'In Lausitzer Textilbetrieben sind die Fäden gerissen', *Berliner Zeitung*, 5 August, p. 29.

Luft, Christa 1991. *Zwischen Wende und Ende. Eindrücke, Erlebnisse, Erfahrungen eines Mitglieds der Modrow-Regierung*, Berlin, Aufbau Taschenbuch Verlag.

Luft, Christa 1992. *Treuhandreport. Werden, Wachsen und Vergehen einer deutschen Behörde*, Berlin and Weimar, Aufbau-Verlag.

Luft, Christa and Faude, Eugen 1989. 'Für außenpolitische Öffnung und internationale Arbeitsteilung', *Neues Deutschland*, 17 November, p. 5.

Luft, Hans 1991. 'Die Treuhandanstalt. Deutsche Erfahrungen und Probleme bei der Transformation von Wirtschaftsordnungen', *Deutschland Archiv*, vol. 24, no. 12, pp. 1270–6.

Maier, Harry 1987. *Innovation oder Stagnation. Bedingungen der Wirtschaftsreform in sozialistischen Ländern*, Cologne, Deutscher-Instituts-Verlag.

Maier, Harry 1991. 'Integrieren statt zerstören. Für eine gemischtwirtschaftliche Strategie in den neuen Bundesländern', *Aus Politik und Zeitgeschichte*, no. 29, pp. 3–12.

Malcolm-Smith, Sally 1993. 'Sitcom holds up an awkward mirror to society', *The European*, 11–14 February, pp. 8–9.

Maron, Monika 1991. 'Writers and the People', *new german critique*, no. 52, pp. 36–41.

Marsh, David 1990a. 'Claims against half E German Property', *Financial*

Times, 22 November, p. 21.
Marsh, David 1990b. 'Two Germanys tackle one environment', *Financial Times*, 21 February, p. 3.
Marsh, David and Colitt, Lesley 1992. 'The lasting legacy of the Treuhand', *Financial Times*, 12 November, p. 23.
Marsh, David and Goodhart, David 1991. 'Murder of an idea', *Financial Times*, 3 April, p. 15.
Matthes, Heinrich 1991. 'Die Bewältigung der Folgen des Sozialismus. Herausforderungen für die deutsche Wirtschaftspolitik', *Wirtschaftsdienst*, vol. 71, no. 12, pp. 609–31.
McAdams, A. James 1993. *Germany Divided: From the Wall to Reunification*, Princeton, New Jersey, Princeton University Press.
MccGwire, Michael 1991. *Perestroika and Soviet National Security*, Washington, The Brookings Institution.
Meer, Horst van der and Kruss, Lothar (eds) 1991. *Vom Industriestaat zum Entwicklungsland?*, Frankfurt on Main, Streitschrift.
Mehr, Max Thomas 1993. 'Die Krise als Chance', *Wochenpost*, vol. 40, no. 4, p. 2.
Meyer, Dagmar 1991. 'Einheitsverliererinnen. Zur Situation ostdeutscher Frauen', *Blätter für deutsche und internationale Politik*, no. 11, pp. 1326–33.
Michel, Jeffrey H. 1987. 'Economic Exchanges Specific to the Two German States', *Studies in Comparative Communism*, vol. XX, no. 1, pp. 73–83.
Miegel, Manfred 1992. 'Die wirtschaftlichen und gesellschaftlichen Perspektiven Deutschlands in den neunziger Jahren', *COMPARATIV. Leipziger Beiträge zur Universalgeschichte und vergleichenden Gesellschaftsordnung*, no. 3, pp. 73–94.
Mit qualitativ neuen Schritten zu höchsten Leistungen. Seminar des Zentralkomitees der SED mit den Generaldirektoren der Kombinate und den Parteiorganisationen des ZK 1986. Berlin, Dietz Verlag.
Mittag, Günter 1991. *Um jeden Preis. Im Spannungsfeld zweier Systeme*, Berlin and Weimar, Aufbau-Verlag.
Mittelbach, Hans 1992. *Strukturwandel in der Landwirtschaft*, Forum Deutsche Einheit, no. 11, Bonn-Bad Godesberg, Friedrich-Ebert-Stiftung.
Mitter, Arnim and Wolle, Stefan (eds) 1990. *Ich liebe euch doch alle! Befehle und Lageberichte des MfS Januar–November 1989*, Berlin, BasisDruck Verlagsgesellschaft.
' "Mrs. Thatchers tadelnder Ton" ' 1990. *Der Spiegel*, 19 February, pp. 160–1.
Müller, Harry and Schubarth, Wilfried 1992. 'Rechtsextremismus und aktuelle Befindlichkeiten von Jugendlichen in den neuen Bundesländern', *Aus Politik und Zeitgeschichte*, no. 38, pp. 16–28.
Müller, Jörg and Vogel, Oskar 1991. 'Erwartungen und Wertorientierungen bei ostdeutschen Bauern', *Utopie kreativ*, no. 5, pp. 40–5.
Müller-Krumholz, Karin 1992a. 'Die wirtschaftliche Entwicklung im Deutschland im ersten Quartal 1992', *DIW Wochenbericht*, vol. 59, no. 20–21, pp. 260–72.
Müller-Krumholz, Karin 1992b. 'Ausgeprägte gesamtwirtschaftliche Verlangsamung', *DIW Wochenbericht*, vol. 59, no. 47, pp. 623–33.

Müller-Krumholz, Karin 1993. 'Rückgang der gesamtwirtschaftlichen Leistung zum Jahresausklang noch gering. Die wirtschaftliche Entwicklung in der Bundesrepublik Deutschland im vierten Quartal 1992', *DIW Wochenbericht*, vol. 60, no. 7, pp. 61–73.

Murmann, Klaus 1992. 'Sozialpakt für den Aufschwung in den neuen Bundesländern?', *Wirtschaftsdienst*, vol. 72, no. 1, pp. 16–18.

Naumann, Gerhard and Trümpler, Eckhard 1990. *Von Ulbricht zu Honecker. 1970 – ein Krisenjahr der DDR*, Berlin, Dietz Verlag.

NEUES FORUM. *Wirschaftsreform der DDR. Internationale Wirtschaftskonferenz des NEUEN FORUMS. Berlin-Buch, 25./26. November 1989. Protokolle und Beiträge* 1990. Berlin, Nikolaische Verlagsbuchhandlung.

Nick, Harry and Radtke, Gerd 1989. 'Gesellschaftliche Entwicklung und sozialistisches Eigentum', *Einheit*, vol. 44, no. 3, pp. 225–32.

Nove, Alex, Höhmann, Hans-Hermann and Seidenstecher, Gertraud (eds) 1982. *The East European Economies in the 1970s*, London, Butterworth.

OECD 1990. *OECD Economic Surveys. Germany 1989/1990*, Paris, OECD.

OECD 1991a. *OECD Economic Outlook*, no. 49, Paris, OECD.

OECD 1991b. *OECD Economic Surveys. Germany 1990/91*, Paris, OECD.

OECD 1992a. *OECD Economic Outlook*, no. 49, Paris, OECD.

OECD 1992b. *OECD Economic Surveys. Germany 1991/92*, Paris, OECD.

Offe, Claus 1992. 'German Reunification as a "Natural Experiment" ', *German Politics*, vol. 1, no. 1, pp. 1–12.

Okun, Bernd 1992. 'Zur mentalitätsgeschichtlichen Dimension des ostdeutschen Transformationsprozesses', *COMPARATIV. Leipziger Beiträge zur Universalgeschichte und vergleichenden Gesellschaftsforschung*, no. 3, pp. 27–41.

Padgett, Stephen 1990. 'British Perspectives on the German Question', *Politics and Society in Germany, Austria and Switzerland*, vol. 3, no. 1, pp. 22–37.

Parkes, Christopher 1993. 'W German growth rate falls to 0.8%', *Financial Times*, 14 January, p. 2.

Parkes, Christopher and Colitt, Leslie 1992. 'Manufacturing falls to 1988 levels', *Financial Times*, 14 February, p. 2.

Paterson, Tony 1992. 'Kohl admits that unity would swamp economy', *The European*, 26–9 March, p. 1.

Paucke, Horst 1990. 'Umweltschutz in der DDR', *wissenschaft und fortschritt*, vol. 40, no. 6, pp. 152–6.

Peel, Quentin 1992a. 'Kohl attacked over economic failure in east', *Financial Times*, 14 February, p. 2.

Peel, Quentin 1992b. 'Poll shows backing for referendum', *Financial Times*, 19–20 September, p. 2.

Peel, Quentin 1992c. 'Symbols of hope and hardship', *Financial Times*, 11 August, p. 12.

Peel, Quentin 1993a. 'Kohl close to deal on "solidarity pact" ', *Financial Times*, 15 January, p. 2.

Peel, Quentin 1993b. 'A long way to go, but little time', *Financial Times*, 21 January, p. 19.

Peel, Quentin 1993c. 'The deal they were condemned to do', *Financial Times*, 15 March, p. 13.

Peel, Quentin and Marsh, David 1993. 'Warning on E German pay pact', *Financial Times*, 18 January 1993, p. 2.

Petschow, Ulrich, Meyerhoff, Jürgen and Thomasberger, Claus 1990. *Umweltreport DDR. Bilanz der Zerstörung, Kosten der Sanierung, Strategien für den ökologischen Umbau*, Frankfurt on Main, S. Fischer.

Piepgas, Ilka 1992. 'Das Geld vom Amt reicht gerade für die Windeln', *Berliner Zeitung*, 28 July, p. 3.

Pilz, Frank and Ortwein, Heike 1992. *Das vereinte Deutschland. Wirtschaftliche, soziale und finanzielle Folgeprobleme und die Konsequenzen für die Politik*, Stuttgart and Jena, Gustav Fischer Verlag.

Plötz, Peter 1985. 'Wirtschaftsbeziehungen der DDR zu den westlichen Ländern', *FS-Analysen*, vol. 12, no. 5, pp. 49–95.

Poldrack, Horst and Okun, Bernd 1992. 'Thesen zum ostdeutschen Transformationsprozeß', *COMPARATIV. Leipziger Beiträge zur Universalgeschichte und vergleichenden Gesellschaftsforschung*, no. 3, pp. 6–17.

Pollack, Detlef 1992a. 'THE TIMES, THEY ARE A-CHANGING', *BISS public*, no. 8, pp. 49–81.

Pollack, Detlef 1992b. 'Systemtransformation als Rationalisierung am Beispiel Ostdeutschlands', *COMPARATIV. Leipziger Beiträge zur Universalgeschichte und vergleichenden Gesellschaftsforschung*, no. 3, pp. 18–26.

Popplewell, Richard 1992. 'The Stasi and the East German Revolution', *Contemporary European History*, vol. 1, no. 1, pp. 37–63.

Presse- und Informationsamt der Bundesregierung (ed.) 1991. *Die Vereinigung Deutschlands im Jahr 1990. Verträge und Erklärungen*, Bonn, Presse- und Informationsamt der Bundesregierung.

Priewe, Jan and Hickel, Rudolf 1991. *Der Preis der Einheit. Bilanz und Perspektiven der deutschen Vereinigung*, Frankfurt on Main, Fischer Taschenbuch Verlag.

Prins, Gwyn (ed.) 1990. *Spring in Winter. The 1989 revolutions*, Manchester and New York, Manchester University Press.

'Privatising East Germany' 1991. *The Economist*, 14 September, pp. 21–2, 24

Przybylski, Peter 1991. *Tatort Politbüro. Die Akte Honecker*, Berlin, Rowohlt.

Przybylski, Peter 1992. *Tatort Politbüro. Volume 2: Honecker, Mittag und Schalck-Golodkowski*, Berlin, Rowohlt.

Pukas, Anna 1993. 'Advance of the ex-Nazi with no regrets', *Daily Mail*, 9 March, p. 10.

Radtke, Gerd-Rainer 1989. 'Wissenschaftlich-technischer und sozialer Fortschrift im Sozialismus', *Einheit*, vol. 44, no. 1, pp. 33–8.

Rae, Nicol C. 1991. 'Die amerikanische und britische Reaktion auf die Wiedervereinigung Deutschlands', *Zeitschrift für Politik*, vol. 38, no. 3, pp. 24–33.

Rein, Gerhard (ed.) 1990. *Die Opposition in der DDR. Entwürfe für einen anderen Sozialismus*, Berlin, Wichern Verlag.

Reinhold, Otto 1989. 'Sozialpolitik, Preise und Subventionen', *Neues Deutschland*, 14 February, p. 3.

Reißig, Rolf and Glaeßner, Gert-Joachim (eds) 1991. *Das Ende eines Experiments. Umbruch in der DDR und deutsche Einheit*, Berlin, Dietz Verlag.

Report of the Central Committee of the Socialist Unity Party of Germany to the 11th Congress of the SED 1986. Rapporteur Erich Honecker, Dresden, Verlag Zeit im Bild.

Report of the Deutsche Bundesbank for the Year 1991 1992. Frankfurt on Main, Deutsche Bundesbank.

Reynolds, David 1991. *Britannia Overruled. British Policy and World Power in the 20th Century*, London and New York, Longman.

Richard von Weizsäcker im Gespräch mit Gunter Hoffmann and Werner A. Perger 1992. Frankfurt on Main, Eichborn Verlag.

Roesler, Jörg 1990. *Zwischen Plan und Markt. Die Wirtschaftsreform 1963– 1970 in der DDR*, Berlin, Haufe Verlag.

Roesler, Jörg 1991. 'The Rise and Fall of the Planned Economy in the German Democratic Republic, 1945–89', *German History*, vol. 9, no. 1, pp. 46–61.

Rudolph, Hermann 1992. 'Die Einheit in der Krise', *Der Tagesspiegel*, 26 July, p. 1.

Sakowsky, Dagmar 1992. 'Probleme des Transformationsprozesses in den neuen Bündesländern. Ein Überblick', *Deutschland Archiv*, vol. 25, no. 12, pp. 1254–65.

'Saying the unsayable about the Germans' 1990. *The Spectator*, 14 July, pp. 8–10.

Schabowski, Günter 1990. *Das Politbüro. Ende eines Mythos. Eine Befragung*, Reinbek bei Hamburg, Rowohlt Taschenbuch Verlag.

'Scheinblüte durch neue Milliarden' 1992. *Der Spiegel*, 15 June, pp. 100–1, 103.

Scheremet, Wolfgang 1992. 'Eine Modellrechnung zur wirtschaftlichen Angleichung zwischen Ost- und Westdeutschland', *DIW Wochenbericht*, vol. 59, no. 7, pp. 80–1.

Scheremet, Wolfgang and Schupp, Jürgen 1992. 'Pendler Migration – Zur Arbeitskräftemobilität in Ostdeutschland', *DIW Wochenbericht*, vol. 59, no. 3, pp. 21–6.

Schneider, Peter 1992. *The German Comedy. Scenes of Life after the Wall*, tr. Philip Boehm and Leigh Harvey, London and New York, I. B. Tauris.

Schneider, Rolf 1990. 'Die politische Moral ist dahin', *Der Spiegel*, 5 February, pp. 29, 31.

Schui, Herbert 1991. *Die ökonomische Vereinigung Deutschlands. Bilanz und Perspektiven*, Heilbronn, Diestel Verlag.

Schulte, Ewald B. 1992. 'Defizit wächst ins Uferlose', *Berliner Zeitung*, 1–2 August, p. 2.

Schulte-Doinghaus, Uli 1990. 'Technik-Antiquariat', *Wirtschaftswoche*, vol. 44, no. 17, pp. 216–19.

Schulz, Werner and Volmer, Ludwig (eds) 1992. *Entwickeln statt abwickeln. Wirtschaftspolitische und ökologische Umbau-Konzepte für die fünf neuen Länder*, Berlin, Ch. Links Verlag.

Schupp, Jürgen 1992. 'Pendler und Migranten – vergleichende Analysen der Daten des Sozio-ökonomischen Panels', *BISS public*, no. 7, pp. 25–36.

Schwarz, Rainer 1991. *Über Innovationspotentiale und Innovationshemmnisse in der DDR-Wirtschaft*, Wissenschaftszentrum Berlin für Sozialforschung, Research Unit Market Research and Corporate Development, Discussion Paper FS IV 91–26.

Schwarze, Johannes and Wagner, Gert 1992. 'Zur Entwicklung der Effektivlohnstruktur in den neuen Bundesländern', *DIW Wochenbericht*, vol. 59, no. 23, pp. 291–5.

Schwenke, Wolfgang 1992. 'Die Scherben kehrt das Arbeitsamt zusammen', *Die Wirtschaft*, vol. 41, no. 4, p. 28.

Seiffert, Wolfgang and Treutwein, Norbert 1992. *Die Schalck-Papiere. DDR-Mafia zwischen Ost und West*, Munich, Goldmann Verlag.

Sherwell, Philip 1992. 'No place to seek asylum', *The Daily Telegraph*, 25 August, p. 15.

'Short-time work: instrument of the "first hour" ' 1992. *Employment Observatory East Germany*, no. 1, p. 6.

Siebert, Horst 1991. 'German unification', *Economic Policy*, vol. 6, no. 13, pp. 287–340.

Siebert, Horst 1992. *Das Wagnis der Einheit. Eine wirtschaftspolitische Therapie*, Stuttgart, Deutsche Verlags-Anstalt.

Siebert, Rosemarie 1991. 'Frauen und ältere Menschen in der ostdeutschen Landwirtschaft', *Utopie kreativ*, no. 5, pp. 35–8.

Singer, Otto 1992. 'The Politics and Economics of German Unification: From Currency Union to Economic Dichotomy', *German Politics*, vol. 1, no. 1, pp. 78–94.

Sinn, Gerlinde and Sinn, Hans-Werner 1992. *Kaltstart. Volkswirtschaftliche Aspekte der deutschen Vereinigung*, 2nd edn, Tübingen, J.C.B. Mohr.

Sinn, Hans-Werner 1992. 'Sozialpakt für den Aufschwung: Noch ist es Zeit', *Wirtschaftsdienst*, vol. 72, no. 1, pp. 11–16.

Smith, Gordon, Paterson William E., and Merkl, Peter H. (eds) 1989. *Developments in West German Politics*, Basingstoke and London, Macmillan.

Smith, Gordon, Paterson, William E., Merkl, Peter H. and Padgett, Stephen (eds) 1992. *Developments in German Politics*, Basingstoke and London, Macmillan.

Smyser, W.R. 1990. 'United Germany: A New Economic Miracle?' *The Washington Quarterly*, vol. 13, no. 4, pp. 159–76.

Smyser, W.R. 1992. *The Economy of United Germany. Colossus at the Crossroads*, London, Hurst.

Sodaro, Michael 1991. *Moscow, Germany and the West from Khrushchev to Gorbachev*, London, I.B. Tauris.

'Sofortmaßnahmen ebenso nötig wie klare in die Zukunft wiesende Lösungen' 1990. *Arbeit und Arbeitsrecht*, vol. 46, no. 1, p. 3.

Stahnke, Arthur A. 1987. 'Kombinate as the Key Structural Element in the GDR Intensification Process', *Studies in Comparative Communism*, vol. XX, no. 1, pp. 27–37.

Stark, David 1992. 'Path Dependence and Privatization Strategies in East Central Europe', *East European Politics and Societies*, vol. 6, no. 1, pp. 17–54.

Statistisches Amt der DDR (ed.) 1990. *Statistisches Jahrbuch der Deutschen Demokratischen Republik '90*, Berlin, Rudolf Haufe Verlag.

Statistisches Bundesamt (ed.) 1992. *Datenreport 1992. Zahlen und Fakten über die Bundesrepublik Deutschland*, Bonn, Bundesanstalt für politische Bildung.

Steinitz, Klaus 1991. *Vom Umbruch zum Aufbruch? Wirtschaftspolitik: Bilanz, Fragen, Vorschläge*, Berlin, PDS.

Steinkühler, Franz 1991. 'Ein Konzept zur solidarischen Finanzierung der deutschen Einheit', *Wirtschaftsdienst*, vol. 72, no. 1, pp. 10–11.

Stent, Angela (ed.) 1985. *Economic Relations with the Soviet Union. American and West German Perspectives*, Boulder and London, Westview Press.

Stinglwagner, Wolfgang 1990. 'Schwere Zeiten für die DDR-Wirtschaft', *Deutschland Archiv*, vol. 23, no. 2, pp. 237–41.

Strohm, Wolfgang 1992. 'Sozialprodukt in Deutschland', *Wirtschaft und Statistik*, no. 1, pp. 11–23.

Strohm, Wolfgang 1993. 'Bruttoinlandsprodukt 1992', *Wirtschaft und Statistik*, no. 1, pp. 11–24.

Suhr, Heinz 1990. *Was kostet uns die ehemalige DDR?*, Frankfurt on Main, Eichborn.

Suhr, Heinz 1991. *Der Treuhandskandal. Wie Ostdeutschland geschlachtet wurde*, Frankfurt on Main, Eichborn.

Suskind, Martin 1990. 'Der schwierigste Balanceakt steht noch bevor', *Süddeutsche Zeitung*, 26 February, p. 3.

Süß, Walter 1990. 'Demokratischer Aufbruch. Auf der Suche nach Profil. Die Wandlungen einer jungen Partei', *Das Parlament*, no. 9–10, 23 February–2 March, p. 17.

taz 1990. *DDR Journal Nr. 2. Die Wende der Wende. Januar bis März 1990. Von der Öffnung des Brandenburger Tores zur Öffnung der Wahlurnen*, Frankfurt on Main, Tageszeitungsverlagsgesellschaft.

Teltschik, Horst 1991. *329 Tage. Innenansichten der Einigung*, Berlin, Siedler Verlag.

Thalheim, Karl C. 1990. 'Der ordnungspolitische Weg der DDR – Entwicklungen und Perspektiven', *Zeitschrift für Wirtschaftspolitik*, vol. 39, no. 1, pp. 77–91.

'The engine of Europe' 1993. *The Economist*, 6 March, pp. 15–16.

'The Treuhand in Berlin: at the centre of the transformation process' 1992. *Employment Observatory East Germany*, no. 1, p. 5.

'The weight on Kohl's mind' 1991. *The Economist*, 6 April, pp. 45–6.

Thomas, Rüdiger 1977. *Modell DDR. Die kalkulierte Emanzipation*, 6th edn. Munich and Vienna, Carl Hanser Verlag.

Tomforde, Anna 1992. 'Bonn bends rules to speed asylum curbs into law', *The Guardian*, 3 November, p. 9.

Torpey, John 1992. 'Exodus and Opposition in the East German Transformation', *German Politics and Society*, no. 26, Summer, pp. 21–42.

Trautmann, Günter (ed.) 1991. *Die häßlichen Deutschen. Deutschland im Spiegel der westlichen und östlichen Nachbarn*, Darmstadt, Wissenschaftliche Buchgesellschaft.

Treuhandanstalt (ed.) n.d. *Promoting the New Germany*, Berlin, Treuhandanstalt.

Treuhandanstalt (ed.) 1991a. *The Chance of the 90's: Investing in Eastern Germany*, 2nd edn, Berlin, Treuhandanstalt.
Treuhandanstalt (ed.) 1991b. *Auftrag, Zwischenbilanz, Grundsätze*, Berlin, Treuhandanstalt.
Ulrich, Ralf 1990. *Die Übersiedlerbewegung in die Bundesrepublik und das Ende der DDR*, Wissenschaftszentrum Berlin für Sozialforschung, Veröffentlichungsreihe der Forschungsgruppe Internationale Beziehungen, P90–302.
Unger, Frank 1991. 'Discourse of Unity and Some Reflections about their Aftermath', *German History*, vol. 9, no. 2, pp. 173–83
'United Germany. They like it and they fear it' 1990. *The Economist*, 27 January, pp. 49–50.
Vesper, Dieter 1991. 'Die öffentlichen Haushalte in Deutschland 1991/92: Anhaltend hohe Finanzierungsdefizite trotz Steuererhöhungen', *DIW Wochenbericht*, vol. 58, no. 38, pp. 539–48.
'Vorgezogenes Altersübergangsgeld. Eine weitere Entlastungsmaßnahme' 1991. *iwd. Informationsdienst des Instituts der deutschen Wirtschaft*, vol. 17, no. 21, p. 2.
Vortmann, Heinz 1990. 'DDR: Verteilungswirkungen von Verbraucherpreissubventionen und indirekten Steuern', *FS-Analysen*, vol. 17, no. 2, pp. 29–50.
Walter, Norbert 1992. 'Country in a state of flux', *Financial Times*, 3 January, p. 12.
Walter, Norbert 1993. 'A year of reckoning', *Financial Times*, 4 January, p. 26.
Wehner, Burkhard 1991. *Das Fiasko im Osten: Auswege einer gescheiterten Wirtschafts- und Sozialpolitik*, Marburg, Metropolis-Verlag.
Weidenfeld, Ursula and Kessler, Martin 1993. 'Wir kaufen nur Zeit', *Wirtschaftswoche*, vol. 47, no. 3, pp. 12–13, 16–17.
Wendt, Hartmut 1991. 'Die deutsch-deutschen Wanderungen – Bilanz einer 40jährigen Geschichte von Flucht und Ausreise', *Deutschland Archiv*, vol. 24, no. 4, pp. 386–95.
'Wer sind die Deutschen?' 1990. *Der Spiegel*, 17 July, pp. 109–12.
'West-Ost Transfers 1992. Grenze in Sicht' 1991. *iwd. Informationsdienst des Instituts der deutschen Wirtschaft*, vol. 17, no. 43, pp. 4–5.
Willgerodt, Hans 1990. 'German Economic Integration in a European Perspective', *Aussenpolitik*, vol. 41, no. 4, pp. 328–38.
Winkler, Gunnar (ed.) 1990. *Sozialreport '90. Daten und Fakten zur sozialen Lage in der DDR*, Berlin, Die Wirtschaft.
Wintour, Patrick 1992. 'Major heaps blame on Bundesbank', *The Guardian*, 18 September, p. 5.
Wolf, Herbert 1991. *Hatte die DDR je eine Chance?*, Hamburg, VSA-Verlag.
Wolf, Martin 1991. 'A nation unified, and yet apart', *Financial Times*, 1 July, p. 14.
Yarranton, Lesley 1992. 'How can this happen to Germans?' *Today*, 30 April, p. 4.
Zapf, Wolfgang 1991. 'Die DDR 1989/1990 – Zusammenbruch einer Sozialstruktur?' *Berliner Journal für Soziologie*, no. 2, pp. 147–55.

Periodicals, magazines, newspapers

Amtliche Nachrichten der Bundesanstalt für Arbeit, Nuremberg, Bundesanstalt für Arbeit, monthly.
Berliner Morgenpost, Berlin, Ullstein, daily.
Berliner Zeitung, Berlin, G+J Berliner Zeitung, daily.
Bild, Hamburg, Axel Springer Verlag, daily.
Daily Mail, Associated Newspapers, London, daily.
Daily Mirror, London, Mirror Group Newspapers, daily.
The Daily Telegraph, London, The Daily Telegraph, daily.
Deutsche Bundesbank, *Monthly Report of the Deutsche Bundesbank*, Frankfurt on Main, Deutsche Bundesbank, monthly.
The Economist, The Economist Newspaper, weekly.
The European, London, The European, weekly.
Express and Star, Wolverhampton, Express and Star, daily.
Financial Times, London, The Financial Times, daily.
Foreign Affairs Bulletin, Berlin, Press Department, Ministry of Foreign Affairs of the German Democratic Republic, every 10 days.
Frankfurter Allgemeine Zeitung, Frankfurt on Main, daily.
The Guardian, London and Manchester, Guardian Newspapers, daily.
Handelsblatt, Düsseldorf, Handelsblatt, daily.
The Independent, London, Newspaper Publishing, daily.
Junge Welt, Berlin, Verlagsanstalt in Berlin, daily.
Mitteldeutsche Zeitung, Halle, Mitteldeutsches Druck- and Verlagshaus, daily.
Neues Deutschland, Berlin, Verlag Neues Deutschland, daily.
Neue Zeit, Berlin, Verlag Neue Zeit, daily.
The Observer, London, The Observer, weekly.
Sächsishe Zeitung, Dresden, daily.
Der Spiegel, Hamburg, Spiegel Verlag, weekly.
Statistisches Bundesamt, *Wirtschaft und Statistik*, Stuttgart, Metzler-Poeschel, monthly.
Statistisches Bundesamt, *Mitteilung für die Presse*, Wiesbaden, Statistisches Bundesamt, irregular.
Süddeutsche Zeitung, Munich, Süddeutsche Zeitung, daily.
The Sun, London, News Group Newspapers, daily.
The Sunday Telegraph, London, The Daily Telegraph, weekly.
The Sunday Times, London, Times Newspapers, weekly.
Der Tagesspiegel, Berlin, Verlag Der Tagesspiegel, daily.
die tageszeitung, Berlin, Freunde der alternativen Tageszeitung, daily.
The Times, London, Times Newspapers, daily.
Today, London News (UK), daily.
Tribüne, Berlin, Tribüne Verlag, daily.
Die Zeit, Hamburg, Zeitverlag Gerd Bucerius, weekly.

Documents

Document 1 Honecker on socialism and the scientific-technical revolution, 1986

Permit me to sum up the essence and content of the economic strategy in a number of priorities.

1. The economic strategy of our party, which covers the period up to the year 2000, is designed to combine the advantages of socialism still more effectively with the achievements of the scientific and technological revolution, which has also entered a new stage. The potential of all economies is being increasingly determined by microelectronics, advanced computer technology, and computer-aided design and manufacturing, and closely linked with these is the spread of other key technologies such as flexible automatic manufacturing systems, new machining techniques and materials, biotechnology, nuclear energy, and laser technology. These represent tremendous challenges and at the same time splendid opportunities for swift product innovation, quality enhancement and cost reductions on a scale previously thought impossible. This is the field in which the rate of growth in labour productivity will be decided, and this in turn will determine the extent to which our economy will be able to satisfy people's needs, cope with the multitude of requirements arising from our country's internal development, and hold its own in the international arena. At the same time, it will give rise to new conditions permitting the role of the working people within the production process to be changed, allowing them to be assigned more interesting and challenging tasks and improving working conditions to levels more appropriate to socialist production conditions.

The rate at which the productive forces on an international scale are developing is increasing, and we are therefore unable to choose our own pace. We will have to succeed in this race against time, leading the field in key areas to achieve major economic and social advances.

2. Our economic strategy aims to raise labour productivity at a faster pace. The wide-spread application of key technologies is the main priority in this context. A growing number of combines are raising labour productivity at

an annual rate of 10 per cent and more, thus setting the pace for years to come. Effective use will have to be made of all factors leading to higher labour productivity. The best economic results are achieved where lower living and materialized labour inputs are combined with higher product quality. This is reflected in net output and national income.

Raising productivity at a faster rate means adhering more strictly to the law of the economy of time. Now that the economy has become, and is to remain, the main arena of the confrontation between the two social systems, time gained is equivalent to a gain in strength for socialism. Manufacturing more high-quality goods with less input, reducing lead times for new products, achieving world standards while operating economically, all this represents time gained for socialism. Maximum economy of time is a challenge that all combines and other firms, in fact all spheres of our national economy, will have to face . . .

10. Our economic strategy up to the year 2000 is designed to promote intensive patterns of production and put them on a lasting basis. The necessity of this stems from the objective laws governing the development of socialism. At the same time, the planned socialist economy of the German Democratic Republic enables advanced technology, primarily key technologies, to be harnessed for the fulfilment of this task. Being the owners of all production and research capacity, our people are turning the marvels of science to better and better use to improve our country's economic potential, add to society's wealth and advance social progress. Every new five-year period will furnish further powerful proof that only socialism is in a position to utilize the immense productive forces brought forth by our century for the benefit of the people.

Source: *Foreign Affairs Bulletin*, vol. 26, no. 12–13, 1986, pp. 99–101.

Document 2 The case for monetary union

At first, many West German economists, myself included, thought it was possible to establish a market economy in the GDR without a monetary union. In that case, the East German currency would have to be stabilised, made convertible and linked to the outside world by flexible exchange rates. After a period of adaptation and restructuring, the exchange rate would have been fixed to the Deutsche mark and a common German currency could have been introduced. Some experts preferred to fix the exchange rate immediately, defending it, if necessary, by imposing controls that could have been gradually removed. Others preferred floating exchange rates and decontrolling foreign exchange transactions step by step.

All of these proposals proved to be unfeasible, not only for political but also for economic reasons:

– Even with a separate currency, East Germans could have compared their real wages with those paid out in West Germany; hence hoping to stop emigration to the Federal Republic by means of a floating exchange rate was unrealistic.

– The opening of the GDR's western border made a floating exchange rate a less useful option in helping East Germany adapt production to free-market conditions than would otherwise have been the case. With the free movement of labour and free trade with the West, real prices would have extended from West Germany to such a degree that changes in the exchange rate would have determined East German real incomes to nearly the same extent as equivalent changes in nominal prices and nominal incomes will in the currency union. Floating exchange rates would not have created enough of an illusion of price and wage stability to make the problem of unemployment and unrealistic wages solvable by Keynesian inflationary measures.

– It is doubtful whether floating exchange rates would have effected the necessary changes to the price structure. Convertibility and free trade with West Germany would inevitably have led to the West German price structure for tradable goods, regardless of the exchange rate. The number of goods traded between the Germanys would have risen sharply and the East German price system would have come to mirror that of the West. Nor would a floating exchange rate have had any advantage as far as non-tradable goods are concerned. Many of them have prices that are artificially low, and in the currency union most of them are bound to rise. Rents, fares, land prices and the like must be raised to free-market levels to ensure the economic use of capital and land neglected for more than 50 years. Although political considerations prevent raising these prices immediately, the introduction of the hard Deutsche mark will at least increase the real value of prices that are being paid. Had the GDR retained its currency, the result could have been inflation and a more distorted price structure by lowering the real value of controlled prices for the non-tradables whose prices would have remained fixed by the government.

– Given the fact that border controls have ceased, the immediate extension of West Germany's price structure to the GDR via the currency union has undermined all plans to protect the East German economy by the continued control of foreign exchange, autonomous tariffs, taxes and quotas.

In sum introducing the Deutsche mark into the GDR is much more than simply a change of currency. It is a lever with which to change the economic and political system in the GDR and switch to a market economy. Adopting the West German price system gives East German companies a reliable base for their economic calculations, which would have been more difficult under flexible exchange rates. Economic policy has a psychological as well as a technical aspect. The Deutsche mark has an international reputation whose influence on economic decisions is uncalculable but definitely positive.

Source: Willgerodt, 1990, pp. 333–4.

Document 3 The State Treaty

Treaty of 18 May 1990 between the Federal Republic of Germany and the German Democratic Republic establishing a Monetary, Economic and Social Union.

CHAPTER I
Basic Principles

Article 1
Subject of the Treaty

(1) The Contracting Parties [German Democratic Republic and Federal Republic of Germany] shall establish a Monetary, Economic and Social Union.
(2) Starting on 1 July 1990 the Contracting Parties shall constitute a Monetary Union comprising a unified currency area and with the Deutsche Mark as the common currency. The Deutsche Bundesbank shall be the central bank in this currency area. The liabilities and claims expressed in Mark of the German Democratic Republic shall be converted into Deutsche Mark in accordance with this Treaty.
(3) The basis of the Economic Union shall be the social market economy as the common economic system of the two Contracting Parties. It shall be determined particularly by private ownership, competition, free pricing and, as a basic principle, complete freedom of movement of labour, capital, goods and services; this shall not preclude the legal admission of special forms of ownership providing for the participation of public authorities or other legal entities in trade and commerce as long as private legal entities are not subject to discrimination. It shall take into account the requirements of environmental protection.
(4) The Social Union together with the Monetary and Economic Union shall form one entity. It shall be characterized in particular by a system of labour law that corresponds to the social market economy and a comprehensive system of social security based on merit and social justice.

Article 2
Principles

(1) The Contracting Parties are committed to a free, democratic, federal and social basis order governed by the rule of law. To ensure the rights laid down in or following from this Treaty, they shall especially guarantee freedom of contract, freedom to exercise a trade, freedom of establishment and occupation, and freedom of movement of Germans in the entire currency area, freedom to form associations to safeguard and enhance working and economic conditions and, in accordance with Annex IX, ownership of land and means of production.
(2) Contrary provisions of the Constitution of the German Democratic

Republic relating to its former socialist social and political system shall no longer be applied . . .

CHAPTER II
Provisions concerning Monetary Union . . .

Article 10
Prerequisites and Principles . . .

(5) To achieve the aims described in paragraphs 1 to 4 above, the Contracting Parties shall, in accordance with the provisions laid down in Annex 1, agree on the following principles for Monetary Union;
– With effect from 1 July 1990 the Deutsche Mark shall be introduced as currency in the German Democratic Republic. The banknotes issued by the Deutsche Bundesbank and denominated in Deutsche Mark, and the federal coins issued by the Federal Republic of Germany and denominated in Deutsche Mark or Pfennig, shall be sole legal tender from 1 July 1990.
– Wages, salaries, grants, pensions, rents and leases as well as other recurring payments shall be converted at a rate of one to one.
– All other claims and liabilities denominated in Mark of the German Democratic Republic shall be converted to Deutsche Mark at a rate of two to one . . .
(6) Following an inventory of publicly owned assets and their earning power and following their primary use for the structural adaptation of the economy and for the recapitalization of the budget, the German Democratic Republic shall ensure where possible that a vested right to share in publicly owned assets can be granted to savers at a later date for the amount reduced following conversion at a rate of two to one.
(7) The Deutsche Bundesbank shall exercise the powers accorded it by the Treaty and by the Deutsche Bundesbank Act in the entire currency area. It shall establish for this purpose a provisional office in Berlin with up to fifteen branches in the German Democratic Republic, which shall be located in the premises of the State Bank of the German Democratic Republic.

CHAPTER III
Provisions concerning Economic Union

Article 11
Economic Policy Foundations

(1) The German Democratic Republic shall ensure that its economic and financial policy measures are in harmony with the social market system. Such measures shall be introduced in such a way that within the framework of the market economy system, they are at the same time conducive to price stability, a high level of employment and foreign trade equilibrium, and thus steady and adequate economic growth.

(2) The German Democratic Republic shall create the basic conditions for the development of market forces and private initiative in order to promote structural change, the creation of modern jobs, a broad basis of small and medium-sized companies and liberal professions, as well as environmental protection. The corporate legal structure shall be based on the principles of the social market economy described in Article I of this Treaty, enterprises being free to decide on products, quantities, production processes, investment, employment, prices and utilization of profits . . .

Article 13
Foreign Trade and Payments

(1) In its foreign trade, the German Democratic Republic shall take into account the principles of free world trade, as expressed in particular in the General Agreement on Tariffs and Trade. The Federal Republic of Germany shall make its experience fully available for the further integration of the economy of the German Democratic Republic into the world economy.

(2) The existing foreign trade relations of the German Democratic Republic, in particular its contractual obligations towards the countries of the Council for Mutual Economic Assistance, shall be respected . . .

Article 14
Structural Adjustment of Enterprises

In order to promote the necessary structural adjustment of enterprises in the German Democratic Republic, the Government of the German Democratic Republic shall, for a transitional period and subject to its budgetary means, take measures to facilitate a swift structural adjustment of enterprises to the new market conditions. The Governments of the Contracting Parties shall agree on the specific nature of these measures. The objective shall be to strengthen the competitiveness of enterprises on the basis of the social market economy and to build up, through the development of private initiative, a diversified, modern economic structure in the German Democratic Republic, with as many small and medium-sized enterprises as possible, and thereby to create the basis for increased growth and secure jobs.

Article 15
Agriculture and Food Industry

(1) Because of the crucial importance of the European Community rules for the agriculture and food industry, the German Democratic Republic shall introduce a price support and external protection scheme in line with the EC market regime so that agricultural producer prices in the German

Democratic Republic become adjusted to those of the Federal Republic of Germany. The German Democratic Republic shall not introduce levies or refunds vis-à-vis the European Community, subject to reciprocity.

(2) For categories of goods in respect of which it is not possible to introduce a full price support system immediately upon entry into force of this Treaty, transitional arrangements may be applied. Pending the legal integration of the agriculture and food industry of the German Democratic Republic into the EC agricultural market, specific quantitative restrictions shall be allowed for sensitive agricultural products in trade between the Contracting Parties.

(3) Without prejudice to the measures to be taken under Article 14 of this Treaty, the German Democratic Republic shall, within the limits of its budgetary means and for a transitional period, take suitable measures to promote the structural adaptation in the agricultural and food industry which is necessary to improve the competitiveness of enterprises to achieve environmentally acceptable and quality-based production, and to avoid surpluses . . .

Article 16
Protection of the Environment

(1) The protection of human beings, animals and plants, soil, water, air, the climate and landscapes as well as cultural and other material property against harmful environmental influences is a major objective of both Contracting Parties. They shall pursue this objective on the basis of prevention, the polluter pays principle, and cooperation. Their aim is the rapid establishment of a German environmental union.

(2) The German Democratic Republic shall introduce regulations to ensure that, on entry into force of this Treaty, the safety and environmental requirements applicable in the Federal Republic of Germany are the precondition for the granting of authorizations under environmental law for new plant and installations on its territory. For existing plant and installations the German Democratic Republic shall introduce regulations to bring them up to standard as quickly as possible . . .

CHAPTER V
Provisions concerning the Budget and Finance
Section I
The Budget

Article 26
Principles underlying the Fiscal Policy of the German Democratic Republic

(1) Public budgets in the German Democratic Republic shall be drawn up by the relevant national, regional or local authorities on their own respon-

sibility, due account being taken of the requirements of general economic equilibrium. The aim shall be to establish a system of budgeting adapted to the market economy. Budgets shall be balanced as regards revenue and expenditure. All revenue and expenditure shall be included in the appropriate budget.

(2) Budgets shall be adapted to the budget structure of the Federal Republic of Germany. The following in particular shall be removed from the budget, starting with the partial budget for 1990 as of the establishment of monetary union:

– the social sector, in so far as it is mainly financed from charges or contributions in the Federal Republic of Germany,

– state undertakings by conversion into legally and economically independent enterprises,

– transport undertaking by making them legally independent,

– the Deutsche Reichsbahn and the Deutsche Post, which will be operated as special funds,

– Government borrowing for housing shall be allocated to individual projects on the basis of their existing physical assets,

(3) National regional and local authorities in the German Democratic Republic shall make every effort to limit deficits in drawing up and executing budgets. As regards expenditure this shall include:

– abolition of budget subsidies, particularly in the short term for industrial goods, agricultural products and food, autonomous price supports being permissible for the latter in line with the regulations of the European Commission, and progressively in the sectors of transport, energy for private households and housing, making allowance for the general development of income,

– sustained reduction of personnel expenditure in the public service,

– review of expenditure, including the legal provisions on which they are based, to determine whether they are necessary and can be financed,

– structural improvements in the education system and preparatory division according to a federal structure (including the research sector) . . .

(d) An inventory shall be made of publicly owned assets. Publicly owned assets shall be used primarily for the structural adaption of the economy and for the recapitalization of the budget in the German Democratic Republic.

Article 27
Borrowing and Debts

(1) Borrowing authorizations in the budgets of the local, regional and national authorities of the German Democratic Republic shall be limited to 10 billion Deutsche Mark for 1990 and 14 billion Deutsche Mark for 1991 and allocated to the different levels of government in agreement with the Minister of Finance of the Federal Republic of Germany. A borrowing limit of 7 billion Mark for 1990 and 10 billion Mark for 1991 shall be established for the advance financing of proceeds expected to accrue from the realization of assets held in trust. In the event of a fundamental change in

conditions, the Minister of Finance of the Federal Republic of Germany may permit these credit ceilings to be exceeded.

(2) The raising of loans and the granting of equalization claims shall be conducted in agreement between the Minister of Finance of the German Democratic Republic and the Minister of Finance of the Federal Republic of Germany. The same shall apply to the assumption of sureties, warranties or other guarantees and for the total authorizations for future commitments to be appropriated in the budget.

(3) After accession, debt accrued in the budget of the German Democratic Republic shall be transferred to the assets held in trust in so far as it can be redeemed by proceeds expected to accrue from the realization of the assets held in trust. The remaining debt shall be assumed in equal parts by the Federal Government and the Länder newly constituted on the territory of the German Democratic Republic. Loans raised by Länder and local authorities shall remain their responsibility.

Article 28
Financial Allocations granted by the Federal Republic of Germany

(1) The Federal Republic of Germany shall grant the German Democratic Republic financial allocations amounting to 22 billion Deutsche Mark for the second half of 1990 and 35 billion Deutsche Mark for 1991 for the specific purposes of balancing its budget. Furthermore, initial financing shall be made available from the federal budget, in accordance with Article 25, amounting to 750 million Deutsche Mark for the second half of 1990 for pension insurance as well as 2 billion Deutsche Mark for the second half of 1990 and 3 billion Deutsche Mark for 1991 for unemployment insurance. Payments shall be made as required . . .

Document 4 The Unification Treaty

Treaty of 31 August 1990 between the Federal Republic of Germany and the German Democratic Republic of Germany on the establishment of German unity (Unification Treaty)

Article 7
Financial System . . .

(2) Article 106 of the Basic Law shall apply to the apportionment of tax revenue among Federation as well as the Länder and communes (associations of communes) in the territory specified in Article 3 of this Treaty with the proviso that
1. paragraph 3, fourth sentence, and paragraph 4 shall not apply up to 31 December 1994; (xi)
2. up to 31 December 1996, the share of income tax revenue received by the communes in accordance with Article 106 (5) of the Basic Law shall be passed on from the Länder to the communes not on the basis of the amount of income tax paid by their inhabitants, but according to the number of inhabitants in the communes;
3. up to December 1994, in derogation of Article 106 (7) of the Basic Law, an annual share of at least 20 per cent of the Land share of total revenue from the German unity Fund (xii) according to paragraph 5, item 1, shall accrue to the communes (associations of communes).
(3) Article 107 (xiii) of the Basic Law shall be valid in the territory [former GDR] specified in Article 3 of this Treaty with the proviso that up to 31 December 1994 the provisions of paragraph 1, fourth sentence, shall not be applied between the Länder which have until now constituted the Federal Republic of Germany and the Länder in the territory specified in Article 3 of this Treaty and that there shall be no all-German financial equalization between the Länder (Article 107 (2) of the Basic Law.
The Land share of turnover tax throughout Germany shall be divided up into an eastern component and a western component in such a way that the average share of turnover tax per inhabitant in the Länder of Brandenburg, Mecklenburg-Western Pomerania, Saxony, Saxony-Anhalt and Thuringia amounts
   in 1991 to 55 per cent
   in 1992 to 60 per cent
   in 1993 to 65 per cent
   in 1994 to 70 per cent
of the average share of turnover tax per inhabitant in the Länder of Baden-Württemberg, Bavaria, Bremen, Hesse, Hamburg, Lower Saxony, North-Rhine/Westphalia, Rhineland-Palatinate, Saarland and Schleswig-Holstein. The share of the Land Berlin shall be calculated in advance on the basis of the number of inhabitants. The provisions contained in this paragraph shall be reviewed for 1993 in the light of the conditions obtaining at the time.
(4) The territory specified in Article 3 of this Treaty shall be incorporated in

the provisions of Article 91 a, 91 b and 104 a (3) and (4) of the Basic Treaty, (xiiia) including the pertinent implementing provisions, in accordance with this Treaty with effect from 1 January 1991.

(5) Following the establishment of German unity the annual allocations from the German Unity Fund shall be distributed as follows:

1. 85 per cent as special assistance to the Länder of Brandenburg, Mecklenburg-Western Pomerania, Saxony, Saxony-Anhalt and Thuringia as well as to Land Berlin to cover their general financial requirements and divided up among these Länder in proportion to their number of inhabitants, excluding the inhabitants of Berlin (West), and

2. 15 per cent to meet public requirements at a central level in the territory of the aforementioned Länder.

(6) In the event of a fundamental change of conditions, the Federation and the Länder shall jointly examine the possibilities of granting further assistance in order to ensure adequate financial equalization for the Länder in the territory specified in Article 3 of this Treaty . . .

Article 23
Debt Arrangements

(1) Upon the accession taking effect, the total debts of the central budget of the German Democratic Republic which have accumulated up to this date shall be taken over by a federal Special Fund without legal capacity, which shall meet the obligations arising from debt servicing. The Special Fund shall be empowered to raise loans:

1. to pay off debts of the Special Fund,
2. to cover due interest and loan procurement costs,
3. to purchase debt titles of the Special Fund for the purposes of market cultivation.

(2) The Federal Minister of Finance shall administer the Special Fund. The Special Fund may, in his name, conduct legal transactions, sue and be sued. The general legal domicile of the Special Fund shall be at the seat of the Federal Government. The Federation shall act as guarantor for the liabilities of the Special Fund.

(3) From the day the accession takes effect until 31 December 1993 the Federation and the Trust Agency shall each repay one half of the interest payments made by the Special Fund.

Repayment shall be made by the first of the month following the month in which the Special Fund has made the payments referred to in the first sentence.

(4) With effect from 1 January 1994 the Federation and the Länder named in Article 1 of this Treaty [the Länder of Brandenburg, Mecklenburg-Western-Pomerania, Saxony, Saxony-Anhalt and Thuringia] as well as the Trust Agency shall take over the total debts which have accumulated in the Special Fund up to 31 December 1993 in accordance with Article 27 (3) of the Treaty of 18 May 1990 between the Federal Republic of Germany and the German Democratic Republic Establishing a Monetary, Economic and Social Union. The distribution of the debts shall

be settled in detail by a separate law in accordance with Article 34 of the Act of 25 July 1990 concerning the Treaty of 18 May 1990 . . . The portions of the total amount for the Länder named in Article 1 of this Treaty to be taken over by each of the Länder named in Article 1 shall be calculated in relation to their number of inhabitants on the date the accession takes effect, excluding the inhabitants of Berlin (West).

(5) The Special Fund shall be abolished at the end of 1993.

(6) Upon the accession taking effect, the Federal Republic of Germany shall take over the sureties, guarantees and warranties assumed by the German Democratic Republic and debited to its state budget prior to unification. The Länder named in Article 1 (1) of this Treaty and Land Berlin for that part in which the Basic Law has not been in force to date shall assume jointly and severally a counter-surety to the amount of 50 per cent of the total debt transferred in the form of sureties, guarantees and warranties to the Federal Republic of Germany. The losses shall be divided among the Länder in proportion to their number of inhabitants on the date the accession takes effect, excluding the inhabitants of Berlin (West).

(7) The German Democratic Republic's share of the Staatsbank Berlin may be transferred to the Länder named in Article 1 of this Treaty. The rights arising from the German Democratic Republic's share of the Staatsbank Berlin shall accrue to the Federation pending the transfer of the share according to the first sentence or a transfer according to the third sentence. The Contracting Parties shall, notwithstanding an examination from the viewpoint of antitrust legislation, provide for the possibility of transferring the Staatsbank Berlin wholly or partially to a credit institution under public law in the Federal Republic of Germany or to other legal entities. In the event that not all assets and liabilities are covered by a transfer, the remaining part of the Staatsbank Berlin shall be wound up. The Federation shall assume the liabilities resulting from the German Democratic Republic acting as guarantor for the Staatsbank Berlin. This shall not apply to liabilities arising after the transfer of the share according to the first sentence or a transfer according to the third sentence. The fifth sentence shall apply mutatis mutandis to new liabilities created by the Staatsbank Berlin during its capacity as guarantor, the burden shall be incorporated upon the accession taking effect into the total debt of the central budget of the German Democratic Republic and be taken over by the Special Fund under paragraph 1 above, which has no legal capacity . . .

Article 25
Assets held in Trust

The Privatization and Reorganization of Publicly Owned Assets Act (Trusteeship Act) of 17 June 1990 . . . shall continue after the accession takes effect with the following proviso:

(1) The Trust Agency shall continue to be charged, in accordance with the provision of the Trusteeship Act, with restructuring and privatizing the former publicly owned enterprises to bring them into line with the requirements of a competitive economy. It shall become a direct institution of the

Federation invested with legal capacity and subject to public law. Technical and legal supervision shall be the responsibility of the Federal Minister of Finance, who shall exercise technical supervision in agreement with the Federal Minister of Economics and the respective federal minister. Stakes held by the Trust Agency shall be indirect stakes of the Federation. Amendments to the Charter shall require the agreement of the Federal Government.

(2) The number of members of the Administrative Board of the Trust Agency shall be raised from 16 to 20, and for the first Administrative Board to 23. Instead of the two representatives elected from the members of the Volkskammer, the Länder named in Article 1 of this Treaty shall each receive one seat on the Administrative Board of the Trust Agency. Notwithstanding Section 4 (2) of the Trusteeship Act, the chairman and the remaining members of the Administrative Board shall be appointed by the Federal Government.

(3) The Contracting Parties reaffirm that publicly owned assets shall be used exclusively for the purpose of activities in the territory specified in Article 3 of this Treaty, regardless of budgetary responsibilities. Revenue of the Trust Agency shall accordingly be used in line with Article 26 (4) and Article 27 (3) of the Treaty of 18 May 1990. As part of the structural adjustment of the agricultural sector, revenue of the Trust Agency may also be used in individual cases for debt relief to agricultural enterprises. First of all, their own assets shall be used. Debts attributed to branches of enterprises which are to be hived off shall be disregarded. Assistance with debt relief may also be granted with the proviso that enterprises pay back the funds granted in whole or in part depending on their economic capabilities.

(4) The power to raise loans granted to the Trust Agency by Article 27 (1) of the Treaty of 18 May 1990 shall be increased from a maximum total of 17 billion Deutsche Mark to a maximum total of 25 billion Deutsche Mark. The aforementioned loans should, as a rule, be repaid by 31 December 1995. The Federal Minister of Finance may permit an extension of the loan periods and, in the event of a fundamental change in conditions, give permission for the loan ceilings to be exceeded.

(5) The Trust Agency shall be empowered, in agreement with the Federal Minister of Finance, to assume sureties, guarantees and other warranties.

(6) In accordance with Article 10 (6) of the Treaty of 18 May 1990 possibilities shall be provided for savers at a later date to be granted a vested right to a share in publicly owned assets for the amount reduced during conversion at a rate of two to one.

(7) The interest and capital payments on loans raised before 30 June 1990 shall be suspended until the adoption of the opening balance in Deutsche Mark. The interest payments due shall be repaid to the Deutsche Kreditbank AG and the other banks by the Trust Agency . . .

Article 28
Economic Assistance.

(1) Upon the accession taking effect, the territory specified in Article of this Treaty shall be incorporated into the arrangements of the Federation existing in the territory of the Federal Republic for economic assistance, taking into consideration the competence of the European Communities. The specific requirements of structural adjustment shall be taken into account during a transitional period. This will make a major contribution to the speediest possible development of a balanced economic structure with particular regard for small and medium-sized businesses.
(2) The relevant ministries shall prepare concrete programmes to speed up economic growth and structural adjustment in the territory specified in Article 3 of this Treaty. The programmes shall cover the following fields:
– measures of regional economic assistance accompanied by a special programme for the benefit of the territory specified in Article 3 of this Treaty; preferential arrangements shall be ensured for this territory;
– measures to improve the general economic conditions in the communes, with particular emphasis being given to the needs of the economy;
– measures to foster the rapid development of small and medium-sized businesses;
– measures to promote the modernization and restructuring of the economy, relying on restructuring schemes drawn up by industry of its own accord (e.g. rehabilitation programmes, including ones for exports to COMECON countries);
– debt relief for enterprises following the examination of each case individually . . .

CHAPTER VII
Labour, Social Welfare, Family, Women, Public Health and Environmental Protection

Article 30
Labour and Social Welfare

(1) It shall be the task of the all-German legislator
1. to recodify in a uniform manner and as soon as possible the law on employment contracts and the provisions on working hours under public law, including the admissibility of work on Sundays and public holidays, and the specific industrial safety regulations for women;
2. to bring public law on industrial safety into line with present-day requirements in accordance with the law of the European Communities and the concurrent part of the industrial safety law of the German Democratic Republic.
(2) Employed persons in the territory specified in Article 3 of this Treaty shall be entitled, upon reaching the age of 57, to receive early retirement payments for a period of three years, but not beyond the earliest possible

date on which they become entitled to receive a retirement pension under the statutory pension scheme. The early retirement payment shall amount to 65 per cent of the last average net earnings; for employed persons whose entitlement arises on or before 1 April 1991 early retirement payments shall be raised by an increment of five percentage points for the first 312 days. The early retirement payments shall be made by the Federal Institute for Employment along similar lines to unemployment pay, notably the provisions of Section 105c of the Employment Protection Act. The Federal Institute for Employment may reject an application if it is established that there is a clear lack of manpower in the region to carry out the occupational duties so far discharged by the applicant. The early retirement payments shall be refunded by the Federation in so far as they reach beyond the period of entitlement to unemployment pay. The provisions on early retirement payments shall be applied to new claims up to 31 December 1991. The period of validity may be prolonged by one year.

In the period from this Treaty taking effect up to 31 December 1990, women shall be entitled, on reaching the age of 55, to receive early retirement payments for a period not exceeding five years.

(3) The social welfare supplement to pension, accident and unemployment payments introduced in the territory specified in Article 3 of this Treaty in conjunction with the Treaty of 18 May 1990 shall be limited to new cases up to 31 December 1991. The payments shall be made for a period not extending beyond 30 June 1995.

(4) The transfer of tasks incumbent upon the social insurance scheme to separate agencies shall take place in such a way as to ensure that payments are made and financed and sufficient staff is available to perform the said tasks. The distribution of assets and liabilities among the separate agencies shall be definitively settled by law.

(5) The details regarding the introduction of part VI of the Social Code (pension insurance) and the provisions of Part III of the Reich Insurance Code (accident insurance) shall be settled in a federal Act.

For persons whose pension under the statutory pension scheme begins in the period from 1 January 1992 to 30 June 1995

1. a pension shall be payable which is in principle at least as high as the amount they would have received on 30 June 1990 in the territory specified in Article 3 of this Treaty according to the pension law valid until that time, without regard for payments from supplementary or special pension schemes.

2. a pension shall also be paid where, on 30 June 1990, a pension entitlement would have existed in the territory specified in Article 3 of this Treaty under the pension law valid at that time.

In all other respects, the introduction should have the goal of ensuring that as wages and salaries in the territory specified in Article 3 of this Treaty are brought into line with those in the other Länder, so are pensions . . .

Notes

xi Article 106 of the Basic Law concerns the apportionment of tax revenue. The provisions which under the Unification Act do not apply concern the proportions of the income tax, corporation tax and turnover tax falling to the Federation and the Länder.

xii On 16 May 1990 the Federal and the State governments set up a fund of DM 115 billion to assist the GDR.

xiii Article 107 of the Basic Law concerns financial equalization. It takes account of the differing financial resources of the federal states.

xiiia These provisions govern the Federation's involvement in fulfilling the responsibilities of the Länder as well as the distribution of expenditure as between the Federation and the Länder.

Document 5 Economic data relating to East Germany, 1991–2

	1991							
Unit	Mar	Apr	May	Jun	Jul	Aug	Sep	Oct
A. New orders (2nd half 1990 = 100)								
Manufacturing industry	92.2	79.8	68.5	75.8	71.3	84.9	71.5	75.2
– Domestic	70.9	70.2	72.1	69.2	70.3	73.2	71.0	70.2
– Foreign	154.1	107.8	58.0	95.0	74.2	121.1	73.1	89.9
– Basic materials/producer goods industry	74.2	68.9	59.2	59.9	64.3	52.7	65.4	72.3
– Capital goods industry	115.1	93.8	78.3	93.7	81.0	122.3	80.0	80.8
– Consumer goods industry	69.2	65.3	62.2	62.3	60.4	57.4	62.0	66.3
Construction industry proper (2nd half 1990 = 100)								
total	103.0	115.0	127.5	161.1	169.0	176.7	199.2	189.4
Building	98.3	106.9	120.0	136.2	144.8	137.3	152.9	152.9
– Residential	80.9	73.3	69.1	103.0	89.0	92.7	87.1	84.2
– Commercial	103.0	111.4	128.1	141.4	154.1	140.1	165.4	177.1
– Public	155.3	145.8	321.0	269.0	363.7	342.2	400.6	388.8
Civil engineering	112.9	132.4	143.8	214.5	221.0	261.6	298.9	267.9
– Road construction	77.8	108.3	153.9	265.8	237.5	315.2	373.6	253.4
B. Net output (until August 1990 on basis of 3rd qtr 1990 = 100; from August 1990 on basis of 2nd half 1990 = 100)								
Manufacturing industry total	65.3	57.9	61.0	63.2	62.6	63.7	68.5	70.8
– Basic materials/producer goods industry	79.4	68.6	68.1	67.1	69.9	74.1	79.4	86.8
– Capital goods industry	51.6	45.6	48.6	52.8	51.0	54.5	58.6	57.6
– Consumer goods industry	73.2	66.6	68.0	72.1	67.9	64.0	73.8	78.8
– Food, beverages and tobacco industry	96.6	87.5	97.0	94.0	96.3	86.9	89.3	96.1
Construction industry proper	–	–	–	–	–	105.3	114.1	119.9
C. Retail sales (3rd qtr 1990 = 100)								
Total	95.2	93.2	–	–	–	–	–	–
D. Foreign trade (DM million)								
Exports	1,180	1,009	1,346	1,074	1,532	1,501	1,255	1,611
Imports	903	752	1,005	870	1,293	918	865	728
Balance of trade	+277	+257	+341	+204	+239	+583	+390	+883
E. Business licences (since beginning of year, in '000)								
Registrations	81.0	112.4	137.4	162.1	188.1	209.7	231.3	253.5
Deregistrations	20.3	28.4	35.1	42.6	51.6	60.1	69.7	79.3

Unit		1991		1992					
		Nov	Dec	Jan	Feb	Mar	Apr	May	Jun
A. New orders (2nd half 1990 = 100)									
Manufacturing industry		78.8	92.4	93.7	65.0	70.9	76.2	59.5	75.1
– Domestic		76.4	71.6	87.6	70.4	74.7	81.5	64.0	79.1
– Foreign		85.9	153.1	111.4	49.3	59.8	60.7	46.4	63.6
– Basic materials/producer goods industry		62.2	71.0	60.7	61.1	63.5	52.4	49.9	56.1
– Capital goods industry		95.7	119.5	113.7	67.1	76.0	99.1	65.4	94.9
– Consumer goods industry		70.0	63.6	80.9	68.2	73.6	66.8	65.0	63.2
Construction industry proper (2nd half 1990 = 100), total		165.5	159.0	147.2	152.8	194.5	189.7	200.7	235.0
Building		132.8	144.1	138.1	154.5	166.3	167.5	180.1	201.1
– Residential		88.6	99.0	96.6	95.1	94.1	108.1	103.5	127.2
– Commercial		139.6	149.3	147.1	178.6	199.8	198.1	210.6	236.4
– Public		310.4	335.7	387.5	294.0	309.4	265.7	364.3	340.0
Civil engineering		235.7	191.0	166.6	149.3	255.2	237.5	245.0	308.0
– Road construction		237.2	176.3	141.2	112.7	193.7	181.0	214.7	263.1
B. Net output (2nd half 1990 = 100)									
Manufacturing industry, total		71.4	67.6	61.8	60.3	67.5	62.1	59.7	63.3
– Basic materials/producer goods industry		87.6	74.4	75.4	75.2	86.2	80.8	77.2	79.1
– Capital goods industry		58.8	59.1	47.5	47.2	51.8	46.1	44.1	49.1
– Consumer goods industry		79.2	71.0	71.9	71.8	79.5	73.5	72.5	71.1
– Food, beverages and tobacco industry		93.9	90.5	93.0	83.5	95.5	92.1	87.9	93.2
Construction industry proper		113.7	82.5	86.2	89.1	108.5	108.0	105.3	116.8
C. Retail sales (3rd qtr 1990 = 100) Total		–	–	–					
D. Foreign trade (DM million)									
Exports		1,914	1,681	1,182	1,194	1,269	1,222	1,074	988
Imports		977	656	724	606	729	713	681	945
Balance of trade		+937	+1025	+458	+588	+540	+509	+393	+43
E. Business licences (since beginning of year, in '000)									
Registrations		273.3	291.4	20.1	39.6	60.6	80.3	97.7	116.0
Deregistrations		89.1	99.1	11.0	20.9	31.3	41.7	50.9	61.7

| | 1992 | | | |
	Jul	Aug	Sep	Oct
A. New orders (2nd half 1990 = 100)				
Manufacturing industry	60.2	64.9	81.7	–
– Domestic	70.3	74.9	85.1	
– Foreign	30.7	35.7	72.0	
– Basic materials/producer goods industry	53.9	50.4	71.1	
– Capital goods industry	65.6	78.5	93.7	
– Consumer goods industry	59.3	59.9	72.8	
Construction industry proper (2nd half 1990 = 100)				
total	219.3	216.4	247.0	
Building	193.9	175.8	203.5	
– Residential	124.7	92.8	128.0	
– Commercial	210.5	220.5	240.9	
– Public	431.3	299.1	337.4	
Civil engineering	274.1	303.7	340.6	
– Road construction	272.2	279.5	314.5	
B. Net output (2nd half 1990 = 100)				
Manufacturing industry, total	61.0	60.5	69.6	
– Basic materials/producer goods industry	77.6	76.7	82.1	
– Capital goods industry	46.8	45.7	56.9	
– Consumer goods industry	65.1	68.1	78.3	
– Food, beverages and tobacco industry	92.5	92.6	96.8	
Construction industry proper	111.3	110.7	118.9	
C. Retail sales (3rd qtr 1990 = 100)				
Total	–	–	–	
D. Foreign trade (DM million)				
Exports	1,158	857	1,100	1,043
Imports	929	713	829	931
Balance of trade	+229	+144	+271	+112
E. Business licences (since beginning of year, in '000)				
Registrations	133.9	147.9	164.3	181.4
Deregistrations	71.7	79.7	89.4	99.5

Sources: Bundesministerium für Wirtschaft, *Monthly Review. The Economic Situation in the Federal Republic of Germany*, nos 1, 6 and 12, 1992.

Document 6 The labour market in east Germany, June 1990–December 1992

The labour market in east Germany, June 1990–December 1990

	June	July	Aug	Sept	Oct	Nov	Dec
Unemployment of which:	142,096	272,917	361,286	444,856	536,800	589,178	642,182
women	69,203	140,481	192,247	244,842	291,081	291,081	351,779
young people under 20 yrs	–	14,447	23,253	28,905	32,480	34,287	37,499
Unemployment rate (%)	1.6	3.1	4.1	5.0	6.1	6.7	7.3
Short-time workers	–	656,277	1,499,872	1,728,749	1,703,782	1,709,899	1,794,032
of which no work done:							
10–25%				431,162	445,727	370,920	328,647
25–50%				739,893	658,226	693,272	724,047
50–75%				352,704	377,951	383,542	445,490
75–100%				204,990	221,878	262,165	295,838
Vocational training registered in month				12,639	23,173	32,730	30,019
Employees in job-creation schemes				4,268	8,417	14,545	20,316

The labour market in east Germany, January–May 1991

	Jan	Feb	Mar	Apr	May	Jun
Unemployment of which:	757,162	786,992	808,349	836,940	842,285	842,504
women	414,950	430,446	446,523	469,129	476,819	482,392
young people under 20 yrs	38,543	40,780	40,551	39,339	38,191	37,017
Unemployment rate (%)	8.6	8.9	9.2	9.5	9.5	9.5
Men (%)	7.6	7.9	8.0	8.2	8.1	8.0
Women (%)	9.6	10.0	10.4	10.9	11.1	11.2
Short-time workers	1,840,639	1,947,059	1,989,815	2,018,907	1,968,477	1,898,937
of which no work done:						
10–25%	282,613	250,806	253,113	270,481	260,384	244,107
25–50%	657,666	643,310	614,848	605,995	578,527	535,672
50–75%	510,408	580,896	607,491	620,562	595,579	579,173
75–100%	389,952	472,047	514,363	521,869	533,987	539,985
Vocational training registered in month	38,154	45,524	55,023	72,977	69,508	81,263
Employees in job-creation schemes:	34,409	46,967	62,549	84,882	113,599	148,235

The labour market in east Germany July–December 1991

	July	Aug	Sept	Oct	Nov	Dec
Unemployment of which:	1,068,639	1,063,237	1,028,751	1,048,527	1,030,719	1,037,709
women	625,493	630,545	617,492	641,366	631,132	634,710
young people under 20 yrs	50,417	49,124	45,169	42,649	39,649	37,256
Unemployment rate (%)	12.1	12.1	11.7	11.9	11.7	11.8
Men (%)	9.8	9.6	9.1	9.0	8.9	8.9
Women (%)	14.5	14.6	14.3	14.9	14.6	14.7
Short-time workers	1,610,775	1,448,847	1,333,362	1,199,875	1,103,449	1,034,543
of which no work done:						
10–25%	216,106	203,466	190,061	174,340	160,230	150,371
25–50%	482,896	411,503	360,218	331,525	297,751	262,792
50–75%	454,263	403,486	377,682	326,761	308,126	297,499
75–100%	457,510	430,392	405,401	367,249	337,342	323,881
Recipients of transitional early retirement benefit	–	206,519	225,885	281,590	305,225	328,813
Vocational training: registered in month	95,614	78,094	85,739	91,893	89,677	88,679
total at end of month	–	324,100	350,500	382,900	410,400	435,200
Employees in job-creation schemes	209,907	261,804	313,029	348,364	371,055	389,861

The labour market in east Germany January–June 1992

	Jan	Feb	March	Apr	May	June
Unemployment of which:	1,343,449	1,290,375	1,220,138	1,195,962	1,149,410	1,123,202
women	827,783	795,703	760,599	752,553	726,070	714,874
young people under 20 yrs	38,306	35,090	31,663	28,823	26,474	26,000
Unemployment rate (%)	16.5	15.9	15.0	14.7	14.6	13.8
Men (%)	12.6	12.1	11.2	10.8	10.3	10.0
Women (%)	21.8	21.0	20.1	19.9	19.2	18.9
Short-time workers	520,591	518,849	493,940	466,263	436,533	417,383
of which no work done:						
10–25%	62,087	76,950	87,580	84,437	77,959	73,993
25–50%	151,724	164,721	154,007	148,165	141,246	137,822
50–75%	153,002	130,969	122,635	112,782	104,248	102,532
75–100%	153,778	146,209	129,718	120,879	113,080	103,036
Recipients of transitional early retirement benefit	443,175	458,227	469,264	472,698	478,593	485,870
Vocational training: total at end of month	446,500	470,900	496,900	507,300	510,300	509,300
Employees in job creation schemes	394,083	399,561	401,471	404,460	404,853	401,880

The labour market in east Germany July–December 1992

	July	Aug	Sept	Oct	Nov	Dec
Unemployment of which:	1,188,234	1,168,732	1,110,751	1,097,452	1,086,464	1,100,749
women	759,949	753,949	718,749	712,525	702,596	703,513
young people under 20 yrs	33,335	32,321	29,257	27,064	24,871	24,019
Unemployment rate (%)	15.1	14.8	14.1	13.5	13.8	13.5
Men (%)	10.4	10.1	9.6	9.4	9.4	9.7
Women (%)	20.1	19.9	19.0	18.8	18.5	18.6
Short-time workers	337,758	287,150	251,476	240,017	236,571	233,431
of which no work done:						
10–25%	63,904	53,547	79,379	79,321	79,015	80,027
25–50%	117,724	102,425	69,084	68,042	66,227	62,225
50–75%	75,568	61,557	36,284	31,582	32,202	33,386
75–100%	80,562	69,621	66,729	61,072	59,127	57,793
Recipients of transitional early retirement benefit	545,468	555,921	560,164	568,605	573,498	578,090
Vocational training: total at end of month	503,700	493,900	490,600	499,200	494,600	479,600
Employees in job-creation schemes	388,692	381,415	374,902	369,701	363,332	354,717

Source: various issues of *Amtliche Nachrichten der Bundesanstalt für Arbeit*

Document 7 Unemployment in east Germany, by region, 1990–2 (%)

	1990	1991						
	Dec	Jan	Feb	Mar	Apr	May	Jun	Jul
Mecklenburg-West Pomerania	8.7	10.9	11.3	11.7	12.1	12.1	11.9	13.9
Brandenburg	7.4	8.4	8.8	9.1	9.4	9.5	9.5	12.1
Saxony-Anhalt	7.0	8.1	8.6	8.9	9.3	9.5	9.7	12.2
Saxony	6.2	7.6	7.8	8.0	8.3	8.3	8.1	10.9
Thuringia	7.3	8.7	9.0	9.1	9.3	9.3	9.4	12.0
East Berlin	9.3	10.1	10.4	10.7	11.1	11.2	11.4	14.0

				1991			1992	
	Aug	Sep	Oct	Nov	Dec	Jan	Feb	Mar
Mecklenburg-West Pomerania	13.9	13.4	13.6	13.6	13.8	19.0	18.4	17.7
Brandenburg	12.2	11.7	11.9	11.6	11.8	16.8	16.3	15.4
Saxony-Anhalt	12.1	12.0	12.2	12.0	11.9	16.9	16.4	15.6
Saxony	10.8	10.4	10.7	10.5	10.5	15.8	15.0	14.1
Thuringia	11.7	11.3	11.5	11.2	11.4	18.0	17.3	16.1
East Berlin	14.1	14.0	14.0	13.8	13.9	17.2	16.4	15.3

					1992				
	Apr	May	Jun	Jul	Aug	Sep	Oct	Nov	Dec
Mecklenburg-West Pomerania	17.6	16.7	16.2	16.8	16.6	15.4	15.4	15.5	15.7
Brandenburg	15.0	14.6	14.4	15.0	14.7	14.1	14.1	14.0	14.2
Saxony-Anhalt	15.5	15.1	14.9	15.5	15.4	14.8	14.6	14.4	14.5
Saxony	13.8	13.2	12.9	14.0	13.7	13.0	12.9	12.7	12.7
Thuringia	15.7	14.8	14.4	15.6	15.5	14.7	14.4	14.1	14.5
East Berlin	14.9	14.3	14.0	14.1	13.8	13.0	12.8	12.7	13.0

Sources: various issues of *Amtliche Nachrichten der Bundesanstalt für Arbeit*.

Document 8 Unemployment and labour-market measures in east Germany, July 1992

	Unemployment			
	Unemployed	Proportion women	Unemployment rate[1]	Duration of unemployment
Länder Employment districts	'000s	%	%	weeks
Mecklenburg-Western Pomerania	164,685	58.7	16.8	43.1
Neubrandenburg	48,056	58.8	19.1	46.0
Rostock	47,236	57.9	16.6	46.9
Schwerin	38,624	61.8	14.6	40.5
Stralsund	30,769	55.8	17.3	40.5
Brandenburg	184,168	63.1	15.0	39.7
Cottbus	43,577	65.3	12.5	37.1
Eberswalde	29,651	59.4	18.3	41.1
Frankfurt (Oder)	28,797	61.7	15.3	39.1
Neuruppin	43,215	62.1	18.0	40.9
Potsdam	38,928	65.8	13.5	40.8
Saxony-Anhalt	221,013	65.2	15.5	44.8
Dessau	21,773	63.9	15.9	36.1
Halberstadt	26,352	66.1	17.9	48.7
Halle	31,992	64.1	12.7	48.6
Magdeburg	54,854	63.7	15.2	50.3
Merseburg	32,070	66.1	16.3	44.1
Sangerhausen	21,969	65.3	17.7	42.9
Stendal	20,457	66.3	16.3	41.7
Wittenberg	11,546	70.5	15.3	33.5
Saxony	325,928	67.0	14.0	38.0
Annaberg	32,765	68.2	19.0	42.6
Bautzen	52,326	67.1	15.7	38.3
Chemnitz	33,310	65.4	12.8	34.0
Dresden	32,153	61.9	9.6	36.2
Leipzig	51,582	66.9	11.0	38.9
Oschatz	15,003	64.9	17.2	37.6
Pirna	28,269	67.4	15.7	38.3
Plauen	20,419	71.3	15.4	32.4
Riesa	16,660	67.8	14.6	44.0
Zwickau	37,853	68.4	18.3	39.0
Thuringia	195,976	67.1	15.6	34.7
Erfurt	37,674	64.1	14.1	34.9
Gera	23,333	67.6	13.9	36.0
Gotha	31,201	69.9	17.9	41.5
Jena	25,271	67.4	13.5	29.3
Nordhausen	26,940	66.6	18.2	37.4
Suhl	40,111	66.7	15.6	32.7
Altenburg[7]	17,034	71.8	19.6	36.8
East Berlin	96,464	55.1	14.1	42.4
East German total	1,188,234	64.0	15.1	39.8
As a comparison: West Germany[8]	1,827,712	46.7	6.7	24.3

Improvement of the labour market as a result of people in:

	Job-creation measures (ABM)		Short-time working		Training measures	
	'000s[2]	%[1]	'000s[3]	%[1]	'000s[4]	%[1]
Mecklenburg-West Pomerania	45,450	4.6	13,693	1.4	54,513	5.6
Neubrandenburg	16,062	6.4	3,059	1.2	14,563	5.8
Rostock	14,698	5.2	2,406	0.8	14,008	4.9
Schwerin	8,359	3.2	3,567	1.7	15,750	6.0
Stralsund	6,331	3.6	3,567	2.0	10,212	5.7
Brandenburg	59,593	4.9	22,191	1.8	59,813	4.9
Cottbus	14,845	4.3	5,857	1.7	12,494	3.6
Eberswalde	10,190	6.3	2,490	1.5	9,401	5.8
Frankfurt (Oder)	9,818	5.2	3,436	1.8	10,125	5.4
Neuruppin	13,016	5.4	5,267	2.2	12,717	5.3
Potsdam	11,724	4.1	5,150	1.8	15,305	5.3
Saxony-Anhalt	90,302	6.3	35,235	2.5	74,906	5.3
Dessau	10,283	7.5	3,559	2.6	8,737	6.4
Halberstadt	10,431	7.1	2,620	1.8	7,175	4.9
Halle	12,036	4.8	4,053	1.6	12,427	4.9
Magdeburg	24,381	6.8	12,653	3.5	18,978	5.3
Merseburg	9,695	4.7	8,071	4.0	10,192	5.0
Sangerhausen	9,395	7.6	2,100	1.7	8,463	6.8
Stendal	9,005	7.2	1,175	0.9	5,453	4.3
Wittenberg	5,076	6.7	1,231	1.6	3,675	4.9
Saxony	101,280	4.4	66,960	2.9	133,624	5.7
Annaberg	11,051	6.4	5,499	3.2	10,120	5.9
Bautzen	17,477	5.2	9,165	2.7	18,610	5.6
Chemnitz	7,422	2.9	10,525	4.0	18,110	7.0
Dresden	5,597	1.7	8,323	2.5	15,753	4.7
Leipzig	25,736	5.5	12,372	2.6	21,862	4.7
Oschatz	3,157	3.6	2,106	2.4	5,460	6.3
Pirna	7,147	4.0	5,428	3.0	10,142	5.6
Plauen	7,618	5.7	2,148	1.6	8,352	6.3
Riesa	8,526	7.5	2,726	2.4	9,850	8.6
Zwickau	6,027	2.9	7,731	3.7	15,428	7.5
Thuringia	64,275	5.1	34,193	2.7	77,739	6.2
Erfurt	8,823	3.3	3,904	1.5	17,600	6.6
Gera	6,535	3.9	6,763	4.0	11,159	6.6
Gotha	10,344	5.9	4,866	2.8	8,642	5.0
Jena	8,856	4.7	4,365	2.3	11,562	6.2
Nordhausen	10,999	7.4	2,614	1.8	9,782	6.6
Suhl	16,248	6.3	10,434	4.1	13,088	5.1
Altenburg	3,992	4.6	2,196	2.5	5,429	6.2
East Berlin	27,792	4.1	6,575	1.0	36,859	5.4
East Germany total	388,692	4.9	178,675	2.3	437,212	5.6
As a comparison: West Germany[8]	80,157	0.3	49,050	0.2	236,500	0.9

Improvement of the labour market as a result of people in:

	Early retirement		Total labour-market measures		per unem-ployed person	Shortage, of 'regular' em-ployment[6]	
	'000s[5]	%[1]	'000s	%[1]		'000s	%[1]
Mecklenburg-West Pomerania	99,061	10.1	212,717	21.7	1.29	377,402	38.5
Neubrandenburg	27,417	10.9	61,101	24.3	1.27	109,157	43.4
Rostock	26,773	9.4	57,885	20.3	1.23	105,121	36.9
Schwerin	25,816	9.8	54,455	20.6	1.41	93,079	35.1
Stralsund	19,055	10.7	39,165	22.0	1.27	69,934	39.3
Brandenburg	134,876	11.0	276,473	22.5	1.50	460,641	37.6
Cottbus	35,764	10.3	68,960	19.8	1.58	112,537	32.4
Eberswalde	17,993	11.1	40,051	24.7	1.35	69,725	42.9
Frankfurt (Oder)	20,672	11.0	44,051	23.4	1.53	72,848	38.7
Neuruppin	28,950	12.1	59,950	25.0	1.39	103,165	43.0
Potsdam	31,497	10.9	63,676	22.1	1.64	102,604	35.5
Saxony-Anhalt	158,113	11.1	358,556	25.1	1.62	579,569	40.7
Dessau	16,535	12.1	39,114	28,6	1.80	60,887	44.4
Halle	17,165	11.7	37,391	25.4	1.42	63,743	43.4
Halberstadt	25,522	10.1	54,038	21.5	1.69	86,030	34.3
Magdeburg	38,627	10.7	94,639	26.2	1.73	149,493	41.4
Merseberg	24,028	11.8	51,986	25.4	1.62	84,056	41.1
Sangerhausen	14,105	11.4	34,063	27.4	1.55	56,032	45.2
Stendal	13,742	10.9	29,375	23.4	1.44	49,832	39.7
Wittenberg	8,389	11.1	18,371	24.3	1.59	29,917	39.5
Saxony	250,480	10.8	552,344	23.7	1.69	878,272	37.7
Annaberg	19,528	11.4	46,298	26.8	1.41	79,063	45.9
Bautzen	40,581	12.2	85,833	25.8	1.64	138,159	41.4
Chemnitz	27,626	10.6	63,683	24.5	1.91	96,993	37.2
Dresden	29,532	8.8	59,205	17.7	1.84	91,358	27.4
Leipzig	47,105	10.0	107,075	22.8	2.08	158,657	33.9
Oschatz	9,707	11.1	20,430	23.4	1.36	35,433	40.6
Pirna	20,812	11.6	43,529	24.2	1.54	71,798	39.8
Plauen	15,834	11.9	33,952	25.6	1.66	54,371	41.1
Riesa	14,910	13.1	36,012	31.6	2.16	52,672	46.3
Zwickau	24,745	12.0	53,931	26.1	1.42	91,784	44.3
Thuringia	138,740	11.0	314,947	25.1	1.61	510,923	40.7
Erfurt	26,269	9.8	56,596	21.2	1.50	94,270	35.4
Gera	18,198	10.8	42,655	25.4	1.83	65,988	39.3
Gotha	19,788	11.4	43,640	25.0	1.40	74,841	42.9
Jena	19,135	10.2	43,918	23.5	1.74	69,189	37.0
Nordhausen	15,895	10.7	39,290	26.5	1.46	66,230	44.8
Suhl	28,347	11.0	68,117	26.5	1.70	108,228	44.2
Altenburg	11,108	12.8	22,725	26.1	1.33	39,759	45.7
East Berlin	52,448	7.7	123,674	18.1	1.28	220,138	32.2
East Germany As a comparison:	833,718	10.8	1,838,297	23.4	1.55	3,026,531	32.2
West Germany (8)	16,000	0.1	381,707	1.4	0.21	2,209,419	8.1

(1) As a % of all dependent civilian labour force
(2) Assisted employed workers
(3) Full-time equivalent of working hours under short-time working (number of short-time workers roughly twice as high)
(4) Participants in full-time further training (excluding people trained on-the-job)

(5) Recipients of early retirement benefits under the *Vog* and *Alüg* early retirement programmes

(6) Unemployed persons plus improvement in the labour market as a result of labour-market policies

(7) Employment Office district Altenburg including districts belonging to Saxony

(8) Data on training measures and early retirement are estimated

Source: 'Trends. Unemployment and labour market policy in the East German regions', *Employment Observatory East Germany*, no. 3–4, September 1992, pp. 14–15.

Document 9 The Board of Economic Advisors to the Federal Economics Ministry explains the collapse of the GDR economy

1. The economic situation in the eastern German Länder continues to be characterised by the structures and production methods inherited from the system of central planning, the inefficiencies of which were revealed when the transition to the market economy began. Other factors have intensified the problems of the unprecedented changes. Sales to western markets which had been subsidised under the old system, now proved uncompetitive under the conditions of a market economy. That was to be expected. What was more serious was that the political and economic changes in central and eastern Europe and the transition of the CMEA countries to convertible currencies meant that sales to these countries were largely reduced to replacement parts for previous equipment exports. Eastern Germany thus lost its export base virtually overnight, and domestic sales collapsed as well. Government demand for goods and services produced in East Germany declined tremendously for a while. Eastern Germany's consumers rejected, temporarily at least, even those eastern German products which could compete with western goods in quality and price.

2. The problems arising from the poor supply-side conditions were inherited from the socialist system, together with the extreme deterioration of sales opportunities. These problems created a challenge which the eastern German producers probably could not have overcome, even if wages had been extremely low. However, this was not the case. After the conversion of wages at a rate of one-to-one in the currency union, and after the subsequent wage agreements, a massive discrepancy developed between the costs and potential revenues of enterprises. The conversion rate was favourable for incomes, but substantially worsened the competitiveness of industry. The first collective wage agreements set the price of labour at about one-third of the going-rate in the West; these contracts were soon followed by other settlements that further increased wages sharply.

The discrepancy between the costs level and the profit potential is the result of the extremely low productivity of an obsolete and overstaffed production structure in the East. The neglect of infrastructure, with its effects on costs, was also revealed, as was the over-exploitation of the environment which had now to be dealt with. Social facilities run by factories for employees also had a negative effect on the ability to compete. In addition to the problem of low productivity, there was also the problem that goods were poor in quality and badly marketed. Many products could only – if at all – be sold at greatly reduced prices. Therefore, according to the traditional value measurements of productivity, the value of the output of each East German worker was much lower than that of his West German counterpart . . . In short, the former GDR, like the other socialist countries, wasted resources in producing goods that were in general not marketable, at least not at the prices charged.

The level of wages which would have made goods marketable would have to have been so low that it would have been unacceptable for a number of reasons . . . Whether or not this situation was inevitable, the level of wages considered 'reasonable' by social standards was so high that many factories were no longer able to cover their operation costs. In other words, without subsidies these factories were on the verge of shutting-down. Their productive capital was worthless in terms of revenue. Any additional wage increase not brought about by higher productivity or any other improvement in the market value of the goods produced could only have increased the number of bankruptcies.

Source: Bundesministerium für Wirtschaft, 1992, pp. 1–3.

Document 10 The Bundesbank advocates a tight fiscal and monetary policy

The integration of the new Länder is presenting a major challenge to fiscal policy in particular. In order to build up a workable infrastructure and socially to cushion the restructuring of public authorities, sizeable transfer payments from western Germany are needed, and boost the public sector deficit. Now, however, there are signs that in 1991 the aggregate public sector deficit (including the social security funds) will probably run at the bottom edge of the range hitherto specified (DM 140 billion to DM 160 billion). Considering that the outflow of funds for capital formation by the east German Länder and local authorities is only gradually getting under way, that expenditure requirements are falling short of the appropriations in numerous areas and that tax revenue is rising steeply, it is not impossible that the DM 140 billion figure may actually be undershot. Even so, the 1991 public sector deficit will probably be equivalent to nearly 5% of GNP, an order of magnitude which was exceeded in the 'old' Federal Republic only in 1975.

Public sector deficits of these dimensions are acceptable only for a brief transitional period, even if their financing has so far turned out to be fairly smooth. Major steps have already been taken towards budgetary consolidation, in the shape of the Federal Government's budget plans for 1992 and its medium-term fiscal planning . . . The consolidation process will be hampered, however, by the deterioration of the financial situation of the pension insurance funds and the statutory health institutions, whose expenditure is showing signs of expanding sharply (in part because of the increase in spending in eastern Germany). This makes it the more important for the central, regional and local authorities at all levels (i.e. including the Länder Governments and local authorities) to reduce their deficits to a durably sustainable figure. In this context, restraint in public spending should have priority over tax increases, which pose problems in terms of anti-inflation and growth policy. Given a basic stance of this kind, fiscal policy can work towards maintaining confidence in the stability of government finance and enhancing market forces. At the same time, this would afford appreciable relief to monetary policy in its task of safeguarding the value of money, both domestically and vis-à-vis the rest of the world.

The Bundesbank tightened its monetary policy stance during the summer. After it had lowered this year's monetary target from the corridor of 4% to 6% to that of 3% to 5% on the occasion of its annual review in July . . . the discount rate was raised from 6.5% to 7.5% and the lombard rate from 9% to 9.25% in mid-August. In taking these measures, the Bundesbank intended to document its determination to abide unchanged by its stability-orientated monetary policy stance, especially since the pace of price rises has accelerated distinctly of late. Although price increases which have occurred cannot be reversed by means of monetary policy action, the Bundesbank must do all it can to prevent lasting expectations of higher inflation rates from emerging (on the basis of the present rising

price trends), since such expectations then become more and more difficult to rectify. Given the buoyancy of aggregate demand, this tightening of
monetary policy is unlikely either to obstruct economic growth in western
Germany or to impede the upswing in eastern Germany, especially since
interest-rate movements are having very little effect on capital formation in
the new Länder in view of the numerous public sector promotional
programmes.

The tightening of monetary policy is also in keeping with the international
environment in which the Bundesbank operates. For instance, the
'anchor' function performed by the Deutsche Mark in Europe calls in a
special way for the defence of price stability in order to prevent partner
economies from importing inflation stimuli from Germany (as they seem
to be doing in some cases at present). Moreover, given the diverse economic policy challenges facing the individual countries, a uniform monetary policy strategy geared to lowering interest rates worldwide would not
be acceptable. Instead, each country must 'keep its own house in order', in
accordance with the specific conditions obtaining in it. For the rest, 'real
rates of interest' in Germany are by no means particularly high by international standards; latterly, indeed, they have declined distinctly.

Source: 'The economic scene in the Federal Republic of Germany in summer 1991 – Overview', *Monthly Report of the Deutsche Bundesbank*, vol. 43,
no. 9, September 1991, pp. 8–9.

Document 11 The Treuhand's evaluation of privatization

Since June 1990 the organisation's objectives have been to privatise – principally through 100 per cent sales – to restructure (with a view to privatising) or to close the companies in its control when necessary. Additionally the Treuhandanstalt has been charged with breaking up the larger combines, so that instead of the original 8,000 industrial companies it now owns about 10,000 having sold 3,000 (July 1991).

Privatisation began hesitantly. This was due to the fact that political unification had not yet been completed, the ownership problem had not been resolved, and immediately after currency union eastern German companies lost much of their domestic market as superior west German goods flooded in. East German companies also lost their east bloc markets due to the shortage of hard currency there.

Treuhandanstalt executives were initially side-tracked into keeping the shell-shocked eastern German companies afloat. A total of DM20bn in liquidity credit was handed out in the first three months after currency union merely to ensure that the companies could pay their wages.

Despite these obstacles, by the end of 1990 the Treuhand had established a lasting structure based around eight central departments each responsible for both industrial sectors and a general function. Department 1, for example, was delegated responsibility for machine building and also had overall responsibility for privatisation policy.

The 15 regional offices were restructured too. Experienced west German managers were brought in to lead them and they were given direct responsibility for all companies in their areas employing fewer than 1,500 people (about two thirds of the 8,000 total).

The privatisation figure, only a couple of hundred at the end of 1990, began to rise sharply at the beginning of 1991. In March the Government responded with a new package of interventionist measures, known as the 'Upswing East'. At the same time the Treuhandanstalt placed great public emphasis on the restructuring of those companies which could not be quickly privatised and intensified closer cooperation with the five east German Länder (states).

Then came a terrible blow. On the night of April 1st as Dr Rohwedder was working in his Düsseldorf home he was murdered by terrorists. Mrs Birgit Breuel, Dr Rohwedder's deputy, and a former Christian Democrat finance minister in the west German state of Lower Saxony, succeeded him.

The strategy remained the same:
– to privatise wherever possible
– to restructure companies with a view to later privatisation
– to close companies who have no chance of surviving in a market economy.

Source: Treuhandanstalt 1991a, p. 9.

Document 12 Privatization of Treuhand firms by region, 1 November 1992

	Number privatized	Not yet privatized	Job guarantees	Investment guarantees (DM bn)
Mecklenburg-West Pomerania	1,378	304	111,953	7.6
Brandenburg	1,750	412	269,921	28.3
Saxony-Anhalt	1,707	488	167,589	15.7
Saxony	2,923	1,160	365,689	38.9
Thuringia	1,877	547	173,789	11.1
Berlin	713	242	229,159	20.5
Total	10,348	3,153	1,318,100	122.1

Source: Treuhandanstalt, *Informationen*, no. 17, December 1992, p. 6.

Document 13 The economic scene in Germany in autumn 1992

Conditions in the German economy have deteriorated distinctly of late. In western Germany the real gross domestic product declined by ½% in the third quarter, after adjustment for seasonal and working-day variations, compared with the second quarter, after having grown relatively strongly throughout the first of the year. In eastern Germany the anticipated self-sustaining, broadly based upswing has still not materialised, although some notable successes have been registered in individual areas. At the same time, the rising price trends in Germany have persisted. What is more, the turmoil in the European Monetary System (EMS) has increased the uncertainty about the further course of business activity. Economic policy is currently facing major challenges on all counts. With the aid of a 'solidarity pact', the Government, enterprises and the trade unions are striving to find new answers in order to pave the way for durable and non-inflationary growth in the whole of Germany. The heavy financial burdens imposed by German unification call for special efforts on the part of fiscal and wage policy. Even in this more difficult environment, the task of monetary policy remains that of ensuring stable underlying monetary conditions, thus facilitating the return to greater price stability and creating conditions permitting sustained economic growth.

Western Germany

The slowdown in economic activity that has occurred in western Germany in autumn 1992 owes a great deal to the sharp decline in foreign demand. Contrary to widespread expectations, a strong recovery of global business activity is not discernible as yet. It is true that the US economy has been expanding vigorously of late. But in most other major industrial countries business activity still remains weak . . .

Given its heavy dependence on foreign trade (after all, west German merchandise exports make up about one-quarter of the gross national product), the west German economy is particularly vulnerable to the risks inherent in the international environment. To be sure, exports have held up comparatively well until very recently. But this has been possible only because exporters have been able to draw on relatively large order backlogs. At all events, the inflow of new orders from abroad dropped sharply in the autumn, primarily because of the sluggishness of foreign demand . . .

It is largely because of the decrease in foreign demand that, according to the findings of the Ifo Institute, capacity utilisation in the manufacturing sector has declined – to a level which has latterly been hardly below the multi-year average. At the same time the pressure on corporate earnings has increased since labour costs have continued to go up sharply while the scope for passing on higher costs in the prices of industrial products has remained strictly limited because of the sluggishness of business activity and the intensification of national and international competition. These trends have dampened the propensity to invest. Both current spending on investment and the inflow of new home market orders to west German capital goods producers dropped distinctly in autumn 1991. However, it is not impossible that the severity of the decline in capital spending is being overstated by certain regional shifts in capital investment. It may well be the case that some west German enterprises have taken advantage of the preference differential in favour of eastern Germany, due to government investment incentives there, rather than at their traditional western locations. In this regard, too, Germany must increasingly be regarded as a uniform economic area, the statistical division of which into two separate regions is becoming ever more questionable . . .

Eastern Germany

The east German economy remains beset by serious adjustment problems. There are still no signs of a vigorous economic recovery. Viewed as a whole, employment is continuing to fall. Particularly in the manufacturing sector, labour has been laid off right up to the present. To date, the level of production in that sector has been rather low; in the autumn, the figure for the comparative period of 1991 was undershot by 2½%. Moreover, the inflow of new orders to industry – seasonally adjusted using west German seasonal factors – dropped again in the third quarter, compared with the second one.

Conditions in the manufacturing sector have been exacerbated by the fact that, following the downturn on domestic markets, Germany's traditional markets in eastern and central Europe have ceased to function as well. Although individual firms are gradually beginning to gain a toe-hold in western markets with new products, their sales successes have been modest so far. The cyclical weakness of demand in many countries is inhibiting any rapid expansion of the sales of east German products in western Germany or other western countries. Moreover, there is often a lack of experience of penetrating highly competitive markets and of making headway in the face of old-established business relations. Another competitive drawback in this connection is the high wage rates that have to be paid in eastern Germany, relative to productivity. In the meantime, the level of wages (excluding ancillary agreements) payable in the new Länder has reached 70% of pay levels in western Germany; next year it might actually go up to 80%, which would in fact constitute a renewed sharp rise in negotiated pay rates. The growth in productivity has not nearly kept pace with the increase in wages, so that labour costs per unit of output in eastern Germany are far higher than in the old Länder. A prolongation of the adjustment of wage rates to west German standards would help to enhance the competitiveness of east German firms in price terms.

Yet there have also been some favourable developments in major sectors of the east German economy, which show that the restructuring of enterprises and public authorities has made significant headway. In the construction sector and related industries the strong upswing is continuing. Output and the order inflow are increasing sharply – not only so as to improve the infrastructure and for industrial construction projects but in the meantime also in the field of residential construction. In numerous service areas which were particularly badly neglected in the former GDR, a notable upswing is likely to be given a major stimulus by ongoing privatisation. Of the original 12,400 enterprises in this field, barely 3,200 are still up for sale. After privatisation, reorganisation of these businesses is often required, entailing considerable capital spending. The time needed to carry out these measures has probably been underestimated so far. The level of investment reached to date (at roughly DM 105 billion in 1992, it is expected to make up about one-quarter of current domestic expenditure) suggests, however, that definite progress has been made along the arduous road from a government command economy to a free-market orientation of east German industry.

The most pressing problem in eastern Germany continues to be the high level of unemployment. In November 1.09 million people were registered as being out of work, and the number of short-time workers came to 235,000. But in this case, too, the situation has improved distinctly compared with the beginning of the year. Since January, the number of unemployed has fallen by 255,000 and the number of short-time workers by 285,000. At the same time, 150,000 more people were involved in labour market policy schemes, such as training and further training courses or early retirement. However, this rise is less steep than the simultaneous decline in unemployment and short-time working.

The year-on-year increase in the cost of living in eastern Germany in November, at 2½%, was less strong than in western Germany. However, this was entirely due to the movement of administratively readjusted rents, which were raised sharply in October 1991 and have been constant ever since, so that they have not affected the year-on-year comparison since October 1992. The rents in eastern Germany are to be raised again from January 1993. This new adjustment to market prices will cause the cost-of-living index to jump upwards again, although the social effects of this increase will be mitigated by the introduction of higher housing allowances.

Source: 'The economic scene in Germany in autumn 1992 – Overview', *Monthly Report of the Deutsche Bundesbank*, vol. 44, no. 12, December 1992, pp. 2–5.

Index